PENGUIN BOOKS

ALCOHOL

Griffith Edwards was born in India, where his father directed the Imperial Institute of Veterinary Research, and was educated at Andover Grammar School, Balliol College, Oxford, and the Medical College of St Bartholomew's Hospital. After qualifying in medicine and with postgraduate qualifications in psychiatry, he has centred his work on the study and treatment of dependence on alcohol and other drugs. He is Emeritus Professor of Addiction Behaviour at the National Addiction Centre (University of London) and editor-in-chief of the scientific journal *Addiction*. A member of WHO's Expert Advisory Panel on Alcohol and Drugs, he has taught and consulted in many different countries. He is editor or author of thirty books, including *Unreason in the Age of Reason* (1971), based on lectures which won him the Stevens Medal of the Royal Society of Medicine; *Alcohol Policy and the Public Good* (1994), which has been translated into eight languages; and *Treatment of Drinking Problems* (1982), which was a Behavioral Science Book Service choice. He was awarded the CBE in 1987 for his contribution to social science and medicine. Married with two grown-up children, Griffith lives with his wife, Sue, in Greenwich, London.

Alcohol

The Ambiguous Molecule

Griffith Edwards

PENGUIN BOOKS

To Sue, Dan and Rose

PENGUIN BOOKS

Published by the Penguin Group
Penguin Books Ltd, 27 Wrights Lane, London W8 5TZ, England
Penguin Putnam Inc., 375 Hudson Street, New York, New York 10014, USA
Penguin Books Australia Ltd, Ringwood, Victoria, Australia
Penguin Books Canada Ltd, 10 Alcorn Avenue, Toronto, Ontario, Canada M4V 3B2
Penguin Books (NZ) Ltd, Private Bag 102902, NSMC, Auckland, New Zealand

Penguin Books Ltd, Registered Offices: Harmondsworth, Middlesex, England

First published in Penguin Books 2000
10 9 8 7 6 5 4 3 2 1

The Twelve Steps of Alcoholics Anonymous are reprinted with permission of the General
Service Board of Alcoholics Anonymous GB Ltd. Extracts from 'Drinking Patterns of the
Bolivian Camba' by Dwight B. Heath are reprinted with permission from *Quarterly Journal of
Studies on Alcohol*, Vol. 19, pp. 491–508, 1958 (presently *Journal of Studies on Alcohol*),
copyright by Journal of Studies on Alcohol Inc., Rutgers Center of Alcohol Studies,
Piscataway, NJ 08854. Extracts from Alan Marlatt's 1983 APA article are reprinted with
permission from APA, Washington.

The moral right of the author has been asserted

Set in 10/12.75 pt PostScript Monotype Joanna
Typeset by Rowland Phototypesetting Ltd, Bury St Edmunds, Suffolk
Printed in England by Clays Ltd, St Ives plc

Contents

Alcohol is a fact of life. Walk down any street in the Western world and before long your feet will kick against an empty beer can, or your attention will be caught by an alluring advertisement which suggests that alcohol can magically transform your lifestyle. You will pass by an off-licence or two, and there will be a bar or a pub at the corner. Over there are young people drinking at a pavement café. Perhaps a sad inebriate will lurch against you. But, in the midst of all the casual pleasures of drink, the problems caused by it are more often indoors – hidden, or known only to the afflicted family.

This book seeks to present a mix of important facts on this pervasive fact of life. Its aim is to stir and inform debate and to engage attention, but not to take sides. To that end a number of different perspectives are explored. The earlier chapters examine aspects of the history of drinking and of social attitudes towards drinking in different eras and cultures. This material is fascinating in its own right, but it is being deployed with a serious purpose. The world's image of alcohol, its love or hate for it, and decisions on what to do about this drug, are profoundly coloured by value-laden perceptions of many kinds. Alcohol is a fact around which are created myths, and those myths themselves then become powerful facts.

The book goes on to describe what recent medical science has revealed about the impact of alcohol on the individual's mind and body, the pleasure it gives and the harm it may do, and why for some people it becomes hideously destructive. Alcohol needs to be looked at both in terms of its effects on the individual and in terms of what it does to populations and communities. The spectrum of sciences involved is wide, and their salient findings are here presented in plain language, and illustrated with case studies.

We turn finally to the question of how, in the light of this knowledge, society might in future make a better attempt to deal with this pleasure-giving, somewhat dangerous and ambiguous molecule. How is society to get its pleasure out of alcohol with less likelihood of mass pain?

Most adults anywhere in the world would probably be able to characterize themselves either as drinkers of alcohol or as non-drinkers. Each of those categories, of course, has within it a great mix of persons. The drinkers may be drinking every day and devotedly, or taking no more than a sipped glass of sherry at Christmas. The non-drinker category will include lifetime abstainers, but also those who have stopped drinking because alcohol has made them ill or addicted.

Society seems at present too often to be ill-informed, misinformed or indifferent to the facts on its favourite drug. That's dangerous. This book is written with respect for everyone's unique personal free choice, but in the hope that the facts it lays out will help readers make choices which are well informed and with the myths distinguished from the science.

Acknowledgements

Margaret Annequin proposed this book. Helpful comments on certain draft chapters or particular points were provided by Christopher Cook, Colin Drummond, Kaye Fillmore, Christine Godfrey, Nick Heather, Faith Jaffe, Timothy Peters, Ron Roizen, Robin Room, Mark and Linda Sobell, Jessica Warner, and Harry and Linda Zeitlin. Eric Appleby, Enoch Gordis and Jim Mosher kindly helped with data. Beyond these identified names, immeasurable gratitude is owed to a much wider group of scientists and scholars who have over the years so often and generously shared their wisdom, and given me their friendship. Dwight Heath has given generous permission for the reproduction of the quotations from his work which appear in Chapter 4, and I am similarly grateful to Alan Marlatt for permission regarding quotations reproduced in Chapter 12. The General Service Board of Alcoholics Anonymous has given permission for the reproduction of AA's Twelve Steps, which are to be found in Chapter 8. Sue Edwards gave nurture and detected errors and omissions; Elda Calderone (librarian, Institute of Psychiatry) and Lindsay May Dearlove and Sarah Dodgson (librarians, the Athenaeum) provided bibliographic assistance. Stefan McGrath of Penguin has given me enormously helpful editorial advice and a lot of his time. Bob Davenport provided the best copy-editing I have ever experienced. Finally, I want specially to thank Patricia Davis for her outstandingly competent and patient secretarial support on which I have relied for many years.

This book will at several points use case histories to make live its arguments. Patients, families and doctors in these case histories are all entirely invented, but absolutely true to life.

1 Alcohol, What is It?

This book is neither for nor against alcohol. It considers a particular mind-acting chemical both as a drug and as a social fact. However, it also deals with the myths that have been so abundantly woven around this molecule. And one doesn't get far into this territory before encountering the many stark contradictions in the way people view a substance which has been declared by the World Health Organization to be a cause of cancer, which for the Catholic Church becomes in sacramental wine the blood of Christ, and which meanwhile continues as Western civilization's favourite recreational drug. Alcohol is a pervasive fact of life, but an extraordinary fact – pleasurable and destructive, anathematized and adulated, and deeply ambiguous. This introductory chapter gives in non-technical language some basic information on what alcohol is – the objective nature of the genie in the bottle.

Alcohol the chemical

Alcohol in terms of its molecular structure is C_2H_5OH and looks like this:

$$
\begin{array}{c}
\text{H} \quad \text{H} \\
| \quad | \\
\text{H}-\text{C}-\text{C}-\text{OH} \\
| \quad | \\
\text{H} \quad \text{H}
\end{array}
$$

Thus to a spine of two carbon atoms are attached five hydrogen atoms and a hydroxyl (oxygen–hydrogen) group. That constitutes a fairly simple structure carrying rather little information, and alcohol has therefore sometimes been referred to disparagingly by biochemists as a 'stupid' molecule. Drawn on a sheet of paper (or more properly projected into three-dimensional space), its structure is much smaller and less interesting than those of such complex mind-acting chemicals as, say, heroin, nicotine or the cannabinol which is the core drug constituent of cannabis.

Alcohol at room temperature is a colourless liquid which in pure form is astringent and unpleasant on the tongue. Dilution makes it less unpalatable, and alcohol and water mix together easily. Spirits are about 40 per cent absolute (pure) alcohol; port, sherry and other fortified wines 15–20 per cent; and wine around 12 per cent. A standard beer will be about 4 per cent alcohol by volume, although strong beers can be anything up to 10 per cent. What gives these various beverages their attractive and distinct tastes is not however their alcohol (diluted or otherwise), but the chemicals which have got into them in the course of production. It is possible to produce a beer from which nearly all the alcohol has been extracted and which still tastes reasonably like beer. But take out even a little of the complex flavouring given by sugar, hops, barley and so on, and the residual drink will be a pale imitation or even a parody of the original. Put unkindly, it is the dirt in the drink which makes it attractive to the nose and the palate, and which turns a mixture of alcohol and water into a good beer, a fine wine or a famous malt whisky. Vodka is relatively free from contaminants, and hence relatively odourless and tasteless.

Before going further, let's get a technical issue out of the way. In ordinary usage the word 'alcohol' refers to the substance we expect to find in alcoholic drinks. That is the way in which the word will be employed in this book. However, for the chemist the correct name for that substance is 'ethyl alcohol' or 'ethanol', while 'alcohol' is the generic name for a class of chemicals of which ethyl alcohol is but one member. The simplest member of the family has only one carbon atom at its core and is CH_3OH, methyl alcohol or methanol. Sometimes known as wood alcohol, it is a constituent of methylated spirits and is highly toxic. The higher alcohols include propyl, butyl and amyl alcohol, with respectively three, four and five carbon chains, but these substances will not figure further in this book.

Fermentation

The ultimate source of all beverage alcohol is the breakdown of naturally occurring carbohydrate (starch or glucose) to ethyl alcohol, water and carbon dioxide, by the action of enzymes. Most commercial beer derives from the action of brewers' yeast on barley or other cereals, with hops added to some beers for flavouring. Commercially available wine derives from the breakdown of the sugar contained in the juice of the grape by the yeasts which are present in the bloom on the fruit's surface, although laboratory-bred yeast may also be used. Cider is made from apples, and perry from pears.

But if those are the materials which form the basis for the fermented alcoholic beverages which most societies drink, there are myriad other plant products which have at some time been employed in the production of alcohol, especially in developing countries. In North America, birch beer has been made from the sap of the same tree that provides covering for canoes, and a birch-based drink has also been drunk in Siberia. Chicha is a fermented drink made from maize, and has been consumed over wide areas of Central and South America from the pre-Columbian era onwards. In many parts of Africa, home production of beer has for centuries been a feature of rural culture, with maize, millet or sorghum the usual basis. Barley-based beers are brewed in the more northern parts of Africa, palm wine is a favourite drink in West Africa, and bananas and many other types of fruit are used for alcohol production within other local traditions. Rice wine is popular in the Far East. Other than in the Arctic regions, there is probably no part of the world where the abundance of nature aided by a kindly enzyme has not resulted in the availability of some sort of alcoholic drink. The flavour of these drinks may not always approach that of a real ale or a chateau-bottled claret – indigenous African beer may to the Western palate taste like a diluted porridge and even have a few dead flies floating in the billycan – but alcohol is alcohol and the common factor the world over.

So simple is the process of producing an alcoholic beverage by fermentation that early humans would have got hold of this technique as soon as it was possible to gather fruit, add water, and wait a few days for enzymatic action to do its work. These conditions probably imply the beginnings of a settled and agricultural way of life rather than a nomadic existence. Having emphasized the extreme simplicity of the basic process, it should be acknowledged that modern production of beer involves advanced technology, and brewing has developed a strong scientific base. Wine production also has its science, but in some ways stays closer to its ancient pre-industrial origins.

However primitive or advanced the technology, there is a limit on the alcohol concentration which can be achieved by any form of fermentation. This is set by the fact that, when the concentration rises to a certain level, the yeast will be inhibited or killed by the alcohol which it has itself produced, and at that point the fermentation process will be shut down. Sake, the national drink of Japan, is produced by the action on rice of a non-yeast micro-organism (Aspergillus), and a concentration of about 17 per cent can be achieved before the fermentation is switched off. And that for practical purposes is probably the top alcohol concentration achievable for any beverage by natural fermentation.

Distilling as amazing innovation

For millennia the simple fact of alcohol-induced self-limitation on fermentation meant that there were ceilings on the strength of the product. To get drunk on a 12 per cent wine or a 4 per cent beer is none too difficult, although some of the traditional alcoholic drinks of the developing world have an alcohol content so low that it would require agricultural and brewing resources beyond that of any village to make widespread intoxication at all likely.

In the sixteenth century the age-old natural barrier to production of higher-concentration beverages was overcome by dissemination across Europe of the technology of distillation. Today we may view the bottles of spirits stacked on the slightly more secure shelves at the off-licence as a familiar part of the great drinks spectrum. But in the sixteenth century distillation must have looked like a revolutionary and threatening technology. Suddenly alcohol was available at more than three times the concentration at which people had previously seen or tasted it. All sorts of old balances between populations and their drinking were destabilized. The very word 'spirits' carried a dangerously magical message.

The origins of distillation go back at least 2,000 years. The process was known to the Greeks as early as the first century AD. In the third century AD, Alexander of Aphrodisias gave a description of how sea water could be distilled to produce drinking water. And in passing he mentioned the possibility of carrying out distillation on wine. As so often happened in the history of science and medicine, this Greek learning was transmitted to the Arab world, and then much later brought back to Spain and thence to the rest of Europe.

By the middle of the sixteenth century the use of distillation to provide concentrated alcoholic drinks had become a widely applied technology across the Continent. At first the resulting preparation was viewed primarily as a medicine, but before long it was the basis for a range of new beverages. The distillation of wine would give brandy to Europe and various similar spirituous drinks. From fermented grain with a little flavouring of juniper came gin – originally from Holland, with London gin a later unsweetened and competitive variety. Whisky is derived from various different cereals according to its country of origin – Scotch whisky, for instance, comes from malt and grain with caramel for colouring, the smoke of peat-fired kilns for flavour, and an esteemed spring water as carrier. Rum emerged as a distilled beverage based on molasses. Kentucky bourbon is a latecomer, dating from towards the end of the eighteenth century, made largely from a fermented maize mash which after distillation is aged in charred oak barrels.

The availability of distilled spirits in Europe had multiple consequences. Concentrated alcoholic drinks rapidly became available to the people of every country, but they were particularly well received in the more northern regions, where climate meant that wine could not be a domestic product. Government attempts to regulate and tax spirits were from early days handicapped by the ease with which illicit stills could be set up or bottles of spirits be smuggled across frontiers. One consequence of distilling was thus the earliest variant of something rather akin to the problem of illicit production of, and trade in, drugs:

less bulky products are better for the black market than bulky products. A further consequence was that the manufacture and marketing of alcohol became more commercialized than had previously been the case with pre-industrial fermented beverages.

In the absence of sales figures from those early days, it is difficult to estimate the extent to which spirits added to, rather than merely substituted for, other types of alcohol consumption. But at least in some countries and in some periods there was quite a lot of addition. Before long Russia had easy access to vodka, and that was quite some competitor to birch beer. Across those great tracts of cold northern Europe where there was no hope of ever growing a grape, raw spirits penetrated the culture and became integral to the way of life, and have remained so right up to modern times. As we will see in Chapter 3, the British gin epidemic of the eighteenth century had several different determinants, but the availability of cheap gin was one of its causes. In time, European exports took spirits to many parts of the world. Distilled spirits did terrible damage to the indigenous people of North America, and were an item of barter in the slave trade with Africa. New drug technologies of any kind can often upset old ecological balances, and distillation in its day was a leap in drug technology: gin palace, opium den, crack house – there is a lineage.

Blood alcohol concentration

So there in its container of whatever kind, with its individual pretty label – or in a bucket off the back of an African pick-up truck – is our diluted and contaminated dose of ethyl alcohol ready for the taking. When swallowed, the alcohol is absorbed from the stomach and the small intestine. Absorption will be slowed by the presence of food, or can be somewhat speeded if the drink has been chilled or has been aerated with bubbles of carbon dioxide. Less concentrated drinks may have their alcohol more rapidly absorbed than stronger ones, so iced champagne drunk on an empty stomach can be an effective way of getting alcohol to the brain quickly. After a preliminary pass through the liver, some of the alcohol will be reaching the brain within minutes. The blood or brain alcohol level will then slowly increase for the next thirty to sixty minutes as the absorption of a single drink is completed. Several drinks taken together or spaced out in a series of drinks will result in the alcohol level going upwards longer and higher. But enormous variation in absorption rates can occur between individuals and on different occasions.

The blood alcohol concentration (BAC) which is achieved after any drink or drinking session will reflect a balance between, on the one hand, how much alcohol is absorbed and over what time, and, on the other hand, how quickly the body is getting rid of alcohol. The larger part of elimination (80 per cent) is achieved by metabolic breakdown in the liver, and a heavy drinker may be able to break down alcohol twice as fast as someone who drinks more lightly or occasionally. Some alcohol is excreted unchanged in the urine, and a little bit is breathed out through the lungs or lost in sweat. But the self-deceiving belief of old-time colonial hands that alcohol is relatively harmless in a hot climate, because it can be prodigiously sweated out, has no scientific basis.

Given all the variations in absorption and elimination which are likely to be brought about by food intake, the type of drink taken and variations in individual physiology, calculations of what BAC will be produced by what kind of alcohol intake can never be exact. As a rough guide, however, one may assume that a single British standard drink (one glass of wine, half a pint of beer, a measure of spirits, each of which contains 8–10 grams of alcohol) will raise the drinker's BAC by about 20 mg% (20 milligrams of alcohol per 100 millilitres of blood).

Here is an illustration of how calculations can be made on the sort of BAC level which may be expected to result from a specific drinking occasion. If someone were to throw back ten drinks in quick time, the arithmetic would suggest that the BAC achieved would be 10 × 20 or 200 mg%. But in the real world no one is likely to take those ten drinks all in the first minute of a party and then sit back. Even as their absorption of spaced drinks is pushing their BAC up, so at the same time elimination will be pulling it down; as noted above, the BAC achieved at any particular moment reflects the net effect of that profit and loss. Alcohol is cleared from the body at a rate equivalent to about 15 mg% of BAC in one hour. If, therefore, we sketch a scenario in which our hypothetical party-goer consumes ten drink between 8 p.m. and 11 p.m., calculations would suggest that when he or she is stopped by a policeman at midnight the breathalyser reading would be at 10 × 20 mg% or 200 mg%, less elimination of 4 × 15 mg% or 60 mg%, thus giving 140 mg% as the likely midnight BAC figure. The outcome would be a bad case of drink driving – 80 mg% is the current British legal driving limit.

In most instances the sort of arithmetic discussed here can give a fair approximation to what is actually likely to happen to a blood alcohol level in given circumstances, but it should be emphasized again that such calculations are not an exact art. For anyone to drive a motor vehicle on the basis of do-it-yourself calculations on what will keep them below the legal BAC limit would be very ill advised. 'Do not drink and drive' is the only safe advice.

When alcohol meets the brain

What happens when the absorbed alcohol gets to the brain is the next question to address. There can be no doubt that, so far as most people are concerned, when alcohol meets the brain the event is received as good news. Something subtly pleasant begins to happen. The average drinker is not likely to sit around and attempt to put into words what he or she is beginning to experience, but after a glass or two something wanted and familiar is usually being sensed. What is experienced psychologically will be modified by personality, previous experience with alcohol, expectations of what alcohol can do for the person concerned, the company and setting, and cultural beliefs. But behind all those important influences is the core fact that when alcohol reaches the brain a mind-acting drug will begin to impact on the brain cells and brain systems in a way which can produce or facilitate pleasurable alterations in mood.

If we look for a word to characterize this experience, 'euphoria' is probably a good summary description, but every drinker will react differently in terms of talkativeness, happiness, enthusiasm, stimulation, sedation, disinhibition, loosening of thought associations, and feelings of power or sexuality. The pleasurable effect of this drug is person-specific, but generally people who have had it happen to them once will go for it again and repeatedly.

Though a change of mood is the the first, obvious, wanted effect produced by alcohol, at the same time there will be produced physiological effects such as increased pulse rate, a rise in blood pressure, and an increased secretion of urine – consequences which are usually of no great immediate importance to the drinker.

There is a dose relationship for many of these effects, so that with more drink the pleasure is increased. Eventually, however, unpleasant effects come into play and drinking becomes aversive. The level of intake at which the response switches from pleasure to aversion varies greatly from person to person, but the wanted euphoria may be replaced by depression and maudlin misery. Nausea and vomiting may be other unwanted physical effects. In addition, there will very soon at ordinary levels of drinking be, with some variation between individuals, a dose-related impairment of reaction time, coordination and balance.

How alcohol acts on the brain and interacts with psychological expectations to produce its impact is a question which has during recent years attracted a great deal of research. A summary conclusion is that alcohol affects brain functioning by its capacity to interfere with the biological system of chemical messengers which is all the time regulating the balance between activity and inactivity in brain cells and brain circuitry. Alcohol does not directly key into receptor sites in the brain as do many other mind-acting drugs, but it produces its effects by cat's-pawing legitimate messengers. Through these mechanisms it will activate structures within the brain whose nerve-cell firing produces pleasure, while through other mechanisms it will dampen firing and produce sedation and impairment of coordination. What we are seeing here is the capacity of a simple molecule to interfere with, or in some way hijack, the functioning of very complex brain systems. The messenger chemicals which are involved in some way or other probably feature in every system known to the brain scientist.

Alcohol as poison

Thus far this chapter has dealt with the idea of alcohol as a chemical, and as a chemical which is a brain-acting drug. To round off the discussion of the basic facts on this molecule, a little needs finally to be said about alcohol as a poison. 'What's your poison?' is a bar-room pleasantry with dark undertones.

Alcohol is potentially a poison in several different ways. The most banal poisonous consequence of drinking alcohol is that it can produce hangover – a state ranging from mild fragility to a thumping headache, nausea, the room spinning round, ghastliness, a short-lived resolve never to touch the stuff again. This state is in part the result of poisoning by the non-alcohol adulterants in the drink (the 'dirt' to which we referred earlier), but dehydration due to the diuretic effect of alcohol also plays a part. It is unpleasant, but no tangible harm is done other than perhaps a morning's work being lost.

Second, let's put in the list of potentially poisonous effects the fact that it is possible to die of an overdose of this drug. That, mercifully, is not too common an occurrence. Nevertheless, the drunk in the police cell has all too often been found dead in the morning as a result of respiratory depression caused by alcohol, complicated perhaps by inhaled vomit, and sometimes also by the capacity of alcohol to lower the blood-sugar level. Death by alcohol overdose occurs rather easily when this drug is mixed with sedatives, tranquillizers or opioids such as methadone or heroin, and many a sad fatality has happened that way.

Third, alcohol is a poison because, either directly or because of the associated malnutrition which tends to go with heavy alcohol use, it can physically damage body tissues and impair body systems. There is hardly any type of tissue which is not vulnerable if excessive drinking is long continued – brain, nerves, muscle, liver, heart . . . the whole anatomy book is there.

Fourth, and as was mentioned at the start of this chapter, chronic exposure to alcohol carries a risk for certain types of cancer.

Fifth and lastly, through its capacity to impair coordination and judgement, alcohol can cause many types of accidents. It may also at times lead to violent behaviour or contribute to the risk of suicide.

Five entries in the downside list produce quite a negative profile for any drug. And, as we will discuss in detail in a later chapter, alcohol is also a drug of addiction – a fact which multiplies the significance of its inherently negative potential. In real life, most people weigh the negatives against the pleasurable positives and deem the balance sheet to be such that drink continues to be their favourite source of chemical fun; but that does not mean that the negatives go away. Alcohol is a stupid molecule which is clever in its ability to play mood music on complex brain systems, but it is an addictive drug with a far from innocent profile. In several respects it is less dangerous than many currently available street drugs, while in other ways it is more dangerous. Alcohol-related deaths currently run at over 200,000 per year in the USA and at 40,000 per year in the UK. Meanwhile in 1995 the total tax take from drink was $17,580 million in the USA and £9,713 million in the UK. Alcohol is fun, the wine of the Eucharist, a profitable and taxable commodity, but a drug among drugs and highly ambiguous in its costs and benefits.

So much for a brief factual description of alcohol the molecule. But the objective facts are, as already noted at the start of this chapter, only a small part of the total meaning which we give to drink. The mystic beliefs which surround the use of this substance are realities of a quite different kind from anything known to the chemist, and are the matters to which we turn in the next chapter.

2 Alcohol, Myths and Metaphors

Alcohol has primary meanings for the individual because of its molecular properties. Those provided the framework within which we analysed its negatives and positives in the preceding chapter. The present chapter is about the capacity of society to imbue alcohol with secondary meanings. At the extreme, such a process results in the mystical place accorded to alcohol in religion, or to the lay transubstantiation of a particular beverage into the soul of the nation (the Gaelic for whisky is *usquebaugh*, or 'water of life'). And beneath those grand levels of totemic magic exist myriad large or small instances of popular culture giving drink, or the act of drinking, meanings far beyond the merely pharmacological. To your health! *Santé! Salud!*

Wine and Christianity

To start our investigation of the processes which can metamorphose the meaning of alcohol, let's examine how Christianity has co-opted this drug into its rituals.

Jesus performed his first miracle at the wedding feast at Cana in Galilee (John 2:3–11). The contents of 'six water-pots of stone' were turned into wine. And that wine was of notable quality:

> When the ruler of the feast had tasted the water that was made wine, and knew not whence it was: (but the servants who drew the water knew;) the governor of the feast called the bride-groom, And saith unto him, Every man at the beginning doth set forth good wine; and when men have well drunk then that which is worse: but thou hast kept the good wine until now.

We are told that through this transformation Jesus 'manifested forth his glory; and his disciples believed on him'.

That was a phenomenal quantity of wine. But, going on to a much later point in Jesus' story, Matthew 26:26–9 gives this account of the Last Supper:

And as they were eating, Jesus took bread, and blessed it, and broke it, and gave it to the disciples, and said, Take, eat; this is my body. And he took the cup, and gave thanks, and gave it to them, saying, Drink ye all of it; For this is my blood of the new testament, which is shed for many for the remission of sins. But I say unto you, I will not drink henceforth of this fruit of the vine, until that day when I drink it new with you in my Father's kingdom.

Water into wine and wine into blood constitute a miracle and mystery of the Christian Church.

The form of the Christian Mass may derive in part from the rituals of the Jewish Sabbath and the Passover supper, but with profound sacramental meaning added. At an early stage in the history of the Christian Church the rules for the performance of the Eucharist had become formalized. The taking of the sacrament not only defined who was or was not a Christian, but by extension gave definition to the role of the priest and to the Church as the guardian of mysteries. And in those early days there was no doubt in the minds of the faithful that the bread really was flesh, while the wine had genuinely and in the fullest sense become the blood of the Saviour – a process which in AD 1215 at the Fourth Lateran Council came to be given the name 'transubstantiation'.

Much controversy at times attached to the doctrine of transubstantiation. About the year AD 500 the Gnostics, with their mystical approach to religion, had tried to argue that the transformation which took place during the sacrament was symbolic rather than actual. But that was seen by others as very near to heresy. The Church firmed up its literal interpretation in the ninth century. In the thirteenth century St Thomas Aquinas argued that the crass externals (the 'accident') of the bread and wine remained unchanged, while their inner essences were transformed. The Reformation brought a parting of the ways between Catholics and Protestants in relation to many aspects of doctrine, including the meaning to be given to the Eucharist. That famous Anglican rule book the Thirty-nine Articles received parliamentary authority in

1571. It declared in Article 31 that 'the sacrifices of Masses, in the which it was commonly said, that the Priest did offer Christ for the quick and the dead, to have remission of pain or guilt, were blasphemous fables, and dangerous deceits'.

Within modern religious thinking the debate around the meaning of the Eucharist has largely moved on from the historical preoccupation with transubstantiation, and now more often concerns the 'real presence' of Christ. But whether the wine is deemed to be the blood of Christ or no more than symbol, it continues to be taken by priest or congregation in Christian ritual. And for many (though not all) denominations the wine must have alcohol in it: unfermented grape juice is generally not acceptable. If a priest develops a drinking problem, permission may have to be obtained from the bishop for non-alcoholic wine to be substituted in that priest's celebration of Mass.

With due respect for Christian beliefs, within an anthropological perspective what the turning of water into wine represents is something akin to the magic translation of the less good and less powerful into the better and more potent. The later metamorphosis of wine into blood seems to be the same kind of magic, but a further development in the chain of mysterious changes: blood is stronger than wine, and wine now becomes fit stuff for a frankly cannibalistic rite of sacrifice. What also needs to be realized is that Christianity is here constructing a ritual around the use of a mind-acting drug, and that is familiar territory for the anthropologist. The Aztecs called their hallucinogenic mushrooms 'teonanactl' or the 'flesh of the gods'; tobacco was used within shamanistic rituals in Amerindian societies; while in Jamaica for the Rastafarians cannabis becomes part of religious ritual, with the priest chopping up and handing round 'the herb'. Alcohol and other drugs become elements in religious magic partly because they are themselves magical in their ability to transform mental states, but also because religion can control, shape and interpret the sensations which they produce.

Alcohol and the Judaic tradition

For the Orthodox Jew the drinking of alcohol is inherent in many types of religious occasion. Wine is taken at rites of passage. At a circumcision the godfather drinks from the cup over which a benediction has been proclaimed, and at eight days the baby may taste its first drop of wine. The drinking of alcohol is integral to the several household ceremonies of the Sabbath, and has a role in the celebration of most Jewish feasts and holy days.

An authoritative codification of Jewish law is to be found in the *Shulchan Aruch*, a work compiled by Rabbi Joseph Kavo of Safed in the sixteenth century. Here are a few examples of the kinds of way in which drinking features in Jewish life, given through quotations from the *Shulchan Aruch*. (Here and below we quote from C. R. Snyder's *Alcohol and the Jews*, published in 1958.)

It is mandatory to say Kiddush [a prayer traditionally recited in a Jewish family before taking wine on a Friday night] upon old wine, it is also mandatory to select good wine, and if possible an effort to obtain red wine should be made . . . If one has no wine, he should say Kiddush upon bread but not on any other beverage.

At the Great Kiddush, another celebration, the choice of drink may, however, be varied:

If . . . one is fond of brandy and he says Kiddush thereon, he has fulfilled his obligation. He should be careful to observe that the glass contains of one and a half egg-shells and he should drink a mouthful without interruption.

A grace should be said after any meal, whatever the day of the week, and here too alcohol is essential:

If three men ate together it is their duty to unite in saying the Grace after meals, and they must say it over a glass of liquor . . . Some authorities are of the opinion that even a single person is required to say Grace over a glass.

But the *Shulchan Aruch* warns against drunkenness:

When one rejoices on a festival one should not prolong in wine drinking, jesting and levity . . . for drunkenness, jesting and levity is not rejoicing but mere foolishness, which is not according to the command.

However, at the feast of Purim drinking to intoxication is seen as permissible:

The sages made it obligatory on one to become drunk, until he should not be able to differentiate between 'Cursed be Haman' and 'Blessed be Mordecai.' At least one should drink more than he is accustomed to of wine or of another intoxicating beverage; one who is of a weak disposition . . . is best not to become intoxicated.

If one compares the Christian and Jewish ritual use of alcohol there is a core similarity in that both religions give drink a place at the heart of their observances. Beyond that important sameness there are considerable differences. For Christians, wine in the Eucharist is either miraculously transformed into Christ's blood or is directly symbolic of his blood, whereas in the Jewish rituals the symbolic meaning accorded to alcohol is diffuse. For Christians the ritual place for alcohol is in the key sacrament which is celebrated in a church, whereas for Jews alcohol is an element in rituals many of which are celebrated within the family circle, rather than in any institutionalized place of worship. Christianity does not rule formally against drunkenness, although many disapprobations of it are to be found in the Bible. Jewish religion cautions against drunkenness, but at Purim licenses a kind of bacchanalia.

The fact that both religions use this drug as an instrument for ritual purposes produces a mindset favourable to the acceptance of alcohol in societies which embrace either of these faiths. No public-relations agency acting for any kind of product could hope to do better than have it embraced in this way by two world religions.

Islam: alcohol abhorred

If Judaism and Christianity exemplify religions which have taken alcohol to their bosoms, Islam is an example of an opposite kind.

Immediately before the time of the Prophet, the Arab world was a patchwork of tribal fiefdoms marked by various shades of brutality and ignorance. There was no unifying religion, but a scattering of various polytheistic and pagan beliefs. It appears also to have been an era of markedly heavy drinking. Wine fermented from dates and other plant products provided the means. Muhammad (c. AD 570–632) was a merchant, but around AD 610 he began to receive revelations from Allah, the one and only true God. These revelations form the basis of the Muslim holy book, the Koran, and over the years a sequence of them related to alcohol. The phasic development in these ordinances has been well described by Taha Baasher, a Sudanese psychiatrist, and we will make use of his analysis.

The first revelation did no more than put alcohol on the agenda, with a statement that

And of the fruits of the date palm, and grapes, whence we derive strong drink and good nourishment. Lo! therein is indeed a portent for people who have sense.

The second revelation was more challenging:

They question thee about strong drink and games of chance. Say: In both is great sin and some utility for men; but the sin of them is greater than their usefulness. And they ask thee what they ought to spend. Say: That which is superfluous.

The move towards greater consciousness of alcohol as a problem was further advanced by the scandal caused by an occasion when a prominent imam became so drunk as to be unable to conduct evening prayers. Following this unhappy event the third revelation declared:

Oh ye who believe! Draw not near unto prayer, when ye are drunken, till ye know that which ye utter.

Given the necessity to pray five times each day, such an ordinance clearly made continued drunkenness difficult for members of this new religion.

Then came the fourth revelation, with a root-and-branch condemnation of alcohol:

Oh ye who believe! Strong drink and games of chance and idols and divining arrows are only an infamy of Satan's handiwork. Satan seeketh only to cast among you enmity and hatred by means of strong drink and games of chance, and to turn you from remembrance of Allah and from his worship. Will you then have done?

Soon after the fourth revelation, Muslims declared consensually that they 'had done', and from then on abstinence from alcohol was to be an unbending tenet of the Muslim faith, other than for the later revisionist tendencies of the Sufis and Omar Khayyám's untroubled acceptance of wine, as expressed in Edward Fitzgerald's famous 1859 translation:

> Here with a Loaf of Bread beneath the bough,
> A Flask of Wine, a Book of Verse – and Thou
> > Beside me singing in the Wilderness –
> And Wilderness is Paradise enow.

A question which then followed the enunciation of the Muslim prohibition was the degree of punishment which should attach to any infringement of the holy law, and over time the religiously prescribed punishment for use of alcohol was escalated from forty to eighty lashes. Eighty lashes with a palm branch indicates a position far distant from wine as the blood of the Redeemer and the essential ingredient of the Eucharist, or from one and a half egg-shells of brandy gulped down by an observant Jew at Great Kiddush.

Let's here note the attitudes of three other religions to alcohol. Buddhism disapproves of it, and within the five precepts of the lay ethic is the requirement to desist from alcohol. Although Hindu teaching is not so categorical on this matter, the observant Hindu is expected to abstain. Sikhism is not against alcohol (but prohibits tobacco).

Drink as emblem of the nation

The secular mythologizing of alcohol can also be very powerful. Different countries have over the centuries often chosen one favoured drink as symbolizing national virtue, while imbuing the equivalent beverages of other people with the supposedly unattractive attributes of those foreigners. The French, for instance, have traditionally seen great merit in the drinking of wine, while stridently denouncing beer and beer drinkers (though in reality the French have always drunk a great deal of beer and spirits). Here is a statement from Professor Henry Babinski, a renowned nineteenth-century French physician, illustrating that kind of nationalistic stance:

L'usage prolongé du vin a certainement contribué à la formation et au développe-ment des qualités fondamentales de la race: cordialité, franchise, gaîté, qui la différencient si profondément des peuples buveurs de bière.

Or, in translation:

The long-time use of wine has certainly contributed to the formation and development of fundamental qualities of the race: cordiality, frankness, gaiety, which differentiate them so profoundly from people who drink beer.

That quotation comes from a 1930s publication which was sponsored by the French wine industry. The book was called *Mon docteur le vin*. It provided a rich collection of statements by the French medical good and great on the benefits of wine drinking, interspersed with copy which identified wine with Frenchness. Marshal Pétain, in a letter placed at the front of the text, emphasized the importance of wine for the triumphal conduct of war by the French army during the years 1914–18. (At the time of writing, Pétain was still the hero of Verdun rather than the tainted leader of Vichy France.) Raymond Poincaré, president of France from 1913 to 1920, contributed a declaration that wine was 'The essence of happiness and health, an extract of the Gallic temperament, a reflection of the gentle country of France.'

And *Mon docteur le vin* went on to suggest that wine was not really alcohol at all. Some kind of specifically French miracle had taken place in the reverse direction to that experienced in Galilee. Thus Professor Armand Gautier, expressing a view which to the present day continues to have currency in France:

Who does not know the ravages of alcoholism? They are terrifying! Body, spirit and morale are all in decline. Drinkers of wine are not drinkers of alcohol. In wine-growing areas one finds very few alcoholics.

Various other French authorities were also mustered by this publication to state that drinking of wine was at the root of French artistic creativity and sporting prowess, the cause of Frenchmen winning Nobel prizes, and an explanation for the beauty of French women.

If France has identified wine as emblem of that country's soul, the British have been equally given to believing that beer is a symbol of their country's nationhood. A book put out in 1948 by Messrs Whitbread (the brewers) had at the front an encomium written by a sixteenth-century author, John Taylor:

It is an Emblem of Justice, for it allowes and yeelds measure; It will put Courage into a Coward and make him swagger and fight; It is a seale to many a good Bargaine. The Physittian will commend it; the Lawyer will defend it, It Neither hurts, nor kils, any but those that abuse it unmeasurably and beyond bearing; It doth good to as many as take it rightly; It is as good as a paire of Spectacles to cleare the Eyesight of an old parish Clarke; And in Conclusion, it is such a nourisher of Mankinde, that if my mouth were as bigge as Bishopsgate, my Pen as long as a Maypole, and my Inke a flowing spring, or a standing fishpond, yet I could not with Mouth, Pen, or Inke, spak or write the true worth and worthiness of Ale.

The author of that book, B. Meredith Brown, updated this praise of beer to his own times in a passage remarkable for the explicitness with which beer drinking was equated with racial superiority:

Beer, then, is predominantly the drink of those branches of the white races of mankind which inhabit Northern and Western Europe (i.e. north of the wine-producing areas) or who have spread thence to the Western hemisphere – the energetic, and progressive and colonizing people who for the last five hundred years have been the social, industrial and political leaders of civilization as we know it today.

In terms of bare-faced chauvinism and misrepresentation of history, Meredith Brown succeeded in exceeding anything offered in *Mon docteur le vin*.

'What two ideas are more inseparable than Beer and Britannia?' asked the Revd Sydney Smith, the famous eighteenth-century wit. Beer has been much extolled in literature and popular verse. Thus these lines from a traditional drinking song, 'Come, Landlord, Fill the Flowing Bowl':

> The man who drinketh small beer,
> And goes to bed quite sober
> Fades as the leaves do fade
> That drop off in October.
>
> The man who drinketh strong beer
> And goes to bed right mellow,
> Lives as he ought to live,
> And dies a jolly good fellow.
>
> But he who drinks just what he likes
> And getteth half-seas over
> Will live until he die
> And then lie down in clover.

And between each verse the jolly beer-swigging topers were expected to sing in rousing chorus:

> For tonight we'll merry merry be,
> For tonight we'll merry merry be,
> For tonight we'll merry merry be,
> Tomorrow we'll be sober.

Beer was also celebrated in one of the more famous Victorian music-hall songs ever to ring out around the public bar or echo from barrel organs in the streets:

> Beer, beer, glorious beer!
> Fill yourselves right up to here!
> Drink a good deal of it – make a good meal of it,
> Stick to your old-fashioned beer!
> Don't be afraid of it – drink till you're made of it,
> Now, altogether, a cheer!
> Up with the sale of it – down with a pail of it,
> Glorious, glorious beer!

Subsequently the Second World War song 'Roll out the Barrel' enjoyed a similar popularity.

Beer drinking has also often been celebrated as a symbol of national virtue by Britain's poets. When G. K. Chesterton's wrote that 'The rolling English drunkard made the rolling English road' it was undoubtedly beer that Chesterton's drunkard had been imbibing.

Alcohol and lay ritual

There are examples of alcohol being given a magical meaning in lay or ordinary social ritual. In *The Golden Bough*, the anthropologist Sir James Frazer described an ancient Russian custom which by present-day societies is, however, likely to be viewed as not quite ordinary. It was believed that if the corpse of a man who had died of drink could be dug up and dropped into a bog, the rains could be made to come. One must assume that with the arrival of vodka in that part of the world there was no shortage of appropriate corpses to aid the working of this rain-making magic.

Far removed from the throwing of deceased inebriates into bogs are phrases such as 'wet the baby's head', indicating the appropriateness of adult drinking to welcome a child at its christening; the decanter of port at a formal dinner being passed ritually clockwise and the sense of harm done if this rule is broken; the 'stirrup cup' or in Scotland the 'deoch an doris' or drink at the door on departure; the loving cup passed around at a feast as one man drank and the other guarded his back against dagger or sword; the requirement at an Oxford college, to drink a sconce, a quart tankard of beer, as a penalty for any offence to male etiquette such as the mention of a lady's name; drinking in rounds to establish the mutuality of the drinking group; the traditional gift to the workmen of a keg of beer when a building is topped out; the boy buying the girl a drink as a symbol of his mastery, while the modern woman buys her own drink as a statement of her emancipation.

And with 'To your health!' we have the most everyday and pervasive example of a drinking ritual with a whiff of magic. By raising our glasses to each other and speaking an incantation such as 'Cheers!' 'Chin chin', 'Down the hatch!', 'Bottoms up!' or, in British fox-hunting circles, 'Here's mud in your eye!', we do each other transient magical good. The necessity of alcohol for this ritual is a widespread and ancient assumption. Thus Edward Spenser (otherwise known as Nathaniel

Gubbins), writing in 1899: 'Do we express our unfeigned joy and thankfulness for having a great and good Queen to reign over us by toasting her in flat soda water? Forbid the deed!' Flat soda water has no lay magic in it and is never likely to be transubstantiated.

Dark myths also

As well as being frequently mythologized for its virtues, drink has also often been pictured as evil incamate. The illustrations to temperance tracts frequently made allegorical use of devils with spiked tails who might be seen shovelling drunkards into the everlasting bonfire. One particularly poignant dark myth which haunted popular imagination in the nineteenth century was that of spontaneous combustion.

Thus Dickens's *Bleak House*. In the vicinity of Chancery Lane, Mr Tony Weevle and Mr William Guppy sit in a back room hatching a rascally plot. The landlord of the premises is a Mr Krook. He is downstairs drinking himself blind drunk, and he's been at the bottle all day. Mr Weevle has an assignation to pick up a bundle of letters from Mr Krook at midnight, and that material is of great interest to the nefarious Guppy. As St Paul's strikes midnight, Mr Weevle is on his way downstairs. Ghastliness awaits him:

I couldn't make him hear, and softly opened the door and looked in. And the burning smell is there – and the soot is there and the oil is there – and he is not there!

On the floor, a cinder with white ashes is all that remains of the erstwhile drunkard. Spontaneous combustion has struck!

Bleak House was published as a magazine serial in 1852–3. Dickens's principal authority for the tale of Mr Krook's sad fate was an article by Pierre-Aimé Lair which had appeared in the *Journal de physique* in 1800 and which had later been printed in English translation. To give a flavour of that article, let's reproduce a couple of its reported cases – first, that of a certain Grace Pitt.

Grace Pitt, the wife of a fishmonger in the parish of St Clement, Ipswich, aged about sixty, had contracted a habit . . . of coming down every night from her bedroom, half dressed, to smoke a pipe. On the night of 9th of April 1744, she got up from her bed as usual. Her daughter, who slept with her, did not perceive she was absent till next morning . . . and going down into the kitchen found her mother stretched out . . . having the appearance of a log of wood consumed by a fire but without apparent flame . . . This woman, it is said, had drunk a large quantity of spirituous liquors in consequence of being overjoyed to hear that one of her daughters had returned from Gibraltar. There was no fire in the grate, and the candle had burnt entirely out . . .

And here from the same text is an account of a French woman combusted:

'Having,' says Le Cat, 'spent several months at Rheims, in the years 1724 and 1725, I lodged at the house of Sieur Millet, whose wife got intoxicated every day. The domestic economy of the family was managed by a pretty young girl . . . This woman (Madame Millet) was found consumed on the 20th of February, 1725, at the distance of a foot and a-half from the hearth of her kitchen . . . Jean Millet, the husband, being interrogated by the judges who instituted the inquiry into the affair, declared, that about eight in the evening, on the 9th February, he had retired to rest with his wife, who not being able to sleep, went into the kitchen, where he thought she was warming herself; that, having fallen asleep, he was awakened about two o'clock by an infectious odour, and that, having run to the kitchen, he found the remains of his wife . . . It was very unfortunate for Millet that he had a handsome servant-maid, for neither his probity nor innocence were able to save him from the suspicion of having got rid of his wife by a concerted plot . . .'

A text entitled *The Anatomy of Drunkenness* would also have been available to Dickens. The author of this book was a Glaswegian doctor, Robert Macnish, and he devoted a chapter to discussion of 'The Spontaneous Combustion of Drunkards'. The condition was said to be commoner among women than men, and was more likely to happen in winter than in summer. With a ghoulish eye for detail, it was noted that 'The body and viscera are invariably burnt, while the feet, the hands, and the top of the skull almost always escape combustion.' Strangely, although the body would be consumed, usually nothing else in the immediate surroundings would be ignited. And – wonder piled upon wonder! – 'Water, so far from extinguishing the flame, seems to give it more activity . . .'

Having reviewed the published evidence in minute detail, Macnish's conclusion was affirmative – spontaneous combustion happened.

As a postscript to the main issue, he also examined the related claim that a drunkard who belched out a gush of heavily spirit-laden breath might sometimes suffer a similarly fiery and horrid fate.

Inflammable eructations are said to occur occasionally in northern latitudes, when the body has been exposed to intense cold after excessive indulgence in spirituous liquors; and the case of a Bohemian peasant is narrated, who lost his life in consequence of a column of ignited inflammable air issuing from his mouth and baffling extinction.

But Macnish was less inclined to an affirmative verdict on this variant of the spontaneous-combustion story:

There is one thing that may be safely denied; and that is the fact of drunkards having been blown up in consequence of their breath or eructation's catching fire from the application of a lighted candle. Those tales are principally of American extraction; and seem elaborated by that propensity for the marvellous for which our transatlantic brethren have, of late years, been distinguished.

Given the mind-boggling wonders that the European literature offered on spontaneous combustion and which Macnish found credible, it is difficult to see why he stigmatized the Americans for their credulity when it came to the idea of a drunkard's breath catching fire.

Despite Mr Krook and Dickens's best efforts, by the latter part of the nineteenth century spontaneous combustion had largely faded from public and professional consciousness. In the present day if the idea occasionally resurfaces it is for a mention in the kind of book which otherwise deals with the Loch Ness Monster, UFOs and little green men. Grace Pitt probably set herself on fire with her pipe; maybe Monsieur Millet got away with murder; no belching Bohemian peasant ever turned into a human blowlamp. And Mr Krook's sad fate was simply the invention of a master storyteller who knew how to feed his audience's taste for the wonderful and shocking.

So how did that curious idea of spontaneous combustion ever get about, and gain its once considerable scientific acceptance? A highly relevant fact which has become evident with modern research is that excessive drinking is frequently a contributory factor in deaths caused by accidental fires. American research shows that in 47 per cent of accidental deaths by fire which occur in the home the victim is intoxicated at the time. The typical scenario is of a cigarette dropped or some other minor act of carelessness while the person is in a drunken stupor. As with Mr Krook, the drinker is frequently living alone, and when the sofa begins to burn there is no one around to take sensible action. Death may occur when a fire escalates to a devastating conflagration or when fumes kill the stuporous drinker. And the end result these days is likely to be a sad column inch in the local newspaper, with no talk of a strange happening.

Stories of spontaneous combustion thus usually had a tragic reality on which to build, and especially so in an age of open fires and candles. There is perhaps a clue here in the fact that winter was deemed to be the dangerous time of year. But whatever the rootedness of the story in the realities of a still all too familiar type of accident, the fact is that a myth was woven around these realities. Myth, properly understood, is of course not a lie but a symbolic statement with a potent inner meaning. It would be a cheapening of the true meaning of myth ever to equate its deep storytelling with silly-season journalism. What we are being invited to see here is the drunkard (especially the woman drunkard) being mythically punished by a spontaneous, personalized, do-it-yourself, hellfire.

Drinking places

Drinking places are as much woven into culture as is drink itself, and the British, or more specifically the English, pub is often portrayed as a treasured national asset and the envy of other nations. Its origins go back to the wooden huts of the Saxon period, which, according to H. A. Monckton, a historian of the English public house, 'were identified by the traditional long pole which had an evergreen bush hanging from it if the establishment sold wine in addition to ale . . . The pole and bush . . . were almost certainly adopted from the Romans.' Alehouses came to be so common that King Edgar (944–75) decided that there were too many of them and ordered their numbers to be cut to one for each village. The alehouse or tavern evolved into the inn, a place which would give board and lodging to the traveller as well as supplying drink. Chaucer's pilgrims set out for Canterbury from the Tabard inn in Southwark, and from then on the cultural importance of drinking places has been cause for frequent mention in English literature.

Monckton offered the following idealized picture of the English inn from William Harrison's Description of England, which was published towards the end of the sixteenth century:

. . . there is no place in the world where passengers may so freely command as in the English Inns and are attended for themselves and their horses as well as if they were at home . . . the world affords not such inns as England has . . . As soon as a passenger comes to an inn the servants run to him and one takes his horse and walks him until he be cold. Another servant takes the chamber and kindles his fire, the third pulls off his boots and makes them clean . . . his meal will cost him sixpence or in some places only four pence (yet this course is less honourable and not used by gentlemen) . . . While he eats, if he has company especially, he shall be offered music, which he may freely take or refuse . . . at parting if he gave some few pence to the Chamberlain and Ostler they wish him a happy journey.

That image of the inn, or later of the pub, as something especially English and a place of intimate hospitality and genial friendship can be traced over the centuries with many variations. Thus Dr Samuel Johnson opined in 1776, 'There is nothing which has yet been contrived by man, by which so much happiness is produced as by a good tavern or inn.' But, for just as long, drinking places have also been stigmatized as dens of debauchery, with condemnatory views on the wickedness of drink being projected on to the locales where the drinking was done. For the nineteenth-century temperance campaigner the public house was a corrupting social evil, and the saloon was similarly decried in America. Whatever the symbolic extremes of the drinking place as quintessential warmth by the fire or alternatively as a latter-day Sodom, the fact remains that such places are products of national culture, and often help make and maintain that culture.

The late-twentieth-century pub, with its children's area, live music, electronic gaming machines, cable television, absence of any division between snug and saloon and public bar, fake horse brasses, and cannabis dealing going on in one corner, is a place which speaks to its era as much as did the Tabard. What actually happens in these institutions and the varieties of social functions which may be associated with them has seldom been objectively studied. One intriguing analysis of what may go on in the bar besides the drinking is, however, to be found in *The Pub and the People*, a book put together in 1943 by Mass Observation, an organization which in its time was a pioneer in presenting a fine-grained study of contemporary society. The book showed the pub as an institution to be comprehended in terms of multiple functions and symbolisms, rather than just as a space where alcohol was sold and consumed. Here are a few examples of what Mass Observation discovered when its pencil-scribbling observers looked at, sat around in and drank at some of the 300 or so pubs of 'Worktown', a North Country British textile-manufacturing town of 180,000 people. The advertising hoardings in the streets of Worktown were at that time proclaiming the unequivocal message that 'Beer is Best.'

These are the things that people do in pubs:

                    SIT and/or STAND
                       DRINK

               TALK   about betting
                              sport
               THINK   work
               SMOKE   people
                              drinking
               SPIT   weather
                              politics
                              dirt

Many PLAY GAMES
                    cards
                    dominoes
                    darts
                    quoits

Many BET

        receive and

        pay out losings and winnings.

PEOPLE SING AND LISTEN TO SINGING: PLAY THE PIANO AND LISTEN
                TO IT BEING PLAYED

      THESE THINGS ARE OFTEN CONNECTED WITH PUBS. . .

    . . . weddings and funerals.

        quarrels and fights.

        bowls, fishing and picnics.

        trade unions.

        secret societies. Oddfellows. Buffs.

        religious processions.

        sex.

        getting jobs.

        crime and prostitution.

        dog shows.

        pigeon flying.

PEOPLE SELL AND BUY

        bootlaces, hot pies, black puddings, embrocation.

Also

        LOTTERIES AND SWEEPSTAKES happen.

        PREJUDICES gather.

  All these things don't happen on the same evenings, or in the same pubs.
But an ordinary evening in an ordinary pub will contain a lot of them.

The molecule transformed

The opening chapter in this book might be seen as a voyage around a
molecule, with the commentary coming from the laboratory sciences.
In the present chapter the journey has been around alcohol as transformed by religion and popular culture. Beer is water, ethanol and a
good deal of 'dirt', but, in an eleventh century poem, St Bridget, an
Irish saint, pictured paradise as a lake of beer with the heavenly family
sipping at it through all eternity.

3 A Short History of Drunkenness

The previous chapter looked at how societies manufacture images of drink. This chapter explores the related but different question of how society has over the centuries responded to the fact of drunkenness. Different countries have had very different histories in this regard. Here we will focus on drunkenness as played out in Britain. That national experience has within it strands which to a greater or lesser degree have also been common in other countries. But in important ways every nation's history of drunkenness is unique.

Drunkenness has been familiar for as long as there has been alcohol for men and women to drink. Rome, Greece and other ancient civilizations all knew and disapproved of inebriety. Famously, Noah was a drunkard. There are a multiplicity of terms which have been used to describe states and shades of inebriety in different languages. Here are a few which at one time or another have entered common English usage: squiffy, tight, sozzled, merry, well oiled, pissed as a newt, paralytic, cut, tipsy, mellow, under the influence, boozed, canned, ploughed, smashed, plastered, pie-eyed, stinko, blotto. The pleasing but now defunct 'gone a peg too low' derived from King Edgar's tenth-century ordinance that drinking vessels should be marked out with pegs. Quite a few of the nineteenth-century synonyms were of nautical origin: four sheets to the wind, main brace well spliced, half-seas-over. Here are some entries from a list compiled by an American author (G. E. Partridge) in 1912: back teeth afloat, been hit by a barn mouse, been lapping the gutter, can't say 'National Intelligence', can't see a hole in a ladder, drunk as a boiled owl, drunk as a brewer's horse, flag of defiance out, fogmatic, gutter-legged, holding up the lamp-post, seeing two moons, smelling of the cork, snakes in the boots.

Whatever the country or century, what characterizes many of the popular synonyms for drunkenness is a sense of the spectators' amusement, of the condition being downplayed or made into a joke, and met with teasing forgiveness rather than condemnation. But if the folk language has tended to take this cosy view of the problem, disapprobation of excessive drinking also has been around for a long time. The man in the street may always have joked about the drunk, but the Church's reactions have born witness to a view of drunkenness as no laughing matter.

The sin of drunkenness

A scholarly account of the Church's stance on alcohol in England, Scotland and Ireland from the sixth to the sixteenth century can be found in *The Discipline of Drink*, a book published in 1876 by the Revd R. E. Bridgett, a Catholic priest. He provided considerable evidence of the Church's concern over drunkenness, both within and outside its own ranks.

Thus the seventh-century Irish priest St Cummian of Fota promulgated an influential penitentiary – a book recommending due levels of penance for different sins – which for many centuries was widely used in Europe. Cummian proposed the following graded levels of sanction directed at the drinker:

If a bishop or any one ordained has a habit of drunkenness, he must either resign or be deposed.

If a monk drinks till he vomits, he must do thirty days' penance; if a priest or deacon, forty days. But if this happens from weakness of stomach, or from long abstinence, and he was not in the habit of excessive drinking or eating, or if he did it in excess of joy on Christmas or on Easter Days, or the commemoration of some saint, and if then he did not take more than has been regulated by our predecessors, he is not to be punished . . .

If a Christian layman vomits through drunkenness, let him do fifteen days' penance. If a priest gets drunk through inadvertence he must do penance seven days; if through carelessness, fifteen days; a deacon or monk, four weeks, a sub-deacon, three, a layman, one week.

He who compels another to get drunk out of evil hospitality must do penance as if he himself had been drunk; if he did it out of hate he must be judged as a homicide.

St Cummian's penitentiary is remarkable for the evidence it provides that, even all those centuries ago, the Church authorities saw it as necessary to respond to drunkenness as a significant problem among both clergy and laity. This penitentiary is also noteworthy for the subtlety of its discrimination. Punishment was by rank within the Church, and was less for a lay person than for a clergyman. And drunkenness was to be judged the more culpable the more it was self-willed. It may be doubted whether modern legislation on drink or drug problems has ever achieved the sophistication of St Cummian's tariff of penances.

Here is Boniface, a Christian missionary of the eighth century, declaiming against drunkenness in Saxon England, in a letter he wrote to Cuthbert, Archbishop of Canterbury:

It is reported that in your dioceses the vice of drunkenness is too frequent; so that not only certain bishops do not hinder it, but they themselves indulge in excess of drink and force others to drink till they are intoxicated. This is most certainly a great crime for a servant of God to do or to have done . . . This is an evil peculiar to pagans and to our race. Neither the Franks, nor the Gauls, nor the Lombards, nor the Romans, nor the Greeks commit it.

The Danes when they arrived in Britain were famously given to heavy celebratory drinking, and when converted to Christianity they took to copiously toasting the saints in substitute for their heathen gods. The Normans looked askance at the drunkenness which they found to be prevalent in England, and it has been suggested that King Harold lost the Battle of Hastings because, when it came to the engagement, his troops were still drunk from the previous night. In its turn, the consumption of wine by Norman knights who engaged in the crusades attracted comment. Here, however, is evidence to show that the saintly Bishop Wulstan could keep his mind on heavenly matters even in difficult circumstances:

In the time of William the Conqueror, he was obliged to maintain a large retinue of men-at-arms, since the Danes were daily expected. He would not dine in private, but sat down in his public hall with his boisterous soldiers; and while they sat drinking for hours together, according to the English fashion, he would keep them company to restrain them by his presence, pledging them when it came to his turn in a tiny cup, which he pretended to taste and in the midst of the din ruminating to himself on the psalms.

Often during those early centuries, the drunkenness which attracted most comment was that associated with public or courtly feastings. These were occasions for large-scale drunkenness, with the ever-present fear of a dagger being drawn. In the thirteenth and fourteenth centuries there are also references to ecclesiastical concern over the excessive drinking which had become a feature of various aspects of ordinary life. A custom which attracted particular criticism was the institution of so-called 'scot-ales'. These seem to have been communal bacchanalias or early versions of a bottle party. In this context the word 'scot' meant 'payment'. A scot-ale was thus a drinking party where people came together at a pre-viously agreed location and paid for their drink when they got there. Scandal occurred when clergy were found to be in the habit of announcing, in church, the time and place of the next scot-ale. Giles of Bridport, Bishop of Salisbury, issued a decree against scot-ales in 1253:

By this synodal approbation we confirm the prohibition of Scot-ales, which has been made for the good both of souls and bodies; and in virtue of obedience we commend rectors, vicars, and other parochial priests, that by frequent exhortations they earnestly induce their parishioners not rashly to violate this prohibition. Should any do so, let them be denounced as interdicted from entering the church or receiving the sacraments . . .

Other types of folk event which attracted concern included bid-ales and help-ales, where someone would try to repair their finances by setting up a pay-when-you-come drinking party. There was also an event called a bride-ale. The clergy from time to time expressed concern about the many excuses for mass drunkenness which were provided by saints' days, and there was repeated anxiety about the carousing which became an expected part of wakes and funerals, as illustrated in the following pronouncement by John Thoresby, Archbishop of York, dating from 1367:

In vigils, men come together in the churches and at funerals, as if to pray, and then turning to a reprobate sense, they indulge in games, and vanities, and even worse by which they greatly offend God and the saints . . . and they make the house of mourning at funerals a house of laughter and excess, to the great ruin of their souls.

These Church records are interesting not only because they show the steady century-by-century efforts made by the Church to curb drunkenness by exhortation and penalty, but also for the insights which are provided into the ways in which convivial drinking and the accompanying drunkenness were integral to many aspects of communal life. But, although the Christian Church was anxious about drunkenness over this long period, it never got anywhere near the prohibition instituted by Islam. After the many hours of fasting and prayer which would have followed his early morning rise from bed, every monk would in those days have expected his tankard of ale to be on the refectory table at 10 a.m.

In the Middle Ages the Church relaxed its system of penances, and in the 1500s the Reformation weakened Church influence on ordinary life. In 1552 public drunkenness for the first time became an offence under the civil law, with punishment by the stocks rather than by penance. From then on its history is traced not by penitentiaries or synods, but by Acts of Parliament and the observations of laymen who wrote about the drinking which they saw going on around them.

What were people drinking?

At this point let's note the kinds of beverage which enjoyed popularity in Britain as time went by. Ale was for many centuries the basic household drink, the stuff of ordinary celebrations, the drink consumed in quantity at great feastings, the drink equally of town and country. Beer differed from ale in that hops had been added to give flavour and as a preservative. In England, this practice was probably introduced in the fifteenth century. Rather earlier than is often realized today, wine made some entry. Imported wine was a favoured drink among the Saxon nobles. It was, however, the British presence in France during the thirteenth century that made French wine increasingly available in England. Froissart, in 1372, described British ships crowding into Bordeaux – 'a fleet of not less than two hundred sail of merchantmen coming for wines' (a precursor, perhaps, of the more recent British penchant for Beaujolais Nouveau). Wine was from then on part of British drinking, but until comparatively recently only a minor element compared to the traditional major dedication to ale or beer.

As for the significance of spirits within the drinking story of the British Isles, a great deal of distilling of spirits was going on in Ireland in the sixteenth century. An Act of the Irish parliament of 1556 tried to curb the manufacture of aqua vitae by introducing a system of licensing. The preamble to this Act indicates the level of official concern:

Forasmuch as aqua vitae, *a drink nothing profitable to be daily drunken and used*, is now universally throughout the realm made, and thereby much corn, grain, and other things consumed, spent and wasted, to the great hindrance, cost and damage of the poor inhabitants of this realm . . .

Despite attempts at legislative control, both in Ireland and Scotland there was from the 1500s onwards an industry dedicated to the illicit production of spirits. Irish settlers brought the art of distilling over to England. But any serious threat to public health posed by spirits lay dormant for a further century.

Drunken high jinks

In the Elizabethan period, drunkenness received adverse notice from various commentators. For Sir Walter Ralegh, drunkenness was a problem because of the potential fixity of the habit – an observation which was much ahead of its time and came close to identification of alcohol as a drug of dependence.

Take special care that thou delight not in wine, for there was not any man that came to honour or preferment who loved it; for it transformeth a man into a beast, destroyeth natural heat, deformeth the face, rotteneth the teeth, and to conclude, maketh a man contemptible, soon old, and despised of all wise and worthy men, hated in thy servants, in thyself and companions . . . it is a bewitching and infectious vice. A drunkard will never shake off the delight of beastliness; for the longer it possesses a man, the more he will delight in it; and the older he groweth, the more he will be subject to it; for it dulleth the spirits, and destroyeth the body, as ivy doth the old tree; or as the worm that engendereth in the kernel of a nut. Take heed, therefore, that such a cureless canker possess not thy youth, nor such a beastly infection thy old age; for then shall all thy life be but as the life of a beast, and after thy death, shalt only leave a shameful infamy to thy posterity, who shall study to forget that such a one was their father.

There are also many references to be found in Stuart times to the evils of drunkenness. Charles I, however, was famed for his sobriety, as shown in this passage from the historian Clarendon:

As he [the King] excelled in all other virtues, so in temperance he was so strict, that he abhorred all debauchery to that degree, that at a great festival, where he once was, being told by one who withdrew from thence, what vast draughts of wine they drank, and that there was one early who had drunk most of the rest down, and was not himself moved or altered, the king said that he deserved to be hanged.

The seventeenth century saw the introduction to Britain of coffee (1650), chocolate (1657) and tea (1660). These dates can only be approximate, but by the end of the century such beverages were widely available and coffee houses had become a feature of London life. Whether these non-alcoholic drinks to any extent substituted for alcohol is uncertain.

A peculiar and most unwelcome hazard attaching to drunkenness was recorded by John Evelyn in his diary for 18 March 1669:

I went with my L: Howard of Norfolke to visite Sir William Ducy at Charleton, where we dined: The servants made our Coach-men so drunk, that they both fell-off their boxes upon the heath, where we were faine to leave them, & were droven to Lond: by two Gent: of my Lords: This barbarous Costome of making their Masters Wellcome, by intoxicating the Servants had now the second time happen'd to my Coachman.

There is a familiar element of shock-horror and 'Oh how awful!' about many of these stories of inebriated high-life bad behaviour. Here, for instance, as later recounted by Lord Macaulay in his *History of England*, is an account of the behaviour of the wit and dramatist Sir Charles Sedley when one night he got drunk with his cronies at the Cock Tavern in Bow Street:

The morals of Sedley were such as even in that age gave great scandal. He on one occasion, after a wild revel, exhibited himself without a shred of clothing in the balcony of a tavern near Covent Garden, and harangued the people who were passing in language so indecent and profane that he was driven in by a shower of brickbats, was prosecuted for a misdemeanour, was sentenced to a heavy fine, and was reprimanded by the Court of King's Bench in the most cutting terms.

Drunkenness was bad behaviour, and gross drunkenness execrably bad. And at the same time the Church – come queen or king or Lord Protector – kept steadily at the message that intoxication was not simply socially reprehensible but also, and more importantly, a sin in the eyes of God. In the following passage, William Beveridge, Bishop of St Asaph in the reign of Queen Anne, is delivering a sermon on 'The Duty of Temperance and Sobriety'. He declares drunkenness to be the father and mother of all sins:

There is no sin but some have committed it in their drink; and if there be any that a drunken man doth not commit, it is not because he would not, but because he could not. He had not an opportunity . . . For a man in such a condition hath no sense of the difference between good and evil; for 'wine' as the prophet speaks (Hos. iv. 11), 'hath taken away his heart'. His reason, his understanding, his conscience, is gone; and therefore, all sins are alike to him. Hence it is that their sin never goes alone, but hath a great train of other sins always following it, insomuch that it cannot so properly be called one single sin, as all sin in one.

Up to about the 1680s the stories which abounded on the subject of English drunkenness seem for the most part to deal with the high jinks of drunken peers, and drunkenness at Court, drunken Members of Parliament who refused to sit down, the excessive habit of toasting, the debauched behaviour of young men at the University of Oxford, the famous drinking of poets and playwrights, the drunkenness at feasts and every kind of celebration – and all this with recurrent discussion of whether the English or the Danes or the Flemish were the worst offenders.

A crucial transformation: alcohol becomes a public-health issue

Over the course of the centuries, many ordinary people must have got drunk without earning for themselves a place in the annals of history, or in the subsequent anthologies of shock and horror put together by Victorian clergymen and nineteenth-century temperance writers. It seems that, until the latter part of the 1600s, although drunkenness was often remarked upon, lamented and sermonized against, and undoubtedly affected all classes, it was not viewed as a problem particularly affecting the urban poor, or as a public-health issue.

Then something changed, and the prime agent of change was probably the sudden widespread availability in Britain of cheap gin. Permission to establish distilleries was first granted by Parliament in 1689, a year after the Glorious Revolution. A licence to set up a distillery could be obtained for a small fee, and at the same time the import of spirits from the Continent was banned. There followed various shifts in taxation and legislative control. An examination of the contemporary data gives a picture of a fluctuating but generally upward trend in gin consumption rather than the precipitate onset of any kind of epidemic. But the following quotation from William Lecky's *History of England in the Eighteenth Century* reflects the devastation which began to be wrought by gin around that time:

Small as is the place which this fact occupies in English history, it was probably, if we consider all the consequences that have flowed from it, the most momentous in that of the eighteenth century – incomparably more so than any event in the purely political or military annals of the country. The average of British spirits distilled, which is said to have been only 527,000 gallons in 1684, had risen in 1727 to 3,601,000. Physicians declared that in excessive gin-drinking a new and terrible source of mortality had been opened for the poor. The grand jury of Middlesex declared that much the greater part of the poverty, the murders, the robberies of London, might be traced to this single cause. Retailers of gin were accustomed to hang out painted boards, announcing that their customers could be made drunk for a penny, dead drunk for two-pence, and have straw for nothing; and cellars strewn with straw were accordingly provided, into which those who had become insensible were dragged, and where they remained till they had sufficiently recovered to renew their orgies.

By 1736 the situation had got so bad that the Grand Jury of Middlesex petitioned Parliament on the harm being done by gin, and a Committee of the House of Commons concluded:

That the low price of spirituous liquors is the principal inducement to the excessive and pernicious use thereof.

That in order to prevent this excessive and pernicious use, a discouragement be given thereto by duty to be laid on spirits sold by retail.

That the selling of such liquors be restricted to persons keeping public brandy-shops, victualling houses, coffee houses, ale-houses, innholders, and to such surgeons and apothecaries as shall make use of it by way of medicine only.

Parliament's intentions found immediate expression in the Gin Act of 1736. This imposed a licence fee of £50 on anyone wanting to engage in the retail sale of gin, together with a tax of £20 per gallon on the product. However, due to various types of evasion – including the sale of spirits under the guise of medicine – this Act failed abysmally in its intentions. By 1742 the sale of spirits had increased to nearly 20 million gallons per year.

In the eyes of many observers, at this period it was still drunkenness that was the central social problem caused by the drink. Blasphemy, rowdiness, insolence, impropriety, ill health, violence and murder were among the frequently decried consequences of intoxication. But at this juncture a very novel entry was added to the previous and age-old list of alcohol-related concerns. Physicians' noting that a 'new and terrible source of mortality had been opened for the poor' marked a crucial transition in public assessment of what was problematic about drink. The urban poor and slum drinking on a large scale had become part of the drink problem, and a threat to the health of the people, in a way never remarked on before. Alcohol had become, in the modern term, a public-health issue.

A picture of the streets

Recently some historians have suggested that the adverse consequences of eighteenth-century gin drinking may at the time have been exaggerated and coloured by an element of moral panic. However, neither the data on gin production nor the many contemporary eyewitness accounts of the sight of London's streets give support to that kind of revisionism. Here is a description of the contemporary scene as given by Lord Lonsdale in a speech made during a House of Lords debate in 1743:

In every part of this great metropolis, whoever shall pass along the streets, will find wretchedness stretched upon the pavement, insensible and motionless, and only removed by the charity of passengers from the danger of being crushed by carriages or trampled by horses, or strangled with filth in the common sewers; and others, less helpless perhaps, but more dangerous, who have drunk too much to fear punishment, but not enough to hinder them from provoking it . . . No man can pass a single hour in public places without meeting such objects, or hearing such expressions as disgrace human nature, – such as cannot be looked upon without horror, or heard without indignation, and which there is no possibility of removing or preventing, whilst this hateful liquor is publicly sold . . . These liquors not only infatuate the mind, but poison the body, they not only fill our streets with madmen and our prisons with criminals, but our hospitals with cripples . . . Nor does the use of spirits, my lords, only impoverish the public by lessening the number of useful and laborious hands, but by cutting off those recruits by which its natural and inevitable losses are to be supplied. The use of distilled liquors impairs the fecundity of the human race, and hinders that increase which Providence has ordained for the support of the world. These women who riot in this poisonous debauchery are quickly disabled from bearing children, or, what is still more destructive to general happiness, produce children diseased from their birth, and who, therefore, are an additional burden, and must be supported through a miserable life by that labour which they cannot share, and must be protected by that community of which they cannot contribute to the defence.

In that passage we can again see that public concern over the drink problem extended far the previous list of prime alcohol-related worries – the profanity associated with drunkenness was still a problem, but now also appeared concern over the multiple types of public expense that drunkenness was causing through hospital costs and loss of the labour force. Debauched women made their appearance, drinking had become a threat to the family, and there was anxiety about what would later be termed national degeneration. Thus the scene was set for the type of discourse about drunkenness which would shape debate and reformist activity throughout the nineteenth century. It was not only the rhetoric that had changed: drunkenness had become objectively a large-scale national problem, and was to be a fixed part of the unaccept-able face of the Industrial Revolution.

Gin remained a popular drink, but by the middle of the eighteenth century the level of gin drinking had been reduced. Following further legislation in 1743 and 1751, annual consumption of spirits was reported by 1760 to be down to about 4 million gallons. In the nineteenth century, the level of spirit drinking again went steeply upwards, to higher peaks than ever previously attained, and in 1828 over 28 million gallons were consumed – a significant per-capita increase even allowing for population growth. But over the same period the consumption of beer declined.

James Silk Buckingham and a radical report

In 1834 a select committee of Parliament reported on 'the problem of drunkenness among the labouring poor'. The chairman of this group was James Silk Buckingham, MP for Sheffield, and a radical who had earlier been involved in the anti-slavery movement. The committee was appointed on 3 June 1834, interviewed fifty witnesses between 9 June and 28 July, and with extraordinary dispatch presented its report on 5 August of that same year. Given Buckingham's previous involvement in petitioning against spirits and his generally maverick reputation, the charge made at the time that his report was biased against drink is probably to some extent fair. Nonetheless, the report remains remark-able for the evidence of its witnesses, the analysis it provided of drunkenness as a social problem, and the range of practical remedies which it proposed.

A central argument of Buckingham's committee was that drunkenness had at that time evolved into being a problem very particularly of the labouring poor. It would take historical analysis of a kind which has not so far been attempted to determine the degree to which that view can be supported objectively. But, fact or fantasy or mixture of the two, the committee's report used precisely that class-based rhetoric of drunkenness which we saw emerging in the 1700s:

It appears to your Committee, from the evidence taken before them, that the vice of intoxication has been for some years past on the decline in the higher and middle ranks of society; but has increased within the same period among the labouring classes and exists at present to a very great extent in the population of England, Scotland, and Ireland, and in the seaport and manufacturing towns as well as in the agricultural districts, including in its victims men, women, and even children.

As an example of the vivid reportage contained in this document, here is a snapshot which it offered of London in 1834:

During this time a woman almost in a state of nudity, with a fine infant at her breast, the only dress being its nightshirt, followed by another child about eight years old, naked except a nightshift, and without either shoes or stockings, followed a wretched-looking man into the house. I saw them struggling through the crowd to get to the bar; they all had their gin; the infant had the first share from the woman's glass; they came back to the outside of the door, and there they could scarcely stand; the man and woman appeared to quarrel; the little child in her arms cried, and the wretched woman beat it most unmercifully; the other little naked child ran across the road; the woman called to it to come back; it came back and she beat it; they all went into the shop again, and had some more gin, apparently to pacify the children.

And here is a Sunday-morning pavement scene of July 1834:

Last Sunday morning I had occasion to walk through the Broadway at a few minutes before eleven o'clock; I found the pavement before every gin-shop crowded; just as church time approached, the gin-shops sent forth their multitudes, swearing and fighting and bawling obscenely; some were stretched on the pavement insensibly drunk, while every few steps the footway was taken up by drunken wretches being dragged to the station-house by the police.

The report deployed these and other eyewitness accounts to build up a stark picture of drunkenness as a social evil which was wrecking the lives of poor people on a scale which is today scarcely imaginable. The persistent images were of the gin palace, seethingness and crowds, bodies on pavements, violence, the shame of women and hurt to children, as well as men brought down. That thick report is today little read, but its images still have the power to conjure up long-gone scenes with a great sense of immediacy.

The suggested list of actions which the report proposed to counter poverty drunkenness was remarkable for the close understanding displayed of the lives of the urban poor. Rather than any retreat to moralizing, what Buckingham's committee offered was a set of achievable action points. For instance, the number of public houses was to be limited, with licences granted by magistrates to be forfeited if there was evidence of repeated disorderly conduct; opening hours were to be restricted; 'the entire separation . . . of the retail sale of spirits from groceries, provisions, wine or beer' was demanded. 'The discontinuance of all issues of ardent spirits to the navy and army' was proposed. A recommendation was made that the practice should be prohibited of paying the wages of workmen at public houses or other places where intoxicating drinks were sold. Wages were to be paid at or before the breakfast hour, so that the wife could go shopping before the husband squandered the week's money. The duties on tea, coffee and sugar were to be reduced. Emphasis was also placed on the need to produce alternative attractions to compete with the pub, through:

The establishment, by the joint aid of Government and the local authorities and residents on the spot, of public walks and gardens, or open spaces for athletic and healthy exercises in the open air, in the immediate vicinity of every town, to an extent and character adapted to its population; and of district and parish libraries, museums, and reading-rooms, accessible at the lowest rate of charge, so as to admit of one or other being visited in any weather and at any time; with the rigid exclusion of all intoxicating drinks of every kind from all such places, whether in the open air or closed.

Finally, under Buckingham's list of 'immediate remedies', there was a call for public education:

A national system of education . . . should embrace as an essential part of the instruction given by it to every child in the kingdom accurate information as to the poisonous and invariably deleterious nature of ardent spirits, as an article of diet, in any form or shape.

The list of proposed actions constituted in totality an enormously broad public-health agenda, and the rootedness of these proposals in down-to-earth social reality is again what particularly deserves note. The committee knew and understood the landscape of contemporary urban working life in every detail. The almost exclusive focus on spirit drinking may today appear curious, but it was still at that time spirits which were viewed by reformers as the dominant evil.

What also should be noted is that there were no medical doctors on Buckingham's committee. There was no talk of drunkenness as a disease, and the remedial measures which were proposed had nothing to say about treatment. If the drinker went insane, there was a sad journey's end for him or her in the lunatic asylum. Many drunkards were going to be imprisoned. But no one at that time was suggesting that the social evil of drunkenness could be treated out of society.

Gin as the Lethe of the miserable

Some of Buckingham's recommendations were implemented, but the problem of drunkenness among the poor remained for nineteenth-century Britain as much an intrinsic part of the urban landscape as the factory chimneys and the pea-soup fogs. Drunkenness was also often a feature of the privileged dining rooms and the gentlemen's clubs, but it was as an inextricable concomitant of urban squalor that it most marked and shamed that century. Here is William Booth, founder of the Salvation Army, writing on drink as a social problem in 1890:

I will take the question of the drunkard, for the drink difficulty lies at the root of everything. Nine-tenths of our poverty, squalor, vice and crime spring from this poisonous tap-root. Many of our social evils, which overshadow the land like so many upas trees, would dwindle away and die if they were not constantly watered with strong drink.

And with Booth too there was an insistence that urban drunkenness had to be understood within the total context of working-class life:

Mere lectures against the evil habit are, however, of no avail. We have to recognise, that the gin-palace, like many other evils, although a poisonous, is still a natural outgrowth of our social conditions. The tap-room in many cases is the poor man's only parlour . . . let us never forget that the temptation to drink is strongest when want is sharpest and misery the most acute. A well-fed man is not driven to drink by the craving that torments the hungry; and the comfortable do not crave for the boon of forgetfulness. Gin is the only Lethe of the miserable.

Lethe was in classical mythology a river which flowed through Hades and whose waters produced forgetfulness of the past.

The problem fades

But even as Booth wrote these words it seems probable that drunkenness as a side effect of poverty and social deprivation had begun to pass its peak — the impact of the Industrial Revolution on urban life was at last beginning somewhat to ameliorate. Rates of arrest for public drunkenness can provide only an approximate indication of the extent of the kinds of drinking behaviour which had perplexed and horrified so many observers of the urban scene from the early eighteenth century onwards; nevertheless, in England and Wales the annual rate for drunkenness arrests, which stood at 85 per 10,000 population in 1875, had by 1890 fallen to 66, while in 1914 it was down to 53.

The First World War killed drunkenness as an issue of public concern, for many years to come. Stringent licensing, shortage of materials for brewing, men away at war, concern about the effect of civilian drinking on the output of armaments, poster campaigns which discouraged the treating of soldiers who were home on leave – all these meant a much different drinking landscape in 1914–18 than had been seen for the previous two hundred years. After the war there were still slums, but the strong connection between poverty and drinking appeared effectively to have been broken. In the 1920s the annual arrest rate per 10,000 for public drunkenness stood on average at a paltry 19. And as the realities of the streets changed so did the rhetoric, with drunkenness no longer being spoken of as the Lethe of the poor. By miraculous redefinition, the pub achieved that popular image of treasured national asset to which we referred in the previous chapter, and the drunk was as likely to be a toff as a working man and was in any case rather funny.

The long story of British drunkenness is of drunkenness always being more or less present as a fact of British life, but for many hundreds of years only as a facet of individual life or perhaps of group carousing – a matter for the most part of men behaving badly. Drunkenness was an individual sin, and the answer to such sinful behaviour was to exact penances and sermonize against it. Then, as we have seen, in the early eighteenth century drunkenness achieved new prominence as a mass event and in every sense a social one, and the remedies proposed became targeted at the social conditions rather than only at the individual drinker. Drunkenness was still the core problem, but the scale had vastly changed and there was an awareness of the extent and variety and huge scale of the health and social consequences which resulted from this behaviour.

That different people can behave in very different ways when intoxicated is a truth evident to any observer. A picture of the various common faces of drunkenness was given four hundred years ago by the Elizabethan writer Thomas Nashe (1567–1601), in his book *Pierce Penilesse*:

The first is Ape drunke, and leapes and sings, and hollowes, and daunceth for the heavens; the second is Lion drunke, and he flings the pots about the house, calls his Hostesse W—, breaks the glass windowes with his dagger, and is apt to quarrell with any man that speaks to him; the third is Swine drunke, heavy, lumpish and sleepie, and cries for a little more drinke, and a fewe more cloathes; the fourth is Sheepe drunke, wise in his own conceit, when he cannot bring forth a right word; the fifth is Mawdlen drunke, when a fellow will weepe for kindness in the midst of his Ale, and kise you, saying, 'By God, Captaine, I love thee, goe thy waies, thou dost not think so often of me as I do of thee. I would (if it pleased God) could I not love thee so well as I do', and then he puts his finger in his ere, and cries; the sixth is Martin drunke, when a man is drunke, and drinkes himself sober ere he stirre; the seventh is Goate drunke, when in his drunkenness he hath no mind but on lechery; the eighth is Foxe drunke, when he is craftie drunke, as many of the Dutch men bee who will never bargaine but when they are drunke.

There is no knowing what type of animal a person may turn into when drunk. In this chapter we will look at a range of conjectures which are commonly advanced in explanation of the varied and unpredictable effects of alcohol on individual conduct. We will start by looking at the idea that alcohol is intrinsically a chemical which can impact on the brain in such a way as to impair self-control and lead to a state of disinhibition. If this rather mechanical 'alcohol disinhibits the brain' formulation is often put forward as an explanation for why a bar-room stool is thrown some evening at closing time, a second theory, which also enjoys wide popular acceptance, is the notion that people when drunk tend to behave like themselves but more so – a psychological explanation in terms of the individual's specific underlying personality. That theory would suggest that the stool is thrown at someone's head because Jimmy is, as his friends will tell you without aid from a psychologist, an excitable and aggressive kind of fellow, who even when sober is apt to rear up at any small or imagined offence.

If the pharmacological and psychological explanations are those for which many people will readily reach, there will probably also be an acknowledgement that cues provided by the immediate environment can also shape what happens. Some kinds of rough, crowded and jostling bars or public houses are places which tangibly invite trouble at closing time. In other locales drunks are expected not to swing punches but to sing songs, laugh loudly and embrace on the pavement. A fourth theory proposes that drunken behaviour is shaped predominantly by the rules and expectations of the individual's culture: Jimmy when intoxicated is a working-class Glaswegian inebriate. And yet another explanation is that some forms of alcoholic drink – particularly spirits – are likely to be more disinhibiting than other kinds of drink: according to that theory, Jimmy might have been less likely to have caused a brawl if he had stayed with the beer and kept off the whisky chasers.

None of those theories on its own is likely to present a complete explanation of what happens in a particular pub on a Saturday night. To understand why one person when drunk throws a stool, another stands up and sings, and yet another tries to kiss the barmaid (with all the rest of Nashe's animal variations probably meanwhile being acted out in the background), we need to put those partial explanations together into a comprehensive whole. How that kind of synthesis is best accomplished is the question which will be addressed in the final section of this chapter.

Drunken behaviour explained as a
pharmacologically induced disinhibition

So to the first, and simplest, explanation: it is the alcohol per se that makes beasts of people. This theory finds its most succinct expression in an old medical-school adage that the moral conscience is that part of the human mental apparatus which is most readily soluble in alcohol. More formal statements within this tradition all make use in one way or another of the neurological concept of 'higher centres' – those parts of the brain which are of later evolutionary origin and which, for instance, mediate self-control. With intoxication, there is the supposed removal of decent civilizing restraint when those centres are anaesthetized by alcohol and the more primitive parts of the brain are then allowed to take over control of behaviour. Often there seems to be more of metaphor than of brain science in this kind of theory.

For endorsement of the theory that alcohol is a chemical which suppresses moral control and releases base and bestial instincts, it would probably be necessary only to consult the nearest policeman. Drinking is implicated in a large percentage of the violent and sexual offences which come before the courts. The penal statistics from many countries suggest that alcohol is involved in 40–50 per cent of murders.

The truth of the matter, however, is that drinking does not at all inevitably or reflexly lead to violent or antisocial behaviour. Drink and drunkenness take different people in different ways, which is exactly what Nashe was insisting on four hundred years ago. Furthermore, and as we will see from evidence presented later in this chapter, different cultures can generate markedly different kinds of drunk. For these and other reasons the seemingly common-sense idea that alcohol is a drug which acts on the brain to dissolve moral conscience has fallen progressively into scientific disfavour. It is too simple by half.

Very recently the brain sciences seem, however, to have breathed new life into the disinhibition theory. Research is beginning to suggest that alcohol releases into the brain a chemical called GABA (gama-amino butyric acid), which can inhibit normally experienced perceptions of external threat. The result may be that the intoxicated drinker becomes buffered against the reactions of the people in his or her surroundings and insulated against the signs of mounting disapproval. At the same time release of another brain chemical, dopamine, may increase the drinker's brain arousal and activity. The combination of decreased sensitivity to other people's responses and increased arousal may be bad news in a crowded bar.

Drunkenness and temperament

Another explanation for the extraordinary diversity in alcohol's effect on human behaviour has for long been that drunkenness is coloured by the individual's temperament. Intoxication is seen as a state in which the drinker reveals his or her real self. Here is an exposition of that kind of theory as given by Dr Thomas Trotter in his 1804 *Essay . . . on Drunkenness*:

The sanguineous and choleric temperaments, I conceive to be the most prone to resentment and ferocity; as may be observed in those whose whole countenance becomes very much flushed or bloated, with their eyes as if starting from their sockets: the former of the two is the most lascivious and amorous. The nervous temperament exhibits most signs of idiotism, and is childish and foolish in its drunken pranks. The phlegmatic temperament is difficult to be roused; is passive and silent, and may fall from the chair before many external signs of inebriety appear. The melancholic temperament . . . shows least of the inebriate in its manner.

Most people would today accept Trotter's hypothesis that drunken behaviour is likely often to be coloured by the drinker's character. The naturally talkative person will become more garrulous after a few drinks, the self-assertive person louder and more dominating, the nasty customer more nasty.

Another conjecture which has from time to time enjoyed popularity is that the person of a refined and educated cast of mind, even in his or her cups, will behave in a more delicate way than the uncultivated person. Trotter again:

The cultivated mind is even seen in drunkenness. It commits no outrage, provokes no quarrel, and turns its ear from insult and offence. But the ignorant and illiterate man is to be shunned in proportion to his excess: it is human nature in its vilest garb, and madness in its worst form.

Drunken behaviour and cueing by the immediate context

The immediate situational cues and the micro-environment of a particular drinking occasion may do much to shape the manner of the individual's intoxicated behaviour. The large backdrop of culture matters, but on the actual day it is what is going on in the room which can powerfully influence whether a fight breaks out. Whatever the country and whatever is being drunk, crowded, noisy, smoke-filled bars with everyone pushing and shoving to get their next drink, and with lots of rather intoxicated patrons knocking against each other's elbows, are likely to provide the kind of setting which invites clumsiness to be taken as obstruction or affront, with ready escalation to a blow being struck or a glass being shoved into someone's face. The police will know that some bars more than others are the places where fights are likely to break out.

Drunkenness shaped by culture

Somewhat akin to Trotter's idea that cultivated persons will keep control of their behaviour when drunk is the self-congratulatory but clearly erroneous belief that 'civilized' nations will drink politely, whereas 'savage' people can be expected to handle their liquor badly and get horribly drunk whenever given the chance. Here are the opinions of a Dr Alfred Hillier, as reported in an article published in 1904 under the title 'The Drinking Habits of Uncivilized and Semi-Civilized Races'. Dr Hillier was giving his views on the behaviour of African labourers.

During a sixteen years' residence in South Africa I have come into contact with natives employed in the towns, on farms, and in very large numbers in the diamond fields and the gold fields, and I have invariably found that where alcohol was accessible to the natives it wrought havoc among them . . . He [the African] is unconscious of any moral obligation on the subject. Alcohol is apparently intended to be drunk, and he drinks with the same natural robust appetite with which he would gorge himself on the flesh of an antelope or an ox . . . When Kaffirs are earning wages, and are enabled to purchase liquor, from 10–20 per cent of them are constantly and continuously incapacitated by drink . . . Moreover, the Kaffir workman is fairly honest, law-abiding and peaceful; drunk, he makes murderous assaults on his fellow natives, and even white men, with all the readiness of a savage instinct no longer restrained by fear of consequences.

Hillier's suggestion that Africans cannot hold their liquor and are likely to act out their supposed savage instincts when drunk has many similarities with American views on Native American drinking from colonial days onwards. American Indians were believed to have a fatal propensity for drunkenness and violence if let near whisky; the contemporary drunken behaviour of the American frontiersmen was glossed over. The theory that whisky will send Native Americans into a reflex orgy of drunkenness has sometimes been referred to as 'the Firewater Myth'. The fact of the matter is that the drinking behaviours and responses to intoxication shown by the indigenous and settler cultures of North America were not nearly so distinct as the myth comfortingly proposed. Many other reports on the drinking and drunkenness of traditional societies have from time to time been used to bolster the idea that civilization provides protection against the likelihood of bestial kinds of drunkenness. Essentially this theory is a variant on the more general Western belief in the benefits of imperialism.

A wide range of anthropological research which has accumulated during recent years can throw light on the question of why different people behave differently when drunk. An influential interpretation of the evidence has been given by two American anthropologists, Craig MacAndrew and Robert Edgerton, who in 1970 published a book called *Drunken Comportment*. MacAndrew and Edgerton deployed a mass of material to show that drinking in traditional societies is not at all necessarily associated with mayhem and can in fact often be rigidly controlled by cultural expectations. One of the most telling case studies that they put forward as evidence derived from field observations made by Dwight Heath on drinking among the Camba of eastern Bolivia, a mestizo people of mixed indigenous and Spanish origin, who have maintained an isolated and traditional way of life since Spanish colonial days. Their favoured drink is a distilled product deriving from fermented sugar cane. This achieves an astonishing 89 per cent of ethyl alcohol and is drunk neat; its name is aptly and simply 'alcohol'. Here is an extract from Heath's account of Camba drinking:

The behavioral patterns associated with drinking are so formalized as to consti-tute a secular ritual. Members of the group are seated in chairs in an approximate circle in a yard or, occasionally, in a hut. A bottle of *alcohol* and a single water glass rest on a tiny table which forms part of the circle. The 'sponsor' of the party pours a glassful (about 300 cc) at the table, turns and walks to stand in front of whomever he wishes, nods and raises the glass slightly. The person addressed smiles and nods while still seated; the 'sponsor' toasts with 'Salud' (health), or 'A su salud' (to your health), drinks half of the glassful in a single quick draught, and hands it to the person he has toasted, who then repeats the toast and finishes the glass in one gulp. While the 'sponsor' returns to his seat, the recipient of the toast goes to the table to refill the glass and to repeat the ritual . . .

Heath went on to describe how the party would progress:

After two or three hours of fairly voluble and warm social intercourse, people tend to become thick-lipped and intervals of silence lengthen. By the fourth hour there is little conversation; many people stare dumbly at the ground except when toasted, and a few who may have fallen asleep or 'passed out' are left undisturbed. Once a band or guitarist starts playing, the music is intermin-able and others take over as individual players pass out.

And then he presented this crucial observation:

Among the Camba drinking does not lead to expressions of aggression in verbal or physical form . . . Neither is there a heightening of sexual activity; obscene joking and sexual overtures are rarely associated with drinking. Even when drunk, the Camba are not given to maudlin sentimentality, clowning, boasting or 'baring of souls'.

Drinking among the Camba, Heath thus tells us, is likely to lead to extreme intoxication, and the social ritual with its multiple toastings in raw spirit is designed to ensure that outcome. But he is describing a remarkably safe, non-violent and even in some ways a 'civilized' kind of drinking party. There are no punch-ups, no furniture thrown, no knives drawn, no evidence of savage disinhibition or ape-like behaviour. Within its own terms this drinking is as polite and formalized as anything to be seen at the black-tie dinner of a gentlemen's club, but with a greater expectation of some passing out.

We should note that, far from MacAndrew and Edgerton contending that drinkers' behaviour is formalized in this sort of controlled way in all the cultures on which anthropologists have reported, their contention was that different cultures are vastly different in the kinds of drinking behaviours which are expected and therefore experienced. *Drunken Comportment* goes on to relate a series of reports by nineteenth-century observers on the violence which had at one period been a frequent and terrifying feature of drinking in Tahiti. This is how William Ellis, a missionary, described a Pacific drinking scene in 1853:

Intemperance at this time prevailed to an awful and unprecedented degree . . . Whole districts frequently united, to erect what might be termed a public still . . . When the materials were prepared, the men and boys of the district assembled in a kind of temporary house, erected over the still . . . In this employment they were sometimes engaged for several days together, drinking the spirit as it issued from the still, sinking into a state of indescribable wretchedness, and often practising the most ferocious barbarities . . . Under the unrestrained influence of their intoxicating draught, in their appearance and actions they resembled demons more than human beings. Sometimes in a deserted still-house might be seen fragments of the rude boiler, and the other appendages of the still, scattered in confusion on the ground; and among them the dead and mangled bodies of those who had been murdered with axes or billets of wood in the quarrels that had terminated their debauch.

If the fact that cultures can differ profoundly in their modes of drunken comportment is one message emerging from MacAndrew and Edgerton's analysis, a further and linked conclusion offered by the authors was that a society which gets drunk according to any particular mode at one point in its history may some time later be found radically to have altered its favoured style of intoxicated behaviour. And that was what happened in Tahiti, where later the habit of riotous mob drunkenness had completely disappeared. In the 1960s some observers reported that 'while most Tahitians get drunk at weekends, their comportment is remarkably amiable in character . . . not only is drunken aggression uncommon, but when it does occur it is a pretty bland affair . . .'

MacAndrew and Edgerton's final conclusion was robustly anthropological. Culture, they proposed, is the total explanation for why different people behave differently when drunk. They suggested that drunken comportment in relatively simple societies, where everyone shares a common view on how to behave when intoxicated, would be uniform and dominated by the expectations of culture and the dictates of the society. In our modern world the parallel expectations are confused and the informal controls uncertain, and drunken behaviour is therefore much more varied and unpredictable. One might see this argument as reflecting back to illuminate Thomas Nashe's quasi-anthropological observations on the drinking behaviour of his contemporaries. Within MacAndrew and Edgerton's theory, the variations in drunken comportment seen by a writer around the taverns of Elizabethan London spoke to the fact that, in the flux and ferment of Nashe's changing world, the drunk was left with the freedom to choose his own mode of drunkenness without any great shaping by cultural expectations.

Bad behaviour and the type of drink taken

The belief that some varieties of alcoholic drink are more likely than others to inflame human passions is found in many cultures. It is, however, a theory with considerable variations between countries and over time as to what have been deemed to be the evident facts. Here, for instance, is Dr G. H. Stockham writing on this topic in 1888:

The alcohol in wine and beer, honestly made from grapes and barley, does not intoxicate to the same degree as an equal amount taken in brandy and whisky. The probable reason of this is that the weightier portions of the wine or beer modify the action of this spirit on the system. Just how this is done, we cannot explain, but that such is its effect, is a demonstrable fact. Wine seems to excite the social and genial traits of character. Though it intoxicates, it seldom renders the individual irritable and combatative . . . Beer dulls and stupefies the brain. Beer is not apt to render the individual belligerent or aggressive. Germans rarely quarrel over their glass and are proverbially a peace-loving, law-abiding people. Their partiality for this drink is a recognized characteristic. When under its influence, they are eminently social and cheerful until the brain becomes overpowered by excessive imbibing, when they become not drunk, but *besotted*. . . Brandy, whisky and spirituous liquors have a more immediate and direct effect on the nerves and the brain . . . a majority of the crimes committed can be traced to the direct or indirect influence of ardent spirits.

That statement is in every detail an essay in myth-making. The lager lout is not rendered loutish specifically by his lager, but by his blood alcohol level coupled with the fact that he and his mates, beer cans in hand, are hanging around the street corner in the hope of a little aggravation. And going back to that Saturday-night drinker, it was not the whisky as whisky that drove him berserk. What matters is that the double shot of spirits which he poured into every pint of beer doubled his evening's alcohol intake.

Bringing explanations together

Alcohol is a drug which has the intrinsic capacity to interfere with brain function and produce a state of intoxication. That capacity is part of the magic in alcohol which is not present in the unfermented juice of the grape. Mayhem has never been reported by anthropologists as a consequence of drinking grape juice, let alone flat soda water. Intoxication is not, however, a fixed and monolithic state; on the contrary, it is an astonishingly *plastic* condition. The concept of plasticity helps synthesize the implications which can be drawn from the diverse types of evidence examined in this chapter. Drunkenness behaviour can be moulded by influences which include the immediate context, the way people react to the drunkenness, the drinker's personality, and the expectations given by culture and society. Drunkenness is more like clay than concrete, and out of that clay can be shaped all the animals of Nashe's menagerie and quite a few other beasts too.

The reason why alcohol is a widely accepted recreational drug is in part that intoxication with this particular substance is remarkably susceptible to cultural prescriptions and proscriptions, all the way from Bolivia to Tahiti. Most people can learn not to behave too offensively when drunk, although there will be situations where society licenses some degree of unrestraint – such as Bacchanalia, Purim, and the stag night. In contrast, intoxication with crack cocaine, or injected amphetamines, or with a heavy dose of LSD, is not so easily shaped, and these are not drugs to which society is ever likely to accord a licit recreational status. Intoxication with alcohol is a temporary chemically induced mental disorder where the intoxicated person is generally not out of touch with reality, but will still respond to what culture dictates.

The final conclusion must be that intoxication with alcohol, although a plastic state and a behaviour which can usually be shaped so as to be more or less socially tolerable, always carries within it some degree of unpredictability. Society wants drink and then has to practise the risk management of drunkenness. Sometimes, however, factors will conspire to mould the drunkenness into antisocial manifestations, violent behaviour breaks through the cultural prohibitions, and then in a moment of lion-drunkenness someone may draw a dagger.

5 Alcohol is a Drug of Dependence

Societies which use alcohol are taking into their midst a drug which has the potential to cause an insidious kind of dependence. For some drinkers, that potential will become a devastating actuality. This chapter will start by describing the human reality of that condition. Something will be said about the psychological and biological basis of the dependence syndrome. We will then go on to the question of why, given the drug's widespread availability, only a minority of people who are exposed to it become dependent. What is it that makes one drinker vulnerable while others appear to be immune? Or are we all really at risk, with no one having a guaranteed immunity against one day waking up to find that their drink controls them rather than that they control the drink?

What alcohol dependence looks and feels like
The experience of being alcohol-dependent does not come in a single form. Its presentation will be influenced by characteristics of the individual, and by the environment and culture in which he or she lives and drinks. Also, early- and late-stage dependence will look different. Psychiatrists describe clinical depression as a disorder with many faces, and it is possible even to have a smiling depression. Similarly, alcohol dependence in the middle-aged and well-heeled managing director may on the surface not look at all like that of the sad drinker begging on the street. Beneath the surface, however, there are elements within the dependence syndrome which occur with great sameness whatever the surface presentation may be like, and whether the person is young or old, male or female, rich or poor, smiling or suicidal.

Before turning to some case examples, let's briefly sketch out the core elements within the alcohol dependence syndrome. These are the signs and symptoms which will allow a clinician to recognize this species of drug dependence whatever its variation on the theme.

Withdrawal symptoms

Because alcohol goes on being broken down and metabolized while the individual is sleeping, the alcohol-dependent person is likely to wake up next morning at least somewhat in withdrawal. The symptoms are in part physiological (shakes, sweats, nausea), and may also in part be psychological (anxiety, depression). They can vary greatly in intensity, according to the stage to which the condition has progressed. For instance, at the early and mild end of the spectrum, withdrawal symptoms may involve only a slight clinking of cup against saucer as the morning tea is sipped, together with a vague sense of nervousness. However, at the extreme, these symptoms can be of appalling severity and make a terrifying beginning to each day. Sufferers will wake drenched with sweat, profoundly nauseous, and so shaky that they cannot lift the first drink of the day to their lips without the assistance of a kind barmaid. At the same time, they may report feelings of anxiety so severe as to approach a panic attack. A sense of bewilderment may overcome such drinkers when they find that drink is beginning to punish them in this cruel way.

The need to take a drink to relieve
the distress of the withdrawal symptoms

Any sensible person afflicted each morning by unpleasant feelings on waking will look for a cure for those symptoms. The ready, quick and astonishingly effective cure for the distress of alcohol withdrawal is to take another drink, and that provides the logic for the morning drink. The person who has progressed only to mild dependence will be able to postpone his or her first drink of the day until lunchtime, albeit with an eye on the clock. The heavily dependent drinker may need a tumbler of whisky before getting out of bed.

Tolerance

The dependent drinker will, as a result of acquired tolerance to the effects of alcohol, show significantly less evidence of intoxication than a light drinker would at the same blood alcohol level. There have been reports of drinkers with a blood level of 800 mg% who have been regarded by people around them as not evidently drunk. But such extreme degrees of tolerance are unusual. Drinkers may proudly claim that they can hold their liquor or drink other people under the table, but what they see as prowess is in fact a symptom of their dependent state. In the later stages, tolerance can begin to fade, with the previously tolerant drinker then unexpectedly becoming drunk and falling down in the street.

Life becomes drink-centred

As a drinker moves into increasingly severe dependence, he or she will typically describe how, step by step, ordinary family and social obligations and the desire for a good reputation gradually lose their significance. Instead, the need to drink, to keep topped up with drink and to secure the supply of drink becomes increasingly important and will in time wipe out responsiveness to every ordinary kind of demand and obligation. Complaints from the family about shortage of money will, for instance, be overruled by the drinker's desperate need to make sure that there is money with which to buy the next drink . . . and the next drink . . . and the next.

An awareness that drink is only uncertainly controllable

Social drinkers enjoy the inner freedom to decide when they will or will not start drinking, and they will also feel that it is comfortably within their power to determine how much they drink and the appropriate moment for them to stop drinking. For such people, drinking feels no more likely to go out of control than their consumption of fruit juice. For dependent drinkers, however, the ability to exert personal control over their drinking is more or less impaired. It will be difficult for them to resist a drink if alcohol is available, and once a session is under way it can be very difficult to set a stopping point short of drunkenness. Words to describe the inner experience are rather difficult to find, but what dependent drinkers seem in essence to experience is that drink has become tricky, unreliable, something which easily runs away with them, an enemy apt to engage in ambush. Drink provokes desire for more drink, and then craving for yet more drink. It is as if the feedback loop which controls the ordinary person's drinking is now malfunctioning.

After a break in the drinking, with restarted drinking the dependence symptoms come back again

Dependent drinkers who have been off drink for a few weeks or months may decide after this break to start drinking again with the firm intention that the old bad experiences will not be repeated. They will insist that they have learned their lesson, and will perhaps try to control their behaviour by giving up spirits and drinking only wine, drinking only in company, and setting themselves sensible limits and counting their drinks. The previously mildly dependent drinker may succeed in these intentions, or perhaps do so at first and then slide slowly back into the old state. The story for the heavily dependent drinker is, in contrast, likely to be one of precipitate reinstatement of severe dependence. Morning shakes which originally took perhaps fifteen years of drinking to develop will, for that kind of drinker, return in full and devastating force after only a couple of days of resumed drinking.

So much for an outline of the elements which together make up the clinical syndrome of alcohol dependence. What needs to be recognized is the extraordinary fact that friendly drink – so easily picked up and put down by most people – can for a minority reveal that alcohol is a drug with the capacity brutally to reduce the drinker to a destructively dependent state. American survey work suggests that about 5 per cent of male and 1 per cent of female drinkers will develop alcohol dependence. From those individuals the statement 'I never believed it could happen to me' can frequently be heard. And meanwhile it would appear that for the most part society itself is not much aware that this problem is among us, and destroying people who never believed it could happen to them.

Alcohol dependence: four case histories

Four case histories, which are true to life but do not derive from particular individuals, will help give human reality to the faces of the dependence syndrome. The selection of these from a vast array of other possible pictures is arbitrary. Between and around these four examples are all manner of other faces of dependence.

The widow who always let the
cat out before taking her first drink

Mrs Isabella Brown was fifty-nine when she fell down the stairs and was admitted to hospital with a skull fracture. Both she and her husband had been schoolteachers; he had died four years previously after a long illness with cancer, and she had for the last year or so of his life retired from her job to look after him. After his death she felt isolated, purposeless and deeply empty, and was left with only her cat for company.

With her husband she had been in the habit of having a gin in the evening, and they would sometimes share a bottle of wine. The idea of drink being a problem or a necessity had never entered their minds. After her husband's death Mrs Brown became clinically depressed. She did not seek any professional help, but one evening she found a bottle of gin left at the back of a cupboard and drank enough to give her a night's sleep. After it had been broached, that bottle lasted her about ten days, but six months later she was regularly drinking half a bottle of gin a day. Drink no longer helped her to sleep, and she was waking feeling sick and with her hands mildly but noticeably shaky. She was resolutely determined not to go straight to the kitchen and open the bottle, but would as a ritual let the cat out and wait for it to come back in before pouring her morning drink. In that way she persuaded herself that her drinking was not compulsive. Only after that drink was she well enough to get on with the day. Drinking was spaced at about three- or four-hour intervals.

Other than the cat and the drink, there was not much else in her life. She did not want people to visit, as that might cut across her drinking schedule, and she did not want her son or daughter to come and stay with her, because 'They didn't understand.' One morning she woke up soaked with sweat and for the first time ever paroxysmally shaking. That is when she fell down the stairs and very nearly killed herself.

Jack the Lad

Jack Mullins, aged twenty-nine, was arrested for attempted robbery of an off-licence. Next morning he was found to be in severe withdrawal, and a police surgeon had to be sent for. The story was of a heavy-drinking father, a depressed mother, a heroin-dependent brother. Jack had grown up on a deprived council estate, had spent a lot of his school years truanting, and after leaving school had never had a regular job. He was glue-sniffing at twelve, smoking cigarettes regularly at thirteen, drinking in pubs at sixteen, and had then gone on casually to use most types of illicit drug. Through every other kind of drug experience, however, ran his attachment to alcohol. His lifestyle was financed by petty acquisitive crime and cannabis dealing. If he ran short of funds he could for a few days stay off drink without ill effect and would sit around indoors.

Up to the age of, say, twenty-five, his drinking could be described as heavy and chaotic, but variable. There was then at age twenty-six to twenty-seven a period of rapid transition, and he himself distinguished between 'drinking like it used to be' and 'this bad drinking'. He moved quickly to consuming up to two bottles of spirits a day, with a special taste for Bacardi, though strong beer was also acceptable. Day and night often merged, but he could wake in the middle of his sleep with intense withdrawal symptoms. He thought about little else but alcohol, and measured out his cash in terms of the drink it could buy. Clubs, pubs, his flat, other people's flats, the streets were all one continuous drinking terrain. The repeated urgent need on waking to douse appalling withdrawal symptoms made a guaranteed beginning to every day.

His intimates were selected as people who drank with the same kind of compulsiveness, and they would drive around together in a car, looking for off-licences to attack. For the robbery we have mentioned, Jack received a two-year prison sentence. On release he was back into all the symptoms of alcohol dependence within twenty-four hours, and inevitably he again engaged in crime to pay for his habit. The picture was remarkably similar to that of his brother, who was robbing to pay for a heroin habit.

A lawyer destroyed

Aged in his mid-fifties, this small-town solicitor was a familiar lunchtime figure in the pub next door to his office. A small, shabby, red-faced man, he would be found in the bar every day from noon to 2.30 or 3.00 p.m., sitting with a little group of heavy-drinking cronies. People knew that Mr Green 'liked his drink' and 'couldn't half put it back', and some described him behind his back as 'a bit of an old soak'. His drinking behaviour was tolerated, however, and he and his law practice staggered on.

What no one realized was that Mr Green was suffering from alcohol dependence to a severe degree, with the drinking dominating his life. His daily schedule during the working week was with monotonous regularity timetabled as follows:

7.30 a.m. – out of bed, hands shaking, no appetite for breakfast, 'terrible bad nerves'.

8 a.m. – get into car, drive around corner and stop, take bottle of vodka out of glove pocket and have a good swig.

8.30 a.m. – arrive at office not feeling too bad, coffee brought in by secretary, get down to work.

10.30 a.m. or thereabouts – shakes threatening to come back, reach for the bottle of vodka kept in a drawer of the desk.

Lunchtime – major drinking session of the day: expect to get through six to eight double vodkas during a few hours.

Afternoon – get on with the work in fuddled state.

6.15 p.m. – stop at another pub on way home: one or two double vodkas quickly thrown back.

6.30 p.m. – home to a couple of self-poured gins before dinner and some whisky after dinner, before usually falling asleep in front of the television, finally going up to bed at 2 a.m.

Mr Green had little interaction with his wife and children, and had effectively excluded himself from all family activities. At weekends he was shut in his study with a bottle. Sometimes there were rows and shouting, and he would then angrily blame his wife for having dragged him into a town where no one appreciated his genius.

Aged fifty-six he vomited blood, cirrhosis of the liver – a classic indicator of alcohol abuse – was diagnosed, and after hospitalization he was off alcohol for six weeks before returning fully to the old drinking pattern. By now his tolerance to alcohol had gone, and at lunchtimes he tended to get embarrassingly drunk in the pub. His behaviour was becoming cause for public scandal. Short of money and with his practice failing, he embezzled funds from clients, and the police called to make inquiries. The next Sunday he drove his car to a secluded spot, fixed a hosepipe to the exhaust, and killed himself. There was an obituary in the local paper which spoke of him as 'a well-known local character', but the fact that alcohol dependence had destroyed him was of course not mentioned.

A vagrant drunk

Patrick Fitzgerald, aged thirty-six, spent the previous night sleeping in a churchyard. Now he was standing outside a cinema and mumbling his plea for 'the price of a cup of tea'. Men like him confront us in every city, begging in the streets, lurching on the subway, or drinking in the park with a bottle gang. Patrick's background was typical. His father and several uncles had severe drinking problems. He came over to England from his native Ireland at seventeen, moved around the country working as a labourer on building sites, never married, sent some money home and drank the rest. He was an exploited and disposable member of a cheap labour force, with no one caring for his welfare and no personal support system. When he developed alcohol dependence he fell out of society, and inevitably drifted into home-lessness. His alcohol dependence was extreme, but physiologically the same disorder as that affecting any other dependent drinker. What marked this man's condition, however, was the intensity of the social complications. He was destitute, unemployable, out of contact with his family, frequently in petty trouble with the law, alienated and stigmatized. The world of homeless drinkers into which he moved taught him survival skills and gave companionship, but it was also a world of unpredictable fights and robberies. And as he stood begging he would be listening to hazy alcohol-induced hallucinatory voices.

Whether they gave him a few pence or walked around him, to most passers-by he was just human flotsam, another sad and hopeless street drunk with no way out. But in fact there can be recovery even from that kind of degradation. One morning when releasing him from the cells, a custody sergeant said to him, 'I think you're too good for this. Get off the treadmill, I don't want to see you in my station again. Here's an address for you – and mind you don't lose it.' A couple of years later Patrick was a valued staff member of the street agency to which he owed his recovery, and he was studying part-time for a social-work qualification.

Mechanisms of the dependence process

What happened to those four people whose cases we have just described, so as to set up and maintain their altered relationship with alcohol?

The crudest explanation runs like this. Some degree of tolerance to alcohol is easily acquired, and occurs to a slight extent even with social drinkers. At a certain stage in a heavy drinker's career, however, withdrawal symptoms will then occur as a kind of biological flip side to tolerance. That is because the alcohol-tolerant brain, when deprived of alcohol, exhibits symptoms of withdrawal overactivity (anxiety, tremor and so on). These symptoms are due to the previous compensation against the sedative action of alcohol now being unopposed and spilling over, producing unwanted excitement. In terms of analogy, a person who has been pushing against someone on the other side of a door will fly through it if the opposition is suddenly removed. With alcohol, that flying-through is the withdrawal state. According to this simple model, the drinker who has developed withdrawal symptoms will have mechanically to go on drinking repeatedly and at a high level to relieve or avoid withdrawal, with the whole cycle thus endlessly repeating itself.

Here is an account given by a dependent drinker which seems to support the explanation of dependence which sees withdrawal as the mainspring of the condition:

Before long I was back on my full amount again . . . same old sweats and nausea. Now up till then I never drank in the morning. Even if I went to sleep and left a glass of whisky – which I often did – I'd always pour it back in the bottle the next morning. Didn't want to touch it. This used to puzzle me – why don't I drink in the morning? – but a few of the old timers used to say, 'It'll come.' Well, some time about July or August, I found that I just couldn't get out of bed. When I put my feet down they were like jelly. And I thought, 'Well, this swig might help me on my way', and I took a swig and was sick a bit but after a few minutes, lovely, back on my legs. It shows you how naive I was at that time, yet I had enough experience of drink – I thought that swig would last me till lunchtime. Well, I'd been up about half an hour and I wanted another one. And when I got to work at 8 a.m. I wanted another. The place where I got it from didn't open till 9 a.m. Jesus, I'll always remember this: I had to wait till 9 a.m. sweating. That's when my morning drinking started.

There are, however, problems with this 'withdrawal as the main-spring' theory. The man who woke with his feet like jelly had been drinking a bottle of whisky a day with great regularity for the ten years before his withdrawal symptoms began. So those symptoms cannot explain post hoc why he chose to drink very heavily in those previous years. The actual quantity drunk did not much change with the arrival of the shakes, although he certainly now had to nurse himself along throughout the day so as to avoid the symptoms coming back. A critic of the idea that it is withdrawal which drives dependence would argue that withdrawal symptoms are for the most part nothing more than belated complications of pre-existing dependence – an effect rather than a cause. They would suggest that what needs to be explained is why this man so much liked drinking and was so greatly attached to his drinking for ten years before the first pang of withdrawal.

The explanation which many psychologists would favour is that dependence is essentially a learned habit, with the instrument for the learning of that habit being the rewardingness of the drink and not the relief from withdrawal. That would put the mechanism of alcohol dependence on the same footing as that of, say, addiction to heroin, where research strongly suggests that it is the pleasure from taking the drug that builds the habit, not the relief from withdrawal. According to this view, it is not withdrawal which is the mainspring, but alcohol itself – alcohol is a drug with which it is possible to build up a drug-taking habit. The label 'dependence', argue the psychologists, has been arbitrarily given to what is simply an ingrained habit.

Which of these two competing explanations of the dependence mainspring is correct remains an open question. It is quite likely that what will ultimately be found is that the effect of alcohol itself contributes to the building of the drink habit, with relief from withdrawal kicking in as a reinforcer of the habit at a certain stage.

Why do some drinkers develop dependence while most do not?

Drinking problems tend to run in families – the children of a heavy drinker are at a greater risk of later having trouble with their drinking than are those of parents for whom drinking has never been a problem. In a large American study published by Deborah Dawson and her colleagues in 1992, interview information was gathered from over 23,000 drinkers drawn from a community sample. The odds of developing a drinking problem were increased by 86 per cent for people who had a parent or sibling with such a problem, while having both a close and a more distant relative put up the odds by 167 per cent. Those findings are in accord with much other research.

However, such data only take understanding so far. All right, 'alcoholism' runs in families, but in many cultures so also does being a tinker, tailor, soldier or sailor. Children follow in their parents' footsteps mostly because of role modelling and opportunity, not because of genetics. Perhaps drinking runs in families not because of anything written into people's genes but because of home influences.

Whatever the condition under study, sorting out how much of any observed 'running in families' is due to nature, and how much to nurture, is a question for the geneticist. The methods that have been deployed with drinking have included twin studies which have compared problem rates among identical and non-identical pairs of twins. If there is a significant genetic predisposition for a problem, concordance rates (both twins of a given pair having a problem, or both not having such a problem) should be higher for identical than for non-identical twin pairs, and that has been the general (but not universal) finding. For instance, in a 1960 study reported from Sweden by Lennart Kaij, 71 per cent of identical twins were concordant for 'chronic alcoholism', but only 32 per cent of non-identical twins.

Another strategy which geneticists have employed has been to compare rates of problem drinking in adult life among children of problem drinkers who were adopted away from their heavy-drinking parent at an early age with rates in various control groups. If the suggestion that drinking problems are to some extent genetically determined is correct, these adopted-away children should when grown up still be at risk of developing a problem, despite the adopted parents offering role models for sobriety. A pioneering study of this kind was published in 1973 by a joint Swedish and American research team led by Donald Goodwin. Compared with controls, a fourfold increase in 'alcoholism' was found in children adopted away before the age of six weeks from families where a parent had at some time been hospitalized for a drinking problem.

There is also a body of research which tends to show that the children of alcoholics, when studied as young adults and at an age before the likely onset of heavy drinking, tend on several laboratory measures to give findings which distinguish them from controls. For instance, in most people a dose of alcohol will increase body sway in the standing subject. An American study published by Marc Schuckit in 1985 suggested that the grown-up but as yet not heavy-drinking children of alcoholics have innate resistance to this sway effect. The implication is that a genetically transmitted ability to adapt to or resist the physiological sway-inducing impact of alcohol may be a marker of a propensity to develop alcohol dependence.

An occurrence within the range of everyday observation is that some people become sweaty and unpleasantly flushed after taking even a small quantity of alcohol, and may turn a bright and embarrassing red. This is a manifestation of a genetic defect in the ability to metabolize alcohol, with a resulting accumulation of acetaldehyde, an organic compound to which alcohol is degraded in the normal course of events as an intermediate step towards its further breakdown in the body.

Such 'flushers' occur sporadically in all populations, but the trait is common among the Japanese. This defect can give a degree of protection against development of alcohol dependence. Truly determined flushers may, however, drink through their discomfort barrier or even resort to premedication with an antihistamine.

Findings from many directions now support the contention that there is something genetic in the predisposition to alcohol dependence. But, paradoxically, an important conclusion to be drawn from genetic research is that genes alone cannot explain everything about the causes of such dependence. Alcohol problems run in families, but on present evidence the likeliest explanations for this finding involve both nature and nurture. Genetics can predispose an individual to alcohol dependence, but, even when there is a strong genetic loading, to turn vulnerability into actuality is likely to require a mix of influences.

Let's look at some non-genetic factors which may explain why some drinkers contract dependence while others (even on occasion their identical twins) do not do. A prime environmental risk factor which enhances vulnerability to development of alcohol dependence is easy access to plenty of alcohol over a good long time. Even with an extreme genetic loading, no one will become dependent on alcohol if they live out their lives in a drink-free desert. But if they live and work in a village famous for its whisky distilleries, and with a free ration of drink that goes with the job, the risk of contracting a drinking problem will be much enhanced above the desert level. Access and thus risk will be heightened by any kind of environment in which drink is cheap and unrestricted, or by a culture which has a permissive attitude towards heavy drinking. Rates for cirrhosis of the liver have over recent years varied by up to a factor of eighteen between different countries in Europe. The same social and cultural features which result in different national cirrhosis rates will have a similar impact on risk of alcohol dependence.

As regards the more personal aspects of environment, factors such as the drinking mores of the family of origin, job, leisure, money in the pocket, and drinking habits of the partner and friends are all likely to protect against or promote levels and styles of drinking which will put the drinker at lesser or greater risk of dependence. With regard to those four case histories quoted earlier, it seems likely that Jack Mullins's development of alcohol dependence was encouraged by his heavy-drinking father and by his association with heavy-drinking friends. Mr Green provides a clear instance of drinking being facilitated by a micro-environment which over many years tolerates and even nurtures excessive drinking. It is unsurprising that publicans should have a cirrhosis rate fifteen times the national average. Although access is probably the dominant explanation for that finding, people with a taste for drink may look for work in a pub or otherwise gravitate somewhat purposefully to situations where alcohol is readily to hand. Patrick Fitzgerald probably had a strong genetic predisposition to alcohol dependence (his father and those uncles), but his lifestyle as a building labourer was also vastly relevant.

Besides access, another common risk factor for alcohol dependence is mental illness. Mrs Brown started to drink her way towards dependence at a time when she was ill with depression. She was socially isolated and had suffered a bereavement, and that kind of situation can lead precipitately to dependence in someone who has no evident genetic vulnerability. Other types of mental illness which can lead to excessive drinking and risk of dependence include manic-depressive illness, with the phases of elation being associated with drinking bouts. Adults who were sexually abused in childhood also have an elevated risk of later alcohol dependence.

Another factor which can contribute to the total level of risk is personality disorder, and that factor stands out in the story of Jack Mullins. His antisocial personality traits underlay his reckless style of drinking, his devil-may-care attitude to the consequences of his drinking, and his willingness to rob in order to fund his habit. There is evidence for some sort of shared genetic predisposition which may underlie the coexistence of this kind of tearaway drinking, personality disorder and criminality in early-onset male alcohol dependence of Jack's kind. Fundamental contributions to this line of research have been made by the American geneticist Robert Clohinger.

It can be anyone

What those four cases histories and the science around them seem persuasively to suggest is that proneness to develop alcohol dependence does not have any single master explanation to cover every individual. It is not a matter of some people being doomed to alcohol dependence by their genes while the rest of us can drink with impunity. And for any one individual no single causal explanation is likely to suffice. The conclusion must be that the reasons why X and not Y develops dependence on this drug will involve the varied contributions of many different factors, acting together or over time. That is the true and complex reality on which society needs to base its responses to the problems which are set by its decision to take into its midst a drug with the potential to produce an insidious kind of dependence.

Society – from the level of individual citizen to the highest reaches of government – should be more aware that alcohol belongs to the class of drugs which can produce dependence. Alcohol is not just one more consumer commodity, like a soap powder to be bought or left on the shelf according to the consumer's free choice. Unlike with soap powder, in relation to alcohol an individual's control over choice can become impaired by dependency. When such a person slips yet another bottle of gin into the supermarket trolley, the purchase will have been made under an inner duress of a kind not experienced with any other item in the shop, save nicotine. Dependence is duress, and that fact should be borne in mind when, for instance, deciding whether or not the government should put another penny on the drink tax, whether to sentence the next young offender to a term of imprisonment or to try to get him or her into treatment, whether to extend licensing hours or hold the line, whether to serve the sodden lawyer with another drink or refuse to serve him and lose trade, whether to blame or pity or mock at the next drunk in the street, and whether to monitor our own level of drinking before one morning the unthinkable happens.

6 **The American Prohibition Experiment**

Here are the basic facts. On 16 January 1920, the United States of America instituted the national prohibition of alcohol, with this regulatory measure being given the status of an amendment to the Constitution – the Eighteenth Amendment. The expectations at that moment were of a new dawn characterized by social harmony, reduced crime, enhanced productivity – the American dream made tangible. On 5 December 1933 the Twenty-first Amendment repealed Prohibition. And the expectations of repeal were the same dreams as had been indulged in when Prohibition had been declared 13 years, 10 months and 20 days earlier.

That a democratic government in the twentieth century should ever have attempted to use the criminal law to cast out from society a substance embedded in national life by myriad ties of traditional usage, cherished symbolism and financial self-interest may to the present age seem an act of lunacy. Prohibition is usually now seen as an unmitigated disaster which did nothing to curb excessive drinking, but which enabled Al Capone to found a criminal empire. And repeal is in turn viewed as marking America's return to sanity.

Why America began to worry about drink

The history of the social forces which eventually led in 1920 to national prohibition go back a long way before that date. The intensely worried reaction of Americans to the national level of drinking and intemperance during the opening decades of the nineteenth century, together with accompanying fears of a continued climb in the upward trajectory of consumption, were·chronicled by the historian W. J. Rorabaugh in his aptly named book *The Alcoholic Republic*. Contemporary witnesses variously described the USA as 'fast becoming a nation of drunkards', as 'hardly better than a nation of sots' and as surpassing all other peoples of the world 'in this degrading, beastly vice of intemperance'.

Rather than taking those kinds of statement at face value, the question which needs to be asked is whether these anathemas signified no more than moral panic as a young nation found and defined itself in the post-revolutionary period, or whether, alternatively, there existed an objective basis for these cries of woe. Whisky consumption had at this period increased steeply, America still had a traditional colonial taste for strong cider, but wine was not popular and what beer was available tended to be weak. To reconstruct from historical records the totality of what was being drunk, in terms of per-capita consumption summed across all beverage types, is very difficult. It is, for instance, impossible to reconstruct how much cider American farming families were producing for their own domestic enjoyment. However, after careful scrutiny of the available data, Rorabaugh felt able to state that total consumption of absolute alcohol 'reached a peak of nearly 4 gallons per capita in 1830'.

Bearing in mind the likelihood that this 4 gallon figure is only a rough approximation, let's consider the probable social implications of that kind of consumption level. Rorabaugh's calculation was based on consumption per head for the population aged over fifteen years. Assuming that the measure used at the time was the imperial rather than the American gallon, 4 gallons converts to approximately 18.2 litres – say 18 litres. On the basis of that conversion we can make a comparison between the 1830s and present-day American drinking. US national per-capita consumption currently runs at about 8.3 litres of absolute alcohol per year. The arithmetic therefore suggests that Americans in 1830 were, on average, drinking at roughly 2.2 times the level of their present-day compatriots. That is a significant differential.

How the total alcohol consumption was spread across the population may have changed over time; for instance, there may have been changes in the proportion of abstainers. Also, prevailing patterns in the way people behave when drunk may have altered. Nevertheless, a per-capita intake of 18 litres would have been accompanied by wide and evident adverse health and social consequences. High levels of alcohol dependence and drunkenness would have been casting an unpleasant shadow over the face of a rapidly changing society in which whisky was cheaper than tea or coffee. Let's extend the basis for comparison a little further. Present consumption is at about 7.6 litres in the UK and 10.8 litres in Spain, with France at the top of the western-European league table at about 12 litres. No modern nation, other than perhaps some countries of the former Eastern Bloc, currently tolerates anything which approaches the level of drinking which America was experiencing at the 1830 peak.

There is likely to have been a measure of got-up panic involved, but these calculations suggest that America in the opening decades of the nineteenth century had good reason to be worried about its drinking. And, curious as it may seem, it was America's experience around that time of an intense concern about its national drinking which helped lead in 1920 to the enactment of Prohibition, for it was that earlier experience of acute anxiety generated by a manifest national drinking problem which stimulated the first wave of temperance activity. From then on the liquor question was to be an issue for American public debate. Whatever the subsequent weaving of fantasies around drink as the evil to be blamed for every American ill, the experience of a drinking epidemic which threatened to make the country into an alcoholic republic shaped national attitudes for decades to come. The national drinking level declined considerably, but tackling the alcohol problem as a symbolic crusade had been given lasting momentum.

Temperance is born

The first stirrings of the temperance reaction to America's drinking occurred very early in the nineteenth century. By 1813 the Massachusetts Society for the Suppression of Intemperance had brought together forty local organizations in common cause. The American Temperance Society (ATS) was founded in 1826, and immediately made itself felt as a powerful force which coordinated a nationwide campaign against spirit drinking, rather than alcoholic drinks more generally. That the temperance movement was riding on a tide of national concern is demonstrated by its recruitment figures: by 1835 the ATS was able to claim a membership of 1.5 million, or about one in five of the free adult population. The clergy took a lead, and doctors became involved in the movement, but the ATS was a lay organization with a strong community base. Eighteen litres per-capita alcohol consumption was to stimulate a wide grass-roots reaction.

The 1830s saw the beginnings of the idea that temperance should demand that its adherents abstain from all alcoholic drinks rather than only spirits. This position became known as 'teetotalism', because those who signed the new 'total' pledge would have the letter 'T' entered by their names. The ATS changed its title to the American Temperance Union, but by the late 1830s arguments over whether the temperance movement should demand total or partial abstinence were causing schism.

In 1840 the Washingtonians emerged in Baltimore as a total-abstinence society which put emphasis on helping the reformed drunkard. This organization can be seen as in several respects a precursor of Alcoholics Anonymous. It spread nationally, held public meetings which were often the best show in town, and put on giant torchlit processions. By 1842 they were claiming to have saved 'at least 100,000 common drunkards and three times that number of tipplers who were on a fair way to becoming sots'. But such were the vicissitudes of the temperance scene that four years after its foundation the Washingtonians were largely a spent force, though in some subtle ways their influence still went marching on.

In the 1830s, parts of Massachusetts voted for what was virtually a system of enforced local prohibition. Over the following years several other states introduced state-wide controls to curb the sale of alcohol. The originally suasionist temperance movement was thus starting to move increasingly towards coercion.

A further shift towards coercion occurred in the 1840s and '50s when, under the political leadership of Neal Dow, sometime mayor of Portland, the state of Maine introduced a series of enactments which put teeth into prohibition of a kind never previously envisaged. An 1851 Act widely known as the Maine Law prohibited the production of alcohol within the state, limited to state agencies the right to sell alcohol (and then only for industrial and medicinal purposes), allowed for searches and seizures, and backed up enforcement with the possibility of heavy fines and imprisonment. When in 1855 these draconian measures led to a riot, Dow ordered the militia to fire on the crowd. One demonstrator was killed and several were wounded. Despite these excesses Maine was seen as a model to be copied, and by 1855 thirteen states had introduced prohibition. So in the 1850s there was already evidence that large tracts of America favoured an absolutist response to drink which to an astonishing degree foreshadowed 1920. The Volstead Act, which later gave national prohibition its statutory basis, might even be viewed as a somewhat watered-down version of these earlier experiments.

The most plausible explanation for the toughness of the American reaction to alcohol during the first half of the nineteenth century must be that when a society feels itself insulted and endangered by the damage which it perceives drink to be causing, that society may turn against alcohol completely. That is what happened centuries earlier in the Islamic world, but absolutist reactions are also to be found within the repertoire of more recent societal responses to alcohol. For instance, from 1919 to 1932 Finland operated a national prohibition. Norway and Sweden also had prohibition experiments around that same time. In northern Canada there have in recent years been several examples of indigenous communities introducing local prohibition to deal with the destruction wrought by heavy drinking. The Micronesian island of Truck provides an instance of a women-led community decision to ban alcohol because of the threat it was posing to the local society. Short of prohibition, there are many examples of societies responding to a dire alcohol problem by instigation of strict controls, with a recent case being Mikhail Gorbachev's draconian but failed attempt to curb drinking in the Soviet Union.

So, when looking for a reason why America responded as it did to alcohol, it is helpful to put that American response into a wider perspective. To some extent the explanation lies perhaps in the riposte 'Why not?' Societies which perceive themselves to be threatened by any drug are apt to respond radically, as seen today in the talk of a war on drugs. But neither in the past nor in the present, for alcohol or any other mind-altering chemical, are the objective dimensions of the problem by themselves a sufficient explanation for the societal reaction.

For a more complete answer one has to look at the nature of the society – its religiosity, for instance; its belief in the law as instrument of social perfection; its wider appetite for 'reform'; the politics of the time – as well as at the dimensions of the problem. Perception is the ultimate determinant of societal response. And in the first half of the nineteenth century sectors of American society came to perceive alcohol negatively. Neal Dow's ordering of the militia to open fire on the crowd cannot be comprehended just by a scanning of the per-capita consumption figures.

The long march

The American temperance movement had by the middle of the nineteenth century become a reality which was not thereafter going to be wiped out, but the further march towards Prohibition was still to be a long one.

In the latter part of the 1850s – partly as a consequence of a decrease in popular and political anxiety about alcohol brought about by the effectiveness of the campaigning and the consequent lower consumption level – the temperance movement for a time lost its momentum. Enforcement of the state-enacted liquor laws began to fall into abeyance. But during the 1870s temperance acquired a new infusion of energy through the large-scale involvement of women in its work. These women seem often to have been possessed of a spontaneous understanding of how to use direct-action techniques. In December 1873 Bethia Ogle marched with a band of women against saloon-keepers and other sellers of liquor in Washington DC. By means of persuasion and not a little intimidation, casks were before long being broken open and drink was flowing in the gutters. A band of praying women drawn from the respectable classes and gathering on their knees on a pavement outside a hapless drink shop was an instrument capable of closing businesses permanently and on a significant scale. Not so respectable was Carrie Nation, who brought 'hatchetize' to the American language as a term to describe her habit of breaking up saloon bars with an axe. Later in her career she joined the vaudeville circuit, and after on-stage demonstrations of her prowess she would sell miniature hatchets to the audience as souvenirs.

Carrie Nation, although a famously outlandish figure in her time, never made more than a minor and embarrassing contribution to the temperance movement. But Bethia Ogle and other like-minded and courageous community activists helped to inspire a highly significant development – the Woman's Christian Temperance Union (WCTU), founded in 1873. Its crusade against drink was later described by Jack Blocker, a historian of temperance, as 'the largest mass movement of women yet seen in the United States'. The WCTU was led for many years by the forceful Mrs Frances E. Willard. With millions of pamphlets published and the capturing of school syllabuses to her credit, she spread across the nation the message that alcohol was an unmitigated poison. She was engaging in rabid propaganda rather than dissemination of the dispassionate truth, but she employed the misrepresentation of science to great effect. Teaching on the evils of alcohol became mandatory across most of America.

Mrs Willard was renowned for her 'do everything' stance. All aspects of society's use of alcohol were her target. By 1890 the WCTU's 7,000 local branches had between them a membership of 150,000, and Willard's leadership was over a period of almost twenty years immensely successful in expanding and holding together WCTU activities. A national Prohibition Party had fielded Neal Dow as a presidential candidate in 1880. This Party, like the WCTU, fought drink on a broad front, while also at times pushing ideas which had nothing to do with the main issue. In 1892 the Party adopted a manifesto which included a demand for government control of the railroads, universal suffrage, a wealth tax, equal pay for women, and the abolition of lynching. Such reformist zeal alienated large sectors of contemporary America and guaranteed the Party's electoral failure.

If the WCTU and the Prohibition Party to which it gave support were handicapped as campaigning organizations by their tendency towards a scatter-gun approach, the founding in 1893 of the Anti-Saloon League was in contrast the emergence of a single-issue campaigning body dedicated to a clear-cut and potentially achievable goal. It was tied to no political party, had no religions affiliation, and was able to win support both from organized labour and from employers. It worked by the simple device of diabolizing the saloon, but that was to be the stalking horse for total national prohibition.

The American saloon of that time was a traditional working-class institution where men gathered to drink and talk. The furnishings might be rich or somewhat bare. Pictures of naked women were favoured. There would probably be one long bar, with most customers taking their drink while standing. Free lunches might be offered to woo patrons. Singers might provide entertainment. Upstairs there could be a political caucus meeting in progress, and the saloon was at times the focus for many types of community activity.

Saloons varied from the well-ordered to places where drunkenness was the norm and the scene on the pavement outside not pretty. There could be links with prostitution and gambling. It seems likely that the spectrum of orderliness and disorderliness in the conduct of saloons would not have been much different from that among contemporary British public houses or the popular drinking places of any other country, or from what Mass Observation saw in the British pub of the 1930s. The aim of the Anti-Saloon League, in furtherance of its single-issue campaign, was, however, to stereotype all saloons as dens of extreme iniquity. Here is how the popular preacher Billy Sunday comprehensively anathematized this American institution:

The Saloon is an infidel. It has no faith in God; has no religion. It would close every church in the land. It would hang its beer signs on the abandoned altars. It would close every public [i.e. non-private] school. It respects the thief and it esteems the blasphemer . . . I tell you that the curse of God Almighty is on the Saloon.

Those words of Billy Sunday's abundantly support the contention that the forces which were slowly pushing America towards Prohibition were not shaped solely by rational reaction to the drink problem or the alcohol-consumption statistics. The rantings of one preacher should not be accorded exaggerated importance, but Billy Sunday's identification of the saloon as an instrument of the Devil is another forceful illustration that societal reactions to alcohol are never likely to be determined by its molecular structure alone. The saloon as desecrator of the altar is a neat contrast to the idea of wine as the blood of Christ.

The Anti-Saloon League developed sophisticated campaigning skills and an ability significantly to influence the political process at national and local levels. When in 1913 it started to campaign for national prohibition, it did so from a well-established organizational and political base. By 1917 a number of states had held referendums and voted for prohibition. Per-capita alcohol consumption was at less than half the level of the 1830s, but the League's intentions were now supported by a subtle but powerful confluence of societal forces. One of these was the increasing industrialization of the country and the demand for a sober workforce. Another was the popular fear of the immigrant and the belief that big cities (and their drinking places) were alien to the traditional American way of life and its imagined rural virtues. Campaigning against drink was also to some extent a campaign for gentrification, for at this period the middle classes did not have alcohol as an important part of their lifestyle. These and other deep currents were helping the prohibition campaign forward when in April 1917 America entered the First World War and the abstinence cause became linked to patriotism.

At the start of America's entry into the war, the Anti-Saloon League used its political influence to secure the passage by Congress of a bill which, in the name of food conservation, forbade the use of grain for distilling. In December 1917 Congress agreed to submit to the vote of individual states a proposal for a constitutional amendment to enforce national prohibition. That the campaign had moved on so far and so fast surprised even the League's most optimistic supporters, but more was to come. In 1918 Congress voted for complete prohibition for so long as the war might last, and for a limited period subsequent to eventual demobilization.

From then on it was for the forces of prohibition a matter of onwards to inevitable victory. The First World War ended in November 1918. In January 1919 individual state legislatures started to vote on whether they would support the Eighteenth Amendment as an instrument of national prohibition. Some legislatures made an immediate decision while others held state-wide referendums, but by the end of that January the majority had given their support to prohibition. In January 1920 the Eighteenth Amendment was ratified and America woke up to find itself officially dry throughout its vast extent.

Prohibition and its realities

Prohibition – initially envisaged as an instrument of the American dream – has by its critics been represented as the American nightmare. Let's try to establish some of the realities. What did the Volstead Act say, and was it ever vigorously enforced? And – from the public-health angle the most crucial question – did this experiment really in any way succeed in reducing drinking or drink-related problems, or was it both crime-positive and health-negative?

Here are the facts on what the Volstead Act actually said. It was 'an act to prohibit intoxicating beverages'. But the possession of beverage alcohol was not an offence, and that was true whether the alcohol came from prescient stockpiling or through purchase of illicit liquor. Neither was it an offence for citizens to brew their own beer or ferment their own wine. The Act made illegal only the commercial manufacture, sale and transport of intoxicating drink (except for cider). The Volstead Act thus fell considerably short of the kind of legislation which the more ardent prohibitionists would have liked to have seen put on the statute book. The degree of control was closer to the level found in relation to cannabis in those present-day jurisdictions which have decriminalized that drug and allowed personal possession than to the usual degree of criminal control exerted by modern-day societies in relation to heroin or cocaine. The Volstead Act was not root-and-branch criminalization of alcohol, and no one was going to be subjected to a street stop and search for alcohol, or be busted for keeping a bottle of bourbon in the closet.

Next there is the question of how the Volstead Act was enforced. The problems with enforcement were several. The federal staff who were entrusted with making it work were insufficient in number, and at both state and city level the exercise was underfunded. Political patronage dictated recruitment of staff, and too many enforcement officers were undereducated, corrupt and criminal. Over a six-year period more than 750 agents were dismissed for a galaxy of charges which included extortion, bribery, illegal disposal of liquor, assault, theft and making false reports.

Prohibition did not look pretty, and that is an incontrovertible fact.

Enforcement agents developed an ugly reputation for excessive violence and too ready use of their guns. In mitigation it may be pleaded that in the course of duty they were often dealing with criminals who were themselves apt to be trigger-happy. However, federal enforcement officers reputedly killed three civilians for every death in their own ranks. Witnesses opposed to Prohibition alleged that over the course of ten years more than 1,000 innocent citizens had been gunned down by agents who were enforcing the Volstead Act. The statistics may have been exaggerated, but appalling killings were headlined in the press, and the reputation of these agents was not helped when on the streets of Washington they seriously wounded the senator for Vermont.

During the Prohibition years, a leakage of liquor to general consumption occurred through the rerouting of communion wine to less than sacramental purposes. This may have been on no great scale, but it helped to create a picture of the law as an ass. In northern Illinois, in 1923, 885,000 gallons of wine were recorded as booked out for ecclesiastical use; a few years later, after stringent attempts to block diversion, the figure had fallen to 60,000 gallons. A similar problem occurred with the widespread abuse of the regulation which allowed every doctor to fill out 100 prescriptions for medicinal whisky in any three-month period. In 1927, 1.8 million gallons of medicinal whisky helped slake the thirst of America and taint the reputation of the medical profession.

Even its champions were forced to admit that Prohibition was an operation which was poorly conceived, administratively flawed, underfunded, outmatched by the forces arrayed against it, and disastrous in its handling of public relations. Before long the noble experiment threatened to turn into an ignoble farce.

Is there factual support for the frequently heard assertion that Prohibition led directly to the burgeoning in America of organized crime of the most pervasive, vicious and corrupting kind? That interpretation was the one which Andrew Sinclair offered in his *Prohibition: The Era of Excess*:

In its practical effects, national prohibition transferred two billion dollars a year from the hands of brewers, distillers and shareholders to the hands of murderers, crooks and illiterates. However badly the liquor trade and shareholders misused their wealth, their middle-class sympathies prevented their money power from spreading a slimy trail of racketeering and corruption everywhere. In politics and in business, in labour unions and employers' associations, in public services and private industries, Prohibition was the golden grease through which organized crime insinuated itself into a position of incredible power in the nation.

Sinclair states that Chester Le Mare, a Detroit gangster, was in a single year able to gross $215 million from his bootlegging.

Although it is undeniable that crime syndicates and the likes of Al Capone waxed rich on the profits which the illicit liquor trade could provide, some historians have argued that it is simplistic to assert that Prohibition was the unique cause for the birth of the crime empires which became a feature of American life in the years between the two world wars. Organized crime had in fact become entrenched in urban America a good fifty years before the enactment of Prohibition, having its roots in the struggle between strong-arm capitalism and the labour organizations. Both of those interests were equally willing to hire professional intimidators, dynamiters and assassins. City politicians had also for many years been happy to contract for intimidation at election time. And there had for long been money to be made out of organized extortion, prostitution and illicit gambling.

There is even evidence to suggest that criminal involvement in the production and distribution of alcohol substantially preceded the Prohibition era. A report from the *Philadelphia Times* of 15 November 1890 speaks to that point:

There are not 100 of the nearly or quite 4,000 speak-easies [illegal drinking places] in operation in Philadelphia that are not known to the police; but instead of closing them and bringing the criminals to punishment, they are protected [and] compelled . . . to vote and work at elections as the police direct them in obedience to orders from the city administration.

Not even the speakeasy, that most evocatively named and filmic icon of the Prohibition era, was in fact a creation of Prohibition. History is thus more complex and contradictory than any of the pro- or anti-Volstead propagandists would have us believe. The claim that the totality of corruption and organized crime in America can be laid at the door of national prohibition is not in accord with the evidence.

The assertion that the Eighteenth Amendment was directly responsible for giving the Mafia its power base in America was, however, repeatedly and forcefully made by the forces which began in the 1920s to campaign against Prohibition, and that canard remains a widely credited popular belief to the present day. A balanced reading of history should probably be that, although between 1920 and 1933 illicit liquor did offer enormously rich pickings for entrepreneurial criminals, this was a temporary and opportunistic diversification by an already well established and thriving multi-sector criminal business network.

There are also facts which need to be sorted out regarding the impact of Prohibition on levels of drinking and on drinking problems. The notion that in January 1920 America became a country in which no one could get a drink is a considerable misreading of the true situation. Many people continued to drink, and in particular the middle classes began to find good-quality bootleg liquor rather glamorous. But, due to the impact of wartime restrictions and the creeping state-by-state restrictions, by 1920 per-capita alcohol consumption had, according to Rorabaugh, probably reached an all-time low of about 2.7 litres absolute alcohol per head, or a little less than half of what it had been in 1900. America was veering towards dryness before the national enactment. Over the total Prohibition period and despite the activities of the illicit trade, consumption remained at a fairly low level, and in 1930, despite ten years of prohibition, consumption was still at exactly the 1920 level. However, by 1935 per-capita intake had climbed to about 5 litres per head – an 85 per cent increase on the 1930 figure.

The conclusions to be drawn about what Prohibition did to American drinking are therefore several. First, 1920 is not the starting point from which to start judging the impact of measures against alcohol. There was no absolute starting point, but a protracted ratcheting-up over a long period. Second, it seems fair to conclude that the total array of controls which began before 1920 and were given salience by Prohibition had the effect of substantially reducing consumption and holding it in check. Third, the repeal of Prohibition was followed quite quickly by a dramatic increase in consumption, although the 1935 figure of 5 litres per head was by modern standards still remarkably low.

Those three conclusions together represent an attempt to summarize what can fairly be extracted from complex and sometimes contradictory evidence. Estimates for illicit alcohol production during the Prohibition years are beset by problems. A report published in 1932 by Clark Warburton usefully complements Rorabaugh's tabulations but stops short before repeal. Any statement on what happened to drinking in America as a consequence of Prohibition and repeal has therefore to be on the basis of a best fit with the available facts, and cannot offer categorical certainty.

Let's turn now from the consumption figures to the number of deaths from cirrhosis of the liver during those years, taking these data as an indicator of the underlying rates for heavy drinking. It should be remembered that a decrease in per-capita alcohol consumption may produce a related fall in cirrhosis deaths only some years later (a lagged rather than an immediate relationship). In America the high point for cirrhosis mortality was in 1907, when the figure stood at 14.8 deaths from that cause per 100,000 persons living. By 1920 the statistic had rather more than halved, being down to 7.1 per 100,000. During the ensuing years of Prohibition there were minor fluctuations in the cirrhosis death rates, but the figure never went above 7.5 per 100,000. The cirrhosis data thus give support to the inferences which can be drawn from the consumption data. Caution is needed in interpreting these data, however, and cirrhosis death rates do not necessarily move exactly in step with consumption.

Looking in the round at the realities of Prohibition, it undoubtedly had its costs as well as its benefits. But inspection of the records repeatedly shows large divergences between what actually happened and the massively negative view of this experiment which is today's common currency.

Why repeal?

National prohibition was enacted in January 1920 and repeal was declared in December 1933. Considering (against the rippling background of gunfire) the flurry of paradoxes surrounding an experiment which was designed to wipe out crime and poverty but which came to be portrayed as cause both of a crime wave and of the Great Depression, an unsympathetic commentator might conclude that America was between those dates determined to live out the script of a political farce. Nearly fourteen years of divisiveness, to whose good? How could a great nation wilfully have done this to its citizens?

Within the story of repeal, as with that of Prohibition, there were a variety of interacting processes at work. Let's look at some of those factors in sequence.

What perhaps most stands out is the lack of evidence for any sustained political will to make Prohibition work, once it was on the statute book. One reason why Prohibition failed seems to be that politically and administratively it was allowed to fail. Until Herbert Hoover took office in 1929, there had been little interest at presidential level in supporting the machinery of Prohibition. Congress was unwilling to legislate large sums for enforcement, due to a fear of alienating voters. Most states were unwilling to make special appropriations. Judges were often unsympathetic to prosecutions, and juries might be unwilling to convict.

J. C. Burnham, an American social historian who has written about this period, suggests, however, that when discussing the success or failure of Prohibition one should be alert to variations across both time and geography. Prohibition was in general more successfully enforced during its earlier years, when it still had significant public support, than during the later period when it had lost much of its credibility. And the degree of support for enforcement varied greatly across the country, with, for instance, the political leadership in New Jersey always treating its responsibilities for enforcement with flagrant contempt. Burnham argues that, given the extent to which the system was under-resourced, its degree of operational success was at times remarkable. The politicians and the voters had at the outset underestimated what it would require to hold in place an effective national system to prohibit the use of a culturally embedded recreational drug.

The story of repeal is also a story about the propaganda machine of the Association Against the Prohibition Amendment. Just as the Anti-Saloon League had in its time shown a brilliant ability to demonize the saloon, so by 1918 there was up and running a propaganda machine bent on demonizing the forthcoming Prohibition. There is a wonderful sense of congruence between these two extraordinarily clever campaigning organizations, which were equally dedicated to distortion of the truth. But the myths created by the Association Against the Prohibition Amendment (AAPA) endure to this day, while the images once so forcefully propagated by the Anti-Saloon League are long forgotten. The world 'knows', for instance, that Prohibition was 'a failure', and that is a direct inheritance from the AAPA's propaganda.

Prohibition put out of operation a previously powerful and legitimate industrial complex concerned with the production, distribution and sale of beverage alcohol, while at the same time triggering an increase in income tax so as to compensate for the loss of the tax revenue from drink. It was not surprising that various interest groups should counter-attack. The AAPA was soon attracting substantial funding from exactly those industrialists who, before they had realized the tax implications, had been backers of Prohibition in the expectation of a beneficial impact on productivity. At one point the Du Pont family virtually took over the running of the AAPA, and the records show them bankrolling the Association to an extraordinarily generous degree. The press moguls came in with their funding and the invaluable and deeply biased support of their newspapers. The AAPA's annual report for 1930 included the following note on the success of its public-relations effort:

Available clippings on file in this office prove that six hundred millions of copies of newspapers containing conspicuous publication of our news were read in almost every community throughout the year; 153,617,704 copies of magazines and periodicals containing articles and editorials attacking Prohibition have been read by the public similarly . . . With the co-operation and consent of the newspapers and artists concerned, a collection of cartoons attacking and ridiculing Prohibition was published and widely circulated.

The purpose of all this attack, ridicule and manipulation was, of course, to persuade legislators and the public that Prohibition was failing, and in the process was guilty of causing crime, social disruption and harm, and economic loss vastly beyond anything that had ever stemmed from the availability of drink. Some of the charges were true at least in part, but the AAPA's rhetoric was a front for the distaste of the Du Ponts and others like them for paying high income tax. The degree to which the AAPA succeeded in gaining national political leverage is shown by the fact that in December 1932 the Speaker of the House, before presenting to Congress the repeal amendment, had checked the wording of that amendment with the offices of the AAPA for approval. Congress gave the appearance of having become the poodle of a pressure group. Indeed, beyond the specifics of repeal history, the AAPA is of interest as an early case study showing what may be achieved by heavily funded special-interest lobbying of a kind which has since had many imitators.

Another important element in the repeal story is that, just as the First World War had hastened the coming of Prohibition, so did the cataclysm of the Great Depression make repeal inevitable. In October 1929 the American stock market collapsed, and by 1930 almost one-third of the adult population was out of work. Public and political debate was dominated by economic imperatives. With an eye on the potential tax revenue from liquor, in the presidential election of 1932 the Democrats adopted repeal as their policy, and Franklin D. Roosevelt triumphed on that platform. One of his first acts on taking office in March 1933 was to slash the funding of the Prohibition Bureau by 60 per cent. A few days later he sent a message to Congress urging the dismantling of the Volstead Act – 'I deem action at this time to be of the highest importance.' The legislative procedures required a separate vote by each state. On the evening of 5 December 1933, immediately after the deciding vote, Roosevelt broadcast to the American people:

I ask the wholehearted co-operation of all our citizens to the end that this return of individual freedom should not be accompanied by the repugnant conditions that obtained prior to the adoption of the Eighteenth Amendment . . . We must remove forever from our midst the menace of the bootlegger, and such others who would profit at the expense of good government, law, and order. I trust in the good sense of the American people that they will not bring upon themselves the curse of excessive use of intoxicating liquors, to the detriment of health, morals and social integrity.

That speech – with its talk of 'repugnant conditions' which obtained prior to Prohibition and the 'curse of excessive use', but with reference

also to Prohibition as a threat to 'good government, law, and order' –
was crafted to please both the dry and the wet factions. But Roosevelt's
real and openly stated motivation was that liquor taxes would help pay
for the $3.3 billion public-works programme which he was about to
launch.

Prohibition and inferences for the present day

With Roosevelt's broadcast, the curtain came down on a play which
in one form or another had been running on the American public stage
for rather more than a century. The cast had included clergymen and
gunmen, bands of praying women, Mafiosi carrying sinister violin
cases, Carrie Nation and Billy Sunday, and the Du Ponts as quick-change
artists, with the Anti-Saloon League and the AAPA providing scripts
and chorus lines. The show's programme was printed and distributed
in millions of WCTU pamphlets and in those AAPA-planted newspaper
stories. Great underlying issues were dramatized which bore on the
relationship between the individual and government, and on the division of power between federal government and the individual states.
And the stage scenery changed as time passed. The America of the
1930s was not the same country as it had been a century before.

One way of viewing this history is to dismiss it as a melodrama of
continuing relevance to the present day only insofar as it provides a
warning against Prohibition as a folly never to be repeated. But an
informed view must surely be less simplistic. There is a great deal
within the totality of that story which is of subtle and continuing
relevance to our modern coexistence with alcohol, and indeed with
other drugs. Let's list some of the core factors which support that
position.

• To expect societal responses to alcohol or other drugs to be strictly and rationally about
  dealing effectively with alcohol and drug problems is to fail to understand the important
  influence of the social and political context. The truth of this contention is to
  be found in every element of the hundred-year story which this
  chapter tells. Rather than lamenting that the way in which society
  deals with alcohol does not appear to be dictated by pure scientific

reason, by empirical analysis of the costs and benefits to society of
drinking, or by objective evidence of whether a policy succeeds in
any of its stated aims, we should be willing to accept positively the
insight that alcohol policies are always likely to be carried forward,
frustrated, shaped or nullified by the total environment of what else
is happening, changing, being believed in or fought about. Alcohol
is in that sense a lightning conductor for other social tensions.

- *On the evidence of this story, stringent controls over alcohol are likely to support the
public-health aim of reducing alcohol-related health problems.* That is an essential
but commonly neglected insight which can be drawn from the
American experience. Whether adding national prohibition and the
Volstead Act to the already considerable apparatus of control was
worth the candle is a separate question, and it is arguable that the
Volstead Act was an exercise in overkill. But the message that controls
on alcohol can benefit public health can fairly be extracted from
those years of turmoil, despite the best efforts of the AAPA to
obfuscate that truth.

- *Whether America's control policies 'worked', or any other alcohol policy works, is
not a question to be judged in terms of any one outcome dimension.* Stringent
controls over alcohol reduced both alcohol consumption and alcohol
problems in America. This may have been particularly true among
the urban poor, whereas the middle classes were after 1920 probably
given a new taste for drink and the pleasures of the cocktail. The
saloon was run out of town, even if illicit drinking places burgeoned.
Treatment centres for the inebriate closed down for lack of clients.
But with the advent of Prohibition these gains were at the cost of
tensions and abuses which must be judged as elements of failure and
which became material for the repeal propagandists. Repeal 'worked'
for Roosevelt because on that promise he won a populist election.
And the coming of repeal ultimately helped transfer power from an
old to a new American elite. Outcome was about much else besides
the flow of alcohol.

- *The experience of controls over alcohol has implications for legal controls over illicit
drugs.* It is the negative image of the American Prohibition experience
which is heavily and repeatedly presented in current debate around
the control of illicit drugs. On the basis of a misreading of history,

the attempted prohibition of alcohol is deemed to have been a catastrophe, and it is then argued as if by axiom that existing controls over illicit drugs should be got rid of. One could in fact draw a precisely opposite inference for drug controls from the alcohol experience, but either kind of simple reading would be equally facile. The truth is that controls work to the health benefit when actively enforced and publicly supported. The lesson is also that controls will have their downside as well as their desired outcomes.

So much for the story of the long march to Prohibition and the much shorter road which was taken to repeal.

Beyond the historically rooted view of drunkenness as the common adverse consequence associated with alcohol, over the ages it must have been evident that some people kept on getting drunk with repeated insult to decent expectations and public order. They failed to respond to being preached against, time in the stocks, or the tears and beseechings of their families. What was to be deemed the problem with alcohol thus gradually moved on from the everyday and outward fact of drunkenness to a realization that there were some people around who showed a fixed propensity to get drunk whenever the opportunity presented. What in essence made these drinkers stand out as different was that they readily lost control over their drinking, and again and yet again drank to the point of gross intoxication, persisting in this behaviour despite every pressure which invited them to reform and repent.

The 'drink crave' and the crave for moralism

The simplest and most time-honoured explanation of what was wrong with these inveterate drunkards was that, rather than being given only occasionally to the sin of drunkenness, they were exceptionally and horribly dedicated to this sin. Within that formulation, the frequency of their offence did not suggest an illness or make their transgressions excusable; on the contrary, their recalcitrance suggested that they needed yet heavier punishment. When, however, society began to lose faith in sin as the all-embracing explanation for human deviance, it was an easy step to conclude that there was something constitutionally wrong with this kind of drinker. Habitual drunkards, the observer of the repeatedly inebriated husband, wife or neighbour might then hypothesize, were men or women who, for reasons within themselves, could not, once they had started on drink, control their drinking by act of will. They were in that sense categorically different from other drinkers, and it was this sadly disordered minority who constituted the real problem with drink. Preaching and punishment ceased to be intelligent answers to the behaviour they presented.

If repeated drunkenness was to be reformulated not as perseverative sin but as disorder residing within the individual, it was easy to assume that the disordered drinker was in the grip of a disease. In Chapter 9 we will discuss the eighteenth-century origins of this belief. By the latter part of the nineteenth century the idea that inebriety was a disease had become the conceptual banner behind which marched those doctors who were crusading for the establishment of inebriate asylums, and for the enactment of legislation for compulsory treatment of habitual drunkards. But nineteenth-century reformers lived happily with having the thing several ways at once: drunkenness was a big problem, habitual drunkenness was a disease which was a problem, and drink itself was the underlying problem because it led both to casual drunkenness and to the disease of habitual drunkenness. On a pick-and-mix basis and according to the particular evening's platform or the immediate facet of the crusade, it was possible to fight against drunkenness, campaign for temperance or prohibition and elimination of drink as the pathogenic agent, or lobby for the establishment of inebriate reformatories in which the diseased person would be treated. Many doctors who called for acceptance of the disease formulation were at the same time temperance advocates who wanted to strike at alcohol root and branch. The alcohol-reform movement of that time was a broad Church which at the end of the nineteenth century was getting along quite nicely with mixed but complementary articles of faith.

There were, however, some doctrinal disputes. Quite a few hardliners saw the idea of inebriety as a disease, and talk of 'the drink crave' as a symptom of this sickness, as constituting no more than making excuses for bad behaviour. A section of the temperance movement viewed the disease concept as a distraction from the need to eliminate drink from society. There were doctors who preferred robust condemnation of the drunkard to any namby-pamby talk of illness. Here is Dr Arthur

Shadwell, a medical doctor who had temperance connections, denouncing in 1902 what he saw as the danger which lay in allowing inebriates to hide behind the excuse of a disease state:

The primary malady is not physical but moral . . . 'Irresistible craving' is one of those phrases with which people intoxicate themselves . . . Every desire which any individual fails to resist is to that individual an irresistible craving, and in no other sense is the drunkard's craving irresistible. He does not resist it because he does not want to do so with sufficient energy . . . to minimize the moral responsibility of the vicious is to encourage vice.

Dr Shadwell commended the 'healthier sentiment' towards the drunkard which was to be found in a recent address given by Dr Wilson, the then superintendent of a Scottish asylum:

Dr Wilson . . . said he would like to see a clause in the Habitual Drunkards Bill, then before Parliament, which would provide for the flogging of drunkards, under appropriate and necessary supervision. The notion of heredity did nothing to help the drunkard, but everything to injure him. The latter felt he was compelled to give way to drink. A young man so influenced should be flogged within an inch of his life, every time he took drink. Another excuse used with great effect by the drunkard was the myth of a crave for alcohol. The crave was a very exceptional thing . . . Drunkards were inveterate idlers, who had to be taught to work; they were untruthful, slanderers, and intensely selfish.

And Shadwell reported Dr Thomas Clouston, a much respected psychiatrist, chipping into a discussion of Dr Wilson's paper with a personal condemnation of the 'mawkish sentimentalism' inherent in much contemporary medical thinking on the drunkard.

The records thus show that, as the nineteenth century turned to the twentieth, the idea of drunkenness as a disease, although by then over 100 years old and the favoured formulation of some specialists, was not a universally accepted idea. Among its implacable enemies were medical practitioners such as Shadwell and Wilson. For them the problem lay not with the drink nor in an invented disease, but with the individual's vicious and self-willed indulgence. Medicine and rampant moralism could go hand in hand.

The disease concept as an element within the mix of explanations of drunkenness largely slipped out of sight during the earlier part of the twentieth century. Inebriate reformatories, which had been established in America and Britain as the tangible product of 'inebriety is a disease', never made much of a contribution to solving the drink problem. They were closed or put to other uses. The generation of doctors who had fought for the disease idea died out, and by the end of the 1930s the disease concept of inebriety was so completely forgotten that it might never have existed.

The 1940s and the disease concept reborn

Then, in the 1940s, something astonishing happened. The disease concept staged a comeback, but this time not as a contested or partial definition of what constituted the drink problem, but as the absolute centre of what was to be deemed problematic about drink. This time round the phrasing had changed, and it was not 'inveterate drinking' or 'inebriety' which were being put forward as candidate for disease status. The centuries-old problem of intractable drunkenness was now renamed 'alcoholism'. The term 'alcoholism' (or 'alcoholismus') had been introduced to this field in 1849 by Magnus Huss, a Swedish physician, but what he meant by the word had little resemblance to the way in which it was now to be used. Huss used the term to describe the spectrum of physical complications which can result from excessive drinking. In the new terminology, 'alcoholism' meant the disorder in the drinking behaviour, not the complications.

This disease concept of alcoholism was rapidly taken up by the medical profession, popularized, and fervently disseminated from its American base to the world at large. The disease of alcoholism was the whole problem, and any other view was a heresy to be preached down. A new movement had apparently been born, with 'alcoholism is a disease' inscribed on its marching banners and with everyone falling in behind that slogan. But to some extent it was simply the rebirth of an old movement, adopting a nineteenth-century word as a new talisman, and indulging in a good deal of historical amnesia.

The immediate origins of the 1940s development were in part an American lay body called the National Council on Alcoholism (NCA), which proselytized for the disease concept as a means of legitimizing access to treatment and supporting a humane view of the troubled drinker. The movement was also carried forward by the proliferating success of Alcoholics Anonymous, which soon after its origins in the 1930s adopted the disease concept as a central tenet of its philosophy. (Alcoholics Anonymous is the subject of Chapter 8.)

The scientific underpinning for a new version of the old disease theory came meanwhile from the Yale Center for Alcohol Studies, which was established in 1942 at Yale University in New Haven, Connecticut. Following the years of Prohibition, scientific interest in alcohol problems had almost completely died out in the USA. The scholars who set up the Yale Center deftly avoided the risk of being deemed prohibitionist or against alcohol (by then a vastly unpopular stance and politically untenable) by making it clear from the beginning that alcoholism, not alcohol, would be the focus of their activity. This ensured that the alcohol industry would not be antagonized. The Yale Center founded a journal, inaugurated an influential summer school, set up a literature archive, launched the Yale Plan treatment clinics, and provided the movers and shakers for the rebirth of American interest in the disease of alcohol. The new Church was a narrow one, with no place for anyone who wanted to propose that alcohol itself was the root problem. So deft and politically astute was the reformulation of the problem that it seems almost like a conjuring trick. A rabbit in the form of a disease was brought out of the hat, and alcohol vanished into thin air.

The Yale Center was the working base for many researchers who were subsequently to become leaders in this field of study, but the most influential of them all was E. M. Jellinek. Born in 1890, Jellinek had no medical training, but he claimed credentials as a plant physiologist, statistician, and psychoanalyst. Before joining Yale, since 1939 he had been employed in New York on a grant which had enabled him to conduct, with others, a comprehensive review of the then extant international scientific literature on drinking problems. This literature ran to a massive 5,000 articles. From the Yale Center, Jellinek published influential research which appeared to confirm the disease status of alcoholism by showing that over time the condition was predictably progressive, with distinct and recognizable phases to its natural history. He devised the Jellinek Estimation Formula, which supposedly allowed an estimate of the number of alcoholics in any given geographical area. With the disease an unquestionable entity, cases able to be counted, and governments confronted with the enormous extensiveness of the disorder, this time around there were no disparaging critics to be heard talking of 'mawkish sentimentalism'.

Jellinek's masterwork, *The Disease Concept of Alcoholism*, was published in 1960. It was a work of outstanding scholarship, written by a supreme and revered authority, and in it, on the basis of a scrupulous consideration of the available evidence, Jellinek declared that certain types of excessive drinking constituted disease. The disease concept had now come of age, was unchallenged, and seemingly unchallengeable – almost a religiously received truth. Anyone who dissented from this definition of reality risked anathema.

The new movement now had its great man as well as its big idea. When Jellinek died, in 1963, the disease concept (as idea and also as book) was seen as his supreme legacy. The fact that he seems to have invented for himself a scientific doctorate which no university ever awarded is disturbing, but the significance of his work for the development of ideas on alcohol remains profound. However, his own writings were often more cautious in tone than the absolute interpretations put upon them by those who read him carelessly, or who wanted to make him the high priest of the disease definition of what counts as the problem with alcohol.

The disease concept as balm for tortured hearts

In the early 1960s, few people in any English-speaking country who were concerned about drinking would have questioned the assertion that alcoholism was a disease, and that that disease was the only problem with alcohol. Although some European countries (particularly France and the Nordic countries) stood out against the Anglo-Saxon consensus, Jellinek's ideas were read everywhere with respect. The disease concept was the working assumption of science and medicine, the credo of Alcoholics Anonymous, the slogan of the American NCA, the message of every public lecturer and all the media. A London-based community campaign in 1963 had a poster with the message 'Alcoholism – not a disgrace but a disease', and alcoholism as disease was an idea taken to the streets in many other campaigns, national and local, and in many countries. Campaigns against alcohol itself were dead and buried, discredited stuff of the Victorian past, and the marching banners of the prohibition movement were never again to be unfurled.

This is how Mrs Marty Mann, the founding president of the American NCA, a friend of E. M. Jellinek and herself a recovered alcoholic, laid out the 'alcoholism is a disease' stall in her immensely popular *Primer on Alcoholism*, first published in 1950:

Alcoholism is a disease which manifests itself chiefly by the uncontrollable drinking of the victim, who is known as an alcoholic. It is a progessive disease, which, if left untreated, grows more virulent year by year, driving its victims further and further from the normal world, and deeper and deeper into an abyss which has only two outlets: insanity or death.

Mrs Mann went on to describe the wide blessings which could flow from the acceptance of the disease concept:

It has come as a revelation to thousands of alcoholics seeking desperately to find a reason for their, to them, inexplicable drinking behaviour; for many of them it has been the greatest single factor leading to eventual recovery from that disease. It has come as healing balm to the tortured hearts of wives, mothers and husbands of alcoholics, who had hopelessly clung to a lonely belief that their alcoholic wasn't the 'bad character' of general opinion, but had 'something' specifically wrong with him that drove him to destructive excess in drinking. Finally, it has come as a constructive tool to the hands of baffled and frustrated would-be helpers, both professional and lay people whose work or inclination led them to deal with alcoholics.

Much of her language reads like the rhetoric of an old-time temperance tract – 'victims', 'abyss' 'healing balm', 'tortured hearts'. But this is the prose of a mid-twentieth-century activist who believed that she was translating the findings of the Yale Center into a scientifically informed public message.

In Britain after the Second World War the same disease message began to appear in text after text, with the American dogma swallowed whole. Dr Lincoln Williams, the proprietor of a private nursing home and later the first president of the British NCA, declared in the opening line of his 1960 text *Tomorrow will be Sober* that 'Alcoholism is a disease.' He stated that 'Alcoholism is not synonymous with drunkenness' but 'a constitutional disease allied to personality disorder . . . the source of the problem is the user of the alcohol and not the alcohol itself'. Dr Williams believed that there was 'a chemical idiosyncrasy in the bodies of those who suffer from alcoholism'. He concluded his exposition with the dramatic testimony of one of his former patients. This man recounted how he had been sober for six years, drank some sherry, and within a fortnight was again drinking two bottles of gin a day:

Once an alcoholic always an alcoholic is one hundred per cent true, and if I ever take a drink, say, in ten, fifteen or twenty years' time, I know with my heart and with my head that I should always react in exactly the same way. Is alcoholism a disease? I know to my cost that it is.

Yale's science, Jellinek's book, the Alcoholics Anonymous message, the American NCA's campaign, the personal testimony of myriad recovered alcoholics had all come together to win acceptance of the disease concept by the media, the medical profession and the man and woman in the street. The science and the personal experience seemed to fit together precisely.

The disease concept and the
dependence syndrome – same or different?

Chapter 5 described the alcohol dependence syndrome. It might reasonably be asked whether that syndrome formulation simply reinvents the idea of 'alcoholism as a disease'. The answer to that question is mostly 'no', with a little bit of 'yes'. No, because dependence is not an all-or-nothing or absolute state like 'the disease', but something which exists in degrees. No, because lesser degrees of dependence are compatible with a return to normal drinking. No, because the dependence concept allows for the involvement of psychological processes in the learning and unlearning of the compulsive drinking behaviour, rather than the condition being viewed simply as an irreversible physical disease in biological terms. No, because the syndrome idea puts emphasis on the drug as well as the person, and sees access to the drug as related to prevalence of the disorder. Yes, because many people who see themselves as suffering from 'alcoholism as a disease' are drinkers who have contracted severe alcohol dependence.

The disease as the thing – what consequences?

Let's now try to summarize the consequences which were likely to flow from the triumph of the refurbished disease concept of alcoholism over all earlier ways of seeing the problem with drink. There were perhaps four main consequences.

First, alcohol was defined as not being at all the problem. The problem was very definitely not in the bottle. Alcohol was a good thing, and alcoholism was an unfortunate disease caused by an unidentified defect within the individual rather than by the drink. The disease formulation meant that everyone not born with the disease could drink without damage, that the quantity drunk was irrelevant to the genesis of the problem, that the drinks industry was out of the firing line, and that governments did not have a responsibility to control the alcohol supply in the interest of public health.

Second, a disease was something which should be treated. Alcoholics Anonymous was seen as an organization which by itself would often be able to provide the entirety of the needed help, but the disease concept had also made medical treatment legitimate. In 1956 the American Medical Association formally declared alcoholism to be a disease. With the dawning of this newly discovered disease, clinics proliferated and governments in many countries expanded the treatment facilities for alcoholics who could not pay the private fees, and there were also positive implications for welfare and insurance provisions. In Britain the National Health Service accepted responsibility for alcoholism treatment and began in 1962 to establish regional alcoholism treatment centres. Medical acceptance of the disease concept was the catalyst for this British development.

The third consequence was that alcoholics became good guys. The disease concept made recovering alcoholics into worthy people who could talk openly about their disease and proudly of their recovery, and be welcomed back into society. The awful stigma of Dr Wilson's denunciation was washed away. This humane consequence of the disease formulation meant that many prominent people in the USA were willing to go on public record and declare that they were alcoholics who had dealt with their problem and were now 'in recovery'. And the Betty Ford Clinic is able to use in its title the name of a former First Lady who had been treated at that centre for the disease of alcoholism.

The fourth and final significant consequence to be put into this listing is that the disease concept of alcoholism offered an unequivocal message that the personal action plan for the alcoholic must be to stop drinking and stay stopped. That same message also powerfully shaped the treatments given by the helping professions. The programme offered at the Betty Ford Clinic focuses on establishing lifelong abstinence, and talk of a return to social drinking would be viewed by its counsellors as profoundly seditious. Paradoxically, even as the disease formulation sought to distance itself from the taint of Prohibition, it at the same time proposes personally determined but absolute prohibition for the not inconsiderable number of members of society who are diagnosed as alcoholics. 'Once an alcoholic always an alcoholic' is the linchpin of the disease concept, the credo of alcoholism as a disease.

It would seem fair to conclude that the disease concept of alcoholism is still alive and well. It remains a central tenet of Alcoholics Anonymous and of twelve-step treatment programmes. For experts suddenly to declare that alcoholism is no longer a disease would cause dismay to many people who find this formulation helpful, and might disenfranchise drinkers from insurance benefits and needed treatment. However, what is to be understood by 'alcoholism' is still not well defined. It is a term which scientists find unsatisfactory and try to avoid. Similarly, what is to be understood by 'disease' is a question to baffle academics, even if Dr Lincoln Williams's patient, and many other people, knew in his heart and head that that is what alcoholism is.

The eleventh of May 1933 was a Sunday. At 11.15 a.m. in Akron, Ohio, William Griffith Wilson, a stock-market analyst, called round by arrangement at the home of a fellow Oxford Group member, Dr Robert Hollbrook Smith. In this chapter we will use 'Bill W.' and 'Dr Bob' as the designations for these two men. It was under those identities that they achieved fame as the founders of Alcoholics Anonymous (AA).

After a devastating drinking history, Bill W. had behind him in May 1933 a few weeks of sobriety which had been accomplished through his involvement with the Oxford Group. This was a Christian movement which had in the 1930s secured a significant presence in the USA, the UK and South Africa. Bill W. on that day still felt himself vulnerable to the danger of relapse. On this visit to Ohio from his home in New York, he was seized with the notion that the only way for him to stay sober was to contact another drunk, and carry to him the Oxford Group message. Dr Bob was a surgeon with a thirty-year history of excessive drinking, and had by 1933 a tally of more than a dozen failed hospital admissions for treatment of his drinking problem. He was amply qualified as a target for Bill W.'s new-found missionary zeal. Dr Bob was that morning once more experiencing withdrawal shakes as he tried to sober himself up for the coming week's surgical commitments.

The two men had not met before, and the meeting had been set up through the local Oxford Group network. Dr Bob had reckoned on getting rid of this none too welcome visitor within fifteen minutes of arrival. In the event, morning tuned to late afternoon, and the two men stayed talking with each other for six hours. Dr Bob was subsequently to say of his afternoon with Bill W., 'He was the first living human with whom I had ever talked who knew what he was talking about in regard to alcoholism.' Within the lore of Alcoholics Anonymous, that day's encounter between two drunks in Akron – one fragile in his early sobriety and the other shaking in withdrawal – is deemed to have been the first ever meeting of AA.

To see the origins of AA as lying solely in the more or less chance encounter between these two subsequently renowned figures would, however, be too simple. For a fuller insight into how AA came into being, at that time and in America, we need to examine the confluence of three significant and complementary factors: the Oxford Group connection, the contemporary situation of the alcohol-dependent person in the USA, and, within those contexts, the personal influences of the two gifted but very different men who met in Akron. This chapter will deal with those matters, and then go on to describe how AA functions and to address the question 'Does it work?'

AA and the Oxford Group

Born in 1878 in Pennsylvania, Frank Nathan Buchman was brought up as a Lutheran and ordained as a priest. At a certain point in his career he came to believe that the state of the world was such as imminently to threaten the collapse of civilization. To avert this dreaded outcome, he instigated in 1921 an organization which he initially called The First Century Christian Movement, and which was afterwards variously known as the Oxford Group, Moral Rearmament or Buchmanism. It operated through a network of groups at whose meetings the participants were required to stand up and publicly confess their shortcomings. All members were expected to go out and proselytize for further recruits, with talk of their own sins and of their salvation through the Oxford Group the favoured recruitment pitch. The movement embraced an essentially Protestant ideology based on divine guidance and the surrendering of self to God, access to God and interpretation of his will without the guidance of a priest, repentance, the making of amends, self-improvement, and commitment to the principles of honesty, purity, unselfishness and love and the overcoming of personal pride. It was a religious movement with political undertones, and it attracted sponsorship from big business and the wealthy middle class. Some of its backers viewed it as a bulwark against the menace of communism. Buchman himself later developed an admiration for National Socialism which did his cause no good.

As already mentioned, Bill W. was by May 1933 a convert to the Oxford Group. He had been introduced by an evangelizing school friend who had recently conquered his own drinking problem. That friend, obedient to the organization's dictates, called around one day on the habitually drunken Bill W. to carry to him the good news of salvation through faith and the works of the Group. Bill W. sobered up, slipped, went into hospital, and while detoxifying saw a flash of light and underwent a revelatory spiritual experience. By the time of his visit to Akron he was himself well into the role of Oxford Group missionary. Unsurprisingly, his special interest was in using this movement as vehicle for saving alcoholics, and he set himself to this task with an all-consuming commitment. The ordinary business of earning a living was put on one side.

Bill W., Dr Bob and the recovering drunks who began to gather around them, at first constituted an informal development within the larger Oxford Group organization. But before long tensions began to arise. The leadership of the parent movement was unhappy with special meetings being held exclusively for alcoholics. They saw this initiative as subversive and as constituting a party within the party. Bill W. and his friends, in their turn, increasingly found aspects of the Oxford Group's ideology and practices not to their liking. By 1939 the split had become absolute, and in that year the designation 'Alcoholics Anonymous' was for the first time employed as the name of the breakaway movement. What at the time must have seemed a minor schismatic offshoot from a well-established evangelical movement had achieved its own identity and a brilliant title, but few would then have wagered on this breakaway group having a long-term future.

AA was born out of a good deal of Protestant ideology and a set of practices which derived from an evangelical movement which knew how to organize. The influence of those factors on the shape which AA was to take were important, but AA was never the prisoner of that heritage. Some of the lasting influences of the Oxford Group on AA include the emphasis on the local group as the organizational unit, and on group meetings as the crucial events. AA members standing up to tell their own stories at each meeting represent an obvious Oxford Group derivative. The turning to God, the surrender of pride, the continued personal working out of an everyday life programme, recovery as process and the search for self-change and spiritual growth, the embracing provision of a mutual-support system – all that is very like Buchmanism. But in AA the talk is of past problems and present recovery, not of sin.

Besides the follow-through of certain obvious specifics drawn from those founding evangelical influences on the form and functioning of AA – the group format and the personal declaration or 'story', for example – it has been suggested that AA, as historically an offshoot of Buchmanism, is in its essence simply another Protestant sect. The hallmark of such Protestantism is seen as evident in the AA emphasis on salvation through surrender to God coupled with repentance and restitution, and the exertion of individual self-control – 'by their works ye shall know them'. Harry Levine, an American sociologist, has charted the worldwide dissemination of AA. He has suggested that its acceptance has been greatest in the dominantly Protestant countries, and in what he calls 'temperance cultures'. Its style fits better with North America and Britain than with the Catholic regions of Europe, or with Latin America. That is not to suggest that AA does not recruit Catholics or operate in Catholic countries (or in non-Christian societies), but only to argue that the ideology of AA in a broad sense reflects the Protestant ethic of its origins.

If there are similarities between AA and the movement from which it originally derived, there are also marked differences. The Oxford Group required belief in a Christian god, while AA settles for 'God as we understood Him'. AA does not offer salvation, but assists the individual towards sobriety 'just for today'. The experienced AA member will go out and help other people, but only on a 'take it or leave it' basis and without intrusive proselytizing. AA is not confrontational but, on the contrary, favours 'easy does it' as one of its informal slogans. AA is for those who want it, but it does not attempt to force recovery on anyone who does not want it, and it is not in the business of saving souls. It steers clear of all political affiliations.

Perhaps the best way to describe the significance of the Oxford Group on AA as we know it today might be to say that without Buchman AA would probably not have come into existence, and the founding influence is still present. But, starting as a schism from an evangelical Christian group, AA has metamorphosed into something quite different and very much of its own kind.

AA's origin in the context of 1930s America

Place and time both had something important to do with how AA came to be born. Bill W. and Dr Bob had as their surroundings a troubled and changing American society. It would be absurd to attempt a full portrait of that national backdrop in a few paragraphs, so we will restrict ourselves specifically to a reconstruction of the context in terms of what it must have felt like to have been a drunk on Mainstreet, USA, in 1933.

In the America of the 1930s, to be an alcoholic was not to occupy a popular social position. The public image of the problem drinker was dominantly unsympathetic and unromantic, with an emphasis on the stereotype of the Skid Row bum. Drunks who had money might get themselves admitted for drying out to a private treatment institution, often on a repeated basis. But, as mentioned in Chapter 6, many long-established homes specializing in the treatment of inebriety had closed down during the Prohibition years. When funds or family patience ran out, there was then the option of long-term commitment to a state institution as a final and disgraced disposal. There was no sympathetic or helpful way of conceptualizing the condition, of talking or feeling about it, or of responding to it. That lack of any positive way of thinking about the disorder affected the drinker, the family, the medical profession and the public at large. AA was revolutionary in its capacity to fill that kind of void, and the fact of that void invited the birth of AA. The bankruptcy, at that time, of medical ideas on how to respond to the drinker was woeful. There was an absence of appropriate methods and techniques, an absence of hope, and an inability to understand and empathize. For the most part what was offered was only various types of banal physical treatment. Hardly anyone knew what they were talking about, and that had been Dr Bob's experience until he met Bill W. and found someone who could talk the talk.

Given the unlikelihood of a dependent drinker in the America of the 1930s encountering an informed medical ear, Bill W. had been supremely lucky in chancing upon an exception to that negative expectation. Dr William Silkworth was to play a significant role in the early history of AA. It was under Silkworth's medical care that Bill W. had his final admission for detoxification, and was so fortunate as to find a doctor who did not dismiss as insanity the spiritual conversion experience he described. Silkworth offered to the founding members of AA the idea that their problem was an innately biological disorder, which he characterized as 'an allergy to alcohol'. There is no scientific validity in such a formulation, but it provided a helpful metaphor at the time. Silkworth gave the newly emerging movement the benefit of his enthusiasm, and he was an example of that special kind of doctor who has a natural sympathy towards people with drinking problems. He had treated about 50,000 alcoholic patients by the end of a long and dedicated career.

The fact that AA was responding to an otherwise unmet need was important, but some wider background social influences of the time were probably also significant. A strong and traditional American belief in anything being possible, something about the American capacity to innovate and a willingness to break with orthodoxies, helped AA to come alive. In 1933 and faced by a crushing recession, Franklin D. Roosevelt had on 4 March declared in his inaugural address 'Let me assert my firm belief that the only thing we have to fear is fear itself.' Bill W. and Dr Bob met in Akron just two months after that address had been delivered, and Roosevelt's statement accidentally but aptly encapsulated the cultural origins of a mutual-help movement which was to offer a pathway to recovery for otherwise stigmatized and seemingly helpless and hopeless drunks.

AA's origins and the personal
influence of its founding members

A 'great man' view of history, which fails to take account of the historical context and the background flow of events, is always likely to be incomplete. That said, Bill W. was absolutely the right man to give this new organization its start, to foster in the early stages its difficult survival, and later to help lead it towards maturity. Dr Bob provided the necessary ballast for his more charismatic and mercurial colleague. What they had in common was alcohol dependence, and the experience of dire personal consequences of a kind which subsequent AA members would designate as 'rock bottom'.

W. G. Wilson (1895–1971) was a man of boundless enthusiasms, but his drinking was such as to have rendered him by his late thirties entirely unreliable. Few people meeting him at that time would believe it probable that he would do other than drink himself to death, while causing a maximum of suffering to his family. His broken promises were legion. As so often happens when recovery from an alcohol problem eventually occurs, however, the man who emerged from this chaos showed that the behaviour which for many years must have appeared to onlookers as the thumbprint of sociopathic character disorder was in fact no more than the side effect of the drinking. With alcohol out of the way, Bill W's enthusiasm was directed with immense creativity to helping his fellow sufferers, even if a wild entrepreneurial streak was still at times manifest – as when at an early stage in his recovery he conceived the idea of setting up a string of for-profit AA-based hospitals.

Bill W.'s leadership was highly important in helping pull AA through its early and inchoate years to a distinct identity, belief system and organizational base. He took a central role in drafting *Alcoholics Anonymous*, often referred to as 'The Big Book', which when published in 1939 first gave AA its definitive form. For someone given to forceful opinions, he had an outstanding capacity to work with and listen to other people. After he achieved sobriety, he experienced repeated depressive illnesses. It is possible that untreated depression had contributed to his previous drinking, and his clinical history may thus have been an early instance of what later came to be called a 'dual diagnosis'. A first-person account of his drinking and his recovery is given in 'The Big Book', which reveals that for a time he had combined his drinking problem with misuse of sedatives – yet another kind of prototypical clinical presentation.

What Dr Bob gave to AA in its early days were qualities of common sense, sound judgement and patience. He was to become intensely involved in the hospital treatment of patients with alcohol dependence, thus strengthening the links between AA and the medical profession.

Against the odds: AA becomes an organizational success

Just as any contemporary observer with a reputation for good sense would have predicted that the drunken stock-market analyst and the drunken doctor who met in Akron would have gone on to drink themselves to death, so it might reasonably have been expected that before long AA itself would crash. Given their previous personal track records, Bill W. and Dr Bob did not look like the most promising of founding fathers for any type of sober enterprise. The prize for sound prognostication would undoubtedly have been expected to go to whoever foretold that a group of inebriates setting up as a go-it-alone offshoot from an evangelical Christian movement at the time of the Great Depression, and with the repeal of Prohibition part of the backdrop, would have had only a short life before falling drunkenly apart. If the Washingtonians had lasted only four years, it would have taken a courageous optimist to have forecast a longer life for this latter-day reincarnation of the mutual-help idea.

Four years into AA's existence, it had not in fact achieved anything like the explosive expansion which the Washingtonians had built over a similar time period: it had only about 100 members, and there had been much backsliding, disappointment and divisiveness along the way. Yet, some sixty further years down the road, AA now has 87,000 groups meeting each week. Its message has spread to 150 countries, and it has claimed 1.7 million total membership worldwide. There are no dues or membership fees, but the General Service Office of AA in New York has an annual budget of $12 million deriving from voluntary contributions.

AA has shown a capacity to adapt to cultures other than the American culture of origin. Alanon is a successful parallel organization for friends or family of people who have drinking problems; Alateen meets the needs of children. In America, the Adult Children of Alcoholics movement is strong, and Narcotics Anonymous is available for people with drug problems. The AA model has been copied by sufferers from numerous other types of trouble, and there are now similar self-help groups available for most of the behaviour problems which can afflict humanity. The 'twelve-step' movement – so called after AA's Twelve Steps (see below) – has become part of the American way of life. Enrolment in twelve-step organizations is seen as chic rather than stigmatizing. Bill W.'s entrepreneurial dreams find a certain kind of fulfilment in that AA has become integrated into the Minnesota Model, America's favourite, money-spinning and widely exported private-treatment approach to drinking problems. The Betty Ford Clinic is the world's most famous institution for the treatment of alcohol dependence, and that kind of clinic is in essence AA institutionalized.

The success of AA as judged by its duration, extensiveness, cultural penetration, imitation and commercialization, and the witness of the 1.7 million people who are willing to vote with their feet, does suggest that AA is an organization with a brilliantly intuitive capacity to go on filling a void.

The language which is talked

On the surface, AA is a room with a man or woman standing up and saying 'My name's Mary [or John], I'm an alcoholic.' Stories are told of drinking and recovery, coffee and biscuits are served afterwards at the back of the hall, and certain simplicities are stated plainly. Beneath that surface, however, AA is a complex psychological apparatus so contrived as to instigate and support in flexible fashion the individual's self-change. AA is about stopping drinking, but it is also about developing the skills, self-knowledge and self-control which will allow the drinking to stay stopped. Nevertheless, many people who walk through AA's doors will go on drinking, relapse and relapse again, and find nothing helpful in AA. Understanding of this organization is not helped by claiming it to be a cure for all comers.

Let's now look at what may happen at any AA meeting (and between meetings), and identify some of the elements which seem commonly to be operating within the totality of the change process which is on offer.

'I'm an alcoholic.'

That ritualized form of words with which all speakers will introduce themselves at a meeting is a statement loaded with implications for personal change. The person who utters those words is engaging in an act of surrender, and is giving up the claim of 'I'm not an alcoholic.' He or she is with that phrase claiming a passport, and bonding with a roomful of listeners who feel safe in using the same formula as password. It is a formulation of the problem, an explanation of past behaviour, the cornerstone for the building of recovery: 'I'm an alcoholic', alcoholism is a disease, there is no escaping that incurable fact, but the disease will stay in remission so long as the first drink is not taken. Those words offer a new definition of what is wrong, and of what has been wrong probably for many painful and perplexing years.

The fellowship

One of the discoveries for anyone newly attending AA is the simple fact that AA is there, it exists, these people in the room are AA. There is no swearing-in or signing of a register, but the new member is instantly part of the fellowship of AA. This fellowship is a resource. Perhaps it will prove to be something to walk out on and revile; but it is there that night, and it will be there tomorrow to come back to. The meeting and the chat afterwards are likely to offer a non-intrusive kind of friendliness, and a message of 'take it easy'. Only afterwards will a new member discover the deeper meaning of belonging to this fellowship, what it can give and the limits of the demands to be put upon it and fellow members, what can and cannot be talked about at a meeting, the pathways of the fellowship. But the discovery made by individuals during their early encounters with AA is that, though their drinking behaviour may previously have led to rejection and exclusion on a grand scale, there is now a fellowship to which they belong.

The abstinence goal

AA is unequivocal in its insistence that abstinence is the only feasible goal for the person who by accident of constitution suffers from Silkworth's 'allergy to alcohol' or 'the disease of alcoholism'. There is no signing of a lifetime pledge but on the contrary an active discouragement of long-term promises. The programme centres on the idea of being sober 'just for today'. Someone who has not drunk any alcohol at all for twenty years will, within the AA tradition, still insist that they are taking their sobriety one day at a time, and dealing only with that day's immediacies. If at an early stage a new member insists that they are not *really* an alcoholic, that they will be able to stop drinking after a couple of drinks, that beer isn't for them really alcohol, there will be a shaking of heads, a murmur of 'That won't work', but an acknowledgement that people must make their own experiments.

Talk of ways and means

AA offers a lot of talk on how to stay sober, and there is also teaching by example. Staying sober, it will be emphasized, must be each individual's priority: avoid dangerous situations and, if the temptation set by the alcohol which will be flowing at a wedding looks like being too threatening, keep away. If the whole world looks too threatening, pull the curtains for a day and stay in bed. Be on the alert for your internal excuse-making and the setting-up of self-deceiving little plans to justify that first drink. Deal with resentments, count to ten and don't rear up, walk away from trouble, guard against unmanageable emotional involvements. AA does not dispense these hints for survival through lectures or seminars but by the ongoing, casual, joking discourse which is the essence of AA talk.

A twelve-step programme, but each
person to take from it what they want

The Twelve Steps which define the shape of AA's recovery programme and which were originally drawn up by Bill W. read as follows:

1. We admitted we were powerless over alcohol – that our lives had become unmanageable.
2. Came to believe that a Power greater than ourselves could restore us to sanity.
3. Made a decision to turn our will and our lives over to the care of God *as we understood* Him.
4. Made a searching and fearless moral inventory of ourselves.

5. Admitted to God, to ourselves, and to another human being the exact nature of our wrongs.

6. Were entirely ready to have God remove all these defects of character.

7. Humbly asked Him to remove our shortcomings.

8. Made a list of all persons we had harmed, and became willing to make amends to them all.

9. Made direct amends to such people wherever possible, except when to do so would injure them or others.

10. Continued to take personal inventory, and when we were wrong, promptly admitted it.

11. Sought through prayer and meditation to improve our conscious contact with God *as we understood* Him, praying only for knowledge of His will for us and the power to carry that out.

12. Having had a spiritual awakening as the result of these steps, we tried to carry this message to alcoholics and to practice these principles in all our affairs.

Starting with Step 1 and its admission of defeat, and going all the way through to Step 12 with its move towards helping other people, those steps will for many AA members provide an initial framework for practical action, but one which later may also become guidance for a spiritual journey.

Some members read and study the meanings to be given to each step, revisit these steps, and engage in focused 'step' discussion groups with others in the fellowship. For each person who has engaged in the programme with that degree of intensity, there are likely to be many who have been to AA for a few times or over a few months, and who perhaps carry a printed card of the Twelve Steps in their pocket or handbag, but do not intend to go to another meeting. They may never have taken the idea of a 'programme' too seriously, but they have found in AA something personally useful. And between the extremes of the most dedicated and the most casual kinds of commitment there are infinite variations.

'God as we understood Him'

Inspection of the Twelve Steps will show that 'God' or 'a Power greater than ourselves' is mentioned in six of these steps, while Step 12 refers to 'spiritual awakening'. The Oxford Group origins and Christianity are seemingly much to the fore. The degree to which religion and spirituality are emphasized at AA meetings in fact varies greatly from country to country, with American AA more theistic than AA in other parts of the world. Whatever the national variations, the fact remains, however, that a belief in God is, through the words of the Twelve Steps, nailed to AA's masthead. Critics have at times suggested that AA is not only religious but also religiose

The truth of the matter would again appear to be that people get from AA what they personally choose to take from it. For some the religious element is highly significant and AA is for them a pathway to spiritual self-development, with sobriety a by-product of spiritual change. For others 'God *as we understood Him*' is no barrier to atheism, and for them the 'Power greater than ourselves' is AA, the fellowship itself.

AA and self-responsibility

Although AA doctrine suggests the need to turn over one's life to 'the care of God *as we understood Him*' as a prerequisite to recovery (Step 3), in reality the programme puts strong emphasis on each individual's self-responsibility. No external person or organization, no pill or therapist or hospital, can substitute for the drinker's own responsibility for the decision to stay sober just for today and not take the first drink. Without contradiction, the process is also recovery through the mutuality of the fellowship. If for some members self-help and mutual help are aided by surrender to God, AA for them becomes a self-help, mutual-help and God-help programme.

AA's management structure

The individual group, with its elected secretary and treasurer, constitutes an organizational unit which enjoys considerable autonomy. It will be expected to operate within AA's Twelve Steps programme, and guidance on how to deal with organizational and business matters is provided by a framework statement known as the Twelve Traditions. There are tiers of local and national integrative groupings, probably a national coordinating office, and at the summit of this widely based pyramid there is the US-based General Service Office. Local groups come into existence as a result of local need and enthusiasm, and may be offshoots of established groups which have grown too big. There is no authentication or inspection procedure. Groups sometimes wind themselves down or quietly disappear. The overall machinery of AA's organization functions with a minimum of fuss and a lot of delegation. AA levies no subscription, and no funding is accepted from external sources; its income derives entirely from collections taken at meetings.

One reason why AA has survived and flourished from early days is that the fellowship succeeded in evolving an organizational formula which cleverly combined some essential centralization with a strong emphasis on a broad membership involvement and local autonomy. That formula also insists on anonymity as a cardinal principal. It discourages too much office-holding or self-aggrandisement. There is no statutory rule book, but only the expectations of the Twelve Steps and the Twelve Traditions. That style of working has over the years proved to be extraordinarily well chosen for AA's type of operation.

AA and the question 'Does it work?'

The question of whether AA in a scientific sense actually *works* is not at all easy to answer. A hard-nosed research scientist is likely to argue that the only acceptable test of efficacy would be a randomized controlled trial between AA and not-AA. But the very nature of a mutual-help organization which operates by self-selection rather than random selection makes that kind of research design impossible. Randomizing people to attendance or non-attendance at a Quaker meeting would not be good science, and would be unlikely to tell us much about the impact of Quakerism on the lives of those people who are non-randomly drawn towards it.

Many researchers who accept controlled trials as the only standard of proof will therefore argue that 'There is no evidence that AA works.' And in strict terms that assertion cannot be contested. The possibility must exist that people who after going to AA stop or ameliorate their drinking, or who improve their health or happiness or social functioning, or who in their own terms achieve spiritual growth, would have achieved all those types of change equally well if they had never sat down in the hall. Perhaps rather than AA being the causative change agent, those changes took place because the time was ripe. Within that perspective, attendance at AA could be read as a mere external marker of personal motivation to change, or as an indicator that the time was ripe, rather than AA itself being the true motivator of change. Others will argue with equal cogency that there is no evidence that AA does not work.

Up to the present, science has not found a research approach to overcome the Quaker-meeting conundrum. Without losing critical dispassion, we can however probably do a bit better than a 'don't know at all' kind of answer. With the lack of full and final proof admitted, but on the basis of the available research, it is not unreasonable to conjecture that AA probably works, in some way or other, for not less than 50 per cent of the troubled drinkers who make contact with it. While we wait for the exact science, it seems evident that the reason why people sit around in church halls, hospitals, prisons and all manner of other settings to attend AA and talk its talk is because this fellowship meets their needs.

9 **In the Name of Treatment**

Over the years, what has been done to people with drinking problems in the name of treatment beggars belief. At times doctors have advocated shutting such people up, perhaps for a lifetime, in asylums. In another era and for the well-heeled, a thousand therapeutic hours on a psycho-analyst's couch might be the advised cure. In part the record is one of treatment as a vehicle for humane compassion, whatever the immediate technologies. But on occasion remedies have been deployed of such brutality as to leave one wondering whether it is possible to distinguish between treatment and torture. An extraordinary variety of drugs has from time to time been prescribed, some of them addictive or otherwise dangerous. An element of comedy has also occasionally been manifest, as when a Dr Shilo in 1961 advocated a regime which necessitated the consumption of 231 lemons, to be taken by the patient over the course of precisely 29 days. All five subjects on whom he reported had, with the lemon cure, developed a complete indifference to alcohol, with the craving stamped out.

The start of the treatment story lies with the 'discovery' of drunken-ness as a disease. When, a little over 200 years ago, the medical profession articulated the view that the drinking habit itself, and not just its complications or the withdrawal symptoms, was a disease which should be treated, excessive drinkers were at a stroke made into people to whom things should be done in the name of treatment. That was a development loaded with consequences for the years to come.

The treatment of the drinking habit starts bravely out

The idea that excessive drinking might at times constitute a condition deserving of medical help emerged as a by-product of the eighteenth-century Enlightenment. A spirit of rationality was in the air, and the notion began to develop among doctors that drunkenness was a human behaviour determined by intelligible processes and capable of being ameliorated by rational human interventions. God was out of the equation. Two medical thinkers can be recognized as having laid the foundations for this reformulation. One was the distinguished American physician Benjamin Rush (1743–1813), who was a signatory to the Declaration of Independence. The other was a Scottish doctor, Thomas Trotter (1760–1832), who included in his curriculum vitae a period of service as a ship's surgeon in the Royal Navy, and who had seen action against the French at the Battle of the Dogger Bank. What these two medical men had in common was that Rush as a young man had on a European tour spent time studying at Edinburgh University, while Trotter gained his medical qualification from that institution. No one has so far traced fully the intellectual influences which shaped Rush's and Trotter's thinking on the nature of drinking behaviour, but they both seem to have been aware of the psychological theories which were being propounded by David Hume (1711–76), the Edinburgh philosopher and historian of huge intellectual fame, who was denied a university chair because of his atheism. Long before the advent of modern psychology with its explanations of how behaviours are learned and shaped by cues in the environment, Hume was advancing very similar ideas.

Rush's 1790 pamphlet entitled *An Inquiry into the Effects of Ardent Spirits* received enthusiastic attention in the USA, and caused him later to be counted as a founding father by the American temperance movement. Trotter's 1804 *Essay . . . on Drunkenness* was a more substantial work than Rush's pamphlet, and yet it never received the same degree of public and professional acclaim.

This quotation from Rush so closely mirrors Hume's psychology as to make one suspect a direct connection:

Our knowledge of the principle of association upon the minds and conduct of men, should lead us to destroy, by other impressions, the influence of all those circumstances, with which recollection and desire of spirits are combined . . . Now by finding a new and interesting employment, or subject of conversation for drunkards at the usual times in which they have been accustomed to drink, and by restraining them by the same means from those places and companions, which suggested to them the idea of ardent spirits, their habits of intemperance may be completely destroyed.

And here is an excerpt which shows Trotter's associationist perspective:

The late Dr Cullen, in his lectures, used to mention a family, all of whom were in the habit of taking a dram at a certain hour before dinner, about one o'clock. When the Doctor expressed his wonder at the practice, it was acknowledged by all, that if the time passed, or if they were from home, and did not get the usual dram, it was attended with a considerable *sense of consciousness*. In plain English, they had got into a very bad habit, and found themselves low-spirited for want of their cordial.

Cullen's use of that little clinical anecdote to illustrate his lecture points with remarkable exactness to the idea which shaped Rush's and Trotter's approach to the treatment of what much later was to be called 'dependence'.

It is tempting to see the writings of these two Enlightenment physicians as evidence of a bright dawn, with the medical profession taking over the ownership of the drunkenness problem, and rational and humane treatments the order of the new day from thenceforth. Sadly, that reading of the unfolding history would be far too optimistic. The psychological insight which Rush and Trotter offered on the nature of the drinking habit and on its treatment had little appeal to their fellow professionals in the years which followed. Instead, the nineteenth century's most influential medical response to the troubled drinker centred on the establishment of special residential institutions. Shutting up the drunkard in a retreat or reformatory was to become the advanced thinking.

Institutions as positive need of the age

It was American doctors who in the nineteenth century took the lead
in pressing for the establishment of institutions for the treatment of
the drunkard, but the British were enthusiastic followers of the American
trend. Benjamin Rush had given support to the institutional idea as early
as 1810, and in the subsequent decades pressure gradually mounted in
the USA for inebriate asylums to be set up. The opening in 1857 of
the Washingtonian Home in Boston was one of a number of similar
innovations which took place around that time in US and Canadian
cities. In 1870 a group of doctors came together in New York City to
form the American Association for the Study and Cure of Inebriety.
This organization claimed to be a learned and scientific society, but it
was also a lobbying group devoted to the proliferation of institutions
for the treatment of the drunkard. Its members campaigned for state
legislation which would allow compulsory seclusion, and the Association was in general markedly keen on the draconian.

This is an extract from a statement which the Association drew up
in 1870 as an expression of its principles and purposes:

1. Inebriety is a disease.
2. It is curable as other diseases are . . .
5. All methods hitherto employed for the treatment of inebriety . . . have
   proved inadequate in its cure: hence the establishment of HOSPITALS for
   the special treatment of inebriety . . . becomes a positive need of the age.
6. In view of these facts, and the increased success of the treatment in inebriate
   asylums, this Association urges that every large city should have its local
   and temporary hospital for both the reception and care of inebriates; and
   that every state should have hospitals for their more permanent detention
   and treatment.

The statement ended with a demand for 'ample legal power of control',
and the authority to retain patients 'a sufficient length of time for their
permanent cure'. And it was the disease idea which gave the doctors
the right to exert such control. That is why 'Inebriety is a disease'
logically ranked as item 1.

What motivated this movement? The Association's manifesto can in part be seen as a compassionate plea that America should respond humanely to the hitherto neglected plight of the inebriate. Furthermore, one should be sensitive to the spirit of the age, and these were times which generally believed in the virtues of the asylum as the place for treating the mentally ill. The rhetoric of the Association often also spoke of drunkenness as a threat to family and society, and as a potential contributor to racial degeneration. The drunk was thus configured as a deviant or alien, with a slide then towards emphasis on control by the benign agents of the state, rather than on treatment.

There was always within the American institutional-treatment campaign an element of class distinction. There was to be a well-articulated therapeutic programme for inebriates drawn from the respectable classes, who would enter an institution in response to a little medical or family persuasion, and who would be able to meet the institution's fees. And then there was to be the locking up of the vast hordes of working-class inebriates who had no ability to pay, and for these people precious little in the way of treatment was in reality ever offered. Compulsion might on occasion be good for the recalcitrant inebriate from the middle classes, but for the underclass the sovereign remedy was to bang them all up – preferably for a very long time – and in boot-camp-like conditions. Here is the American Association pressing for that type of institution as a cure for the contemporary urban ill of working-class drunkenness.

. . . the great centres of pauperism and criminality will be broken up. This will be accomplished by the establishment of work-house hospitals, where the inebriate can be treated and restrained. Such places must be located in the country, removed from large cities and towns, and conducted on a military basis . . . They should be military training hospitals, where all the surroundings are under the exact care of the physician, and every condition of life is regulated with steady uniformity.

The recommended duration for such treatment was 'from five to ten years and life'. The concept of the doctor as workhouse master or as camp commandant of the total institution was as far from the Enlightenment dawn as can be imagined; indeed, coming after Rush and Trotter, it seems to herald a new dark night. Such, however, were the fruits of the Association's proselytizing that by 1893 it was able to claim widespread success in the USA, albeit without the degree of compulsion which was seen as optimal. The Association's message had also been carried internationally:

In Europe, over sixty hospitals for the physical care and treatment of inebriates are in active operation today. There are two in Australia, one in China, two in India, one in Ceylon, three in Africa, and one in Mexico.

How's that for the imperial power of ideas? The cause was throughout advanced by talk of science, and the language of progress.

Britain in the nineteenth century saw the energetic building of lunatic asylums as vast red-brick edifices on the edge of every big city, and contact between American and British experts on inebriety sparked a campaign for the establishment in Britain of similar institutional treatment for the inebriate on the American model. Again, a two-tier service was proposed, with retreats and sanatoria for the more privileged class of person and reformatories for the poor. Residents at retreats and sanatoria might sign themselves in for a compulsory stay or could be there on an entirely voluntary basis without the sham of self-committal. But for the reformatory cases there was only compulsion. The desirability of inebriate legislation was first raised in Parliament in 1870. The Habitual Drunkard Act became law in 1879, with further and strengthened Inebriates' Acts in 1888 and 1898. Every Act in this sequence was welcomed as a victory by the British campaigners, but none of these measures was ever seen as sufficiently stringent in the compulsion provided.

The campaign in Britain for the institutional formula was led by the British Society for the Study and Cure of Inebriety, founded in 1884. This body not only aped the American Association's name but faithfully copied its ideology and rhetoric. The confidence with which the benefits of institutional treatment were promulgated and preached knew no bounds. Dr Norman Kerr, the founding president of the Society, declared in 1888 that 'there is nothing equal to a lengthened abode in a genuine and well-conducted home or Retreat for Inebriates'. Dr T. N. Kelynack, another stalwart of the Society and for many years editor of its journal, wrote in 1907 of 'the urgency of the necessity to provide legislative powers whereby not only the inebriate may be rationally cared for and reasonably controlled, but the interests of his family and friends protected and loss to the state so far as possible prevented or mitigated'.

Dr J. W. Astley Cooper, medical superintendent and licensee of the Ghyllwood Sanatorium in Cumberland, published in 1913 a book on the treatment of 'Pathological Inebriety'. His endorsement of institutional treatment was full-blooded: 'Without fear of contradiction . . . we say that for the thorough treatment of inebriety, the special sanatorium stands alone.' As for libertarians who might object to shutting inebriates up, Astley Cooper rejected their arguments as specious:

One has only to work among inebriates, no matter to what class in society they belong, to know that this fear of interfering with the liberty of a subject who has no real liberty, in that he is a slave habitually or periodically to the drink craze, results in the interference of the liberty of all those who have to put up with his irresponsible behaviour . . . leading to untold misery and wretchedness . . . Amended Inebriates' Acts are nearly as important as are the Lunacy Laws.

He went on to call for yet tougher powers of control than the 1898 Act provided.

Having got the inebriates into an institution, there was then the matter of what to do with them. So far as the retreats and sanatoria were concerned, the formula on either side of the Atlantic was remarkably similar. The charge per week in Britain was likely to be around £5, paid quarterly in advance. For this fee, pleasant accommodation and good food would be provided, with opportunity for golf and escorted country walks. Daily prayers and religious services were mandatory. In the evenings there might be music. A well-stocked library was regarded as essential. Into this country-house scene were then injected the specifics of therapy, which could include Turkish baths, electric stimulation, a course of strychnine injections, and other physical treatments. Here is an extract from the text published in 1893 by the American Association, describing the range of treatments it advised for deployment in this type of institution:

Prolonged hot baths are of the utmost service in the treatment of inebriety . . . The preparations of hyoscyamus, conium, stramonium, camphor, hops, aconite, ether and chloroform are all of great service if given with judgement . . . Milk heated to boiling is very valuable . . . If there are decided signs of cerebral congestion the occasional application of a leech behind the ear is good practice . . .

Some physicians were keen on the use of hypnosis with retreat patients. All authorities stressed the singular importance of the morally uplifting influence which should be expected from the medical director. Whatever element in the advised treatment mix was being discussed, the talk was always of its wonderful efficacy, with never any tinge of doubt.

Meanwhile, the scene in the reformatory was likely to be starkly prison-like. The punctilious rules prepared by the Home Office for the conduct of state inebriate reformatories defined an intention to crush. Residents were referred to as 'inmates', and they had to wear clothes 'of such pattern as may be prescribed'. All letters to and from an inmate would be read by the governor, and objectionable passages would be erased. From breakfast of cocoa with bread and butter through to oatmeal gruel at bedtime, nearly every item of diet was regulated to the exact ounce. At 6 a.m. the inmates would 'rise, clean cells etc.' Lights out was at 8.30 p.m., with six to eight hours of individual work to be performed every weekday. The Home Department regulations prescribed the use of the strait waistcoat for men, and for women the use of handcuffs and ankle straps 'under the conditions laid down in Standing Orders for Local Prisons'. That this regime differed significantly from that of a prison seems unlikely, and punishment for infringement of the rules was by solitary confinement with bread and water. Such was the way to treat deviants and aliens. A drunkard could be confined in a state inebriate reformatory by sentence of a court for a period of up to three years if found to have committed an offence when drunk, or with drunkenness a contributing cause. There also existed a parallel system of certified reformatories, which were privatized versions of essentially the same kind of institution, although slightly less rigorous in their regimes.

The enthusiasm for seclusion of inebriates in retreats or reformatories was, however, to last for only a few decades. In the early years of the twentieth century, official confidence in and support for the institutional formula faded on both sides of the Atlantic. The locking up of inebriates had proved to be very expensive, and the contribution it made to solving the problem of drunkenness could never be commensurate with the problem's true extensiveness. It thus came to be seen as an approach which combined ineffectiveness with unacceptable costs – a losing formula. The institutional movement had in its day been the cause for passionate campaigns, but it died unmourned, leaving scarcely a trace other than the buildings turned to other purposes, or a few retreats or nursing homes that went on operating on a voluntary basis. The relevant legislation was either repealed or left to gather dust.

The reasons for the demise of the institutions were several. The retreats and sanatoria were unable to find enough members of the middle classes who were willing to sign themselves in for a year, and dissenting medical voices began to be heard which were critical of the idea of long seclusion. The reformatories failed because they came to be widely seen as ineffective and as places which were being left to cope with a high proportion of detainees who were mentally ill or otherwise untreatable. Thus T. N. Kelynack, quoting in 1907 from the annual report of Her Majesty's Inspector of Inebriate Reformatories:

It will scarcely be surprising to find that many committals are in the lowest possible state of unimprovable degradation, and that it has become necessary to set apart some of our institutions as little better than moral refuse heaps, for the detention of the hopelessly defective, at the lowest possible cost to the country.

And it was the establishment of these 'moral refuse heaps' for which American and British doctors had earlier been crying out, as a moral and reformist cause.

In America, Prohibition and the fall in national alcohol consumption in the lead-up to the enactment of Prohibition did much to remove potential business from the institutions, and the decline in drinking which occurred in Britain during and after the First World War must have assisted similarly to kill off the British fervour for institutional treatment of the inebriate. The nearest to this movement's ever enjoying a return to fashion was probably seen in America, when in the 1930s and onwards enthusiasm developed, in the name of treatment, for the large-scale incarceration of heroin addicts in various kinds of prison-like institution.

Treatment in an era of anything goes

With the decline in the medical faith in institutional seclusion, no new consensus emerged on the remedy for inebriety. Instead, the period up to, say, the end of the 1960s was for the most part characterized by fragmentation. Individual practitioners championed any one from the ever-widening range of physical treatments which were being offered as the cure for alcoholism. As in the previous century, the lack of objective evidence for efficacy never damped the keenness of the advocacy. The American Association went out of business, while the British Society for the Study of and Cure of Inebriety, renamed the Society for the Study of Addiction, became an eccentric paper-reading club and a home for lost causes. A previously emergent medical speciality which had in its time been thrusting, ambitious and well organized seemed to have fallen into premature decay. It was an era of unbridled enthusiasms, big claims, little evidence, and virtually 'anything goes'.

One of the British enthusiasts of this period was Dr J. Yerbury Dent, who was the dedicated champion of apomorphine treatment. Apomorphine is an opioid type of drug which, during the 1930s, came to be used as an agent to produce vomiting in the course of aversion treatment of the kind which was being practised in Seattle and to which we will refer again shortly. But Dr Dent's belief in the therapeutic value of this substance went far beyond anything to do with its use in aversion therapy. Instead, Dent saw it as, in effect, the philosopher's stone of alcoholism treatment. By its specific action on certain areas of the brain, he believed, this drug could cure alcoholism. He started offering this treatment in 1923, and, although continuing as a general practitioner, built up a substantial specialist practice around the use of apomorphine. He claimed success, 'meaning teetotal for at least a year', in 60–70 per cent of his cases. Apomorphine treatment could be augmented by getting patients to read aloud out of a newspaper while the doctor walked around the room and inserted beneficial suggestions into the distracted mind. When Dent's views were challenged at a meeting of the Society for the Study of Addiction, the response he gave was unbending:

If apomorphine depended for its success mainly upon the establishment of aversion and was not, as I think, a treatment for anxiety, why should pushing apomorphine up the nostrils of some forms of hysterical dogs stop their hysteria? Why should it cure wool eating in sheep or cut short the mania in mothers following childbirth?

Dent was a charismatic and much respected figure, and his personal faith in his methods probably helped many patients. But apomorphine as used by him was a vehicle for therapeutic suggestion, rather than ever an objectively effective drug treatment. One commentator summed up the matter in the remark that 'Dent without apomorphine would be more therapeutically powerful than apomorphine without Dent.'

Dent is far from being the only example of an enthusiast becoming personally identified with claims for the supremacy of a particular cure for alcoholism. In France in the 1940s and '50s, Dr Raoul Lecoq championed a proprietary preparation (Curéthyl) which had as its constituents alcohol, liver extract, B vitamins and glucose. This, when given intravenously, was said to stimulate specific antibodies to alcohol and produce 'une véritable immunité'. The all-time prize for the design and marketing of a cure must, however, go to Dr Leslie E. Keeley, an American who had qualified in Chicago. In the 1870s he invented an approach impressively called the Double Chloride of Gold treatment, which was heavily advertised and involved the patient taking a course or courses of Keeley's patent medicine. By the 1890s there were 118 Keeley Institutions franchised across the USA, and the technique had also spread to Europe. A mail-order business was founded. The profits to the parent company from this extended business were at times running at about half a million dollars a year for a treatment of no scientific worth. The last Keeley Institute did not close its doors until the 1960s.

Whether or not a named doctor was associated with a particular treatment, what characterized this period in treatment history was the willingness to throw, at some time or other, almost any drug at the alcohol-dependent patient, in the name of treatment. Here, in date order, are some examples:

1935 Drs Charles Shadel and Walter Voegtlin established in Seattle a sanatorium to treat alcoholics by a Pavlovian method described as 'conditioned aversion'. By the 1980s over 30,000 patients had been treated by an approach which, unusually in the contemporary arena, had some scientific basis.

1938 Drs F. S. Macy and W. D. Silkworth wrote in the *Lancet* on the benefits of 'Colloidal Gold and Colloidal Iodine in Chronic Alcoholism'.

1941 Dr W. Bloomberg, an American doctor, described his experience in prescribing amphetamine sulphate to fifty-five 'chronic alcoholics'. For this ill-advised treatment he claimed benefit in over 80 per cent of his patients.

1947 Writing from Ecuador, Dr C. A. Pareja reported a series of sixteen alcoholics treated by the injection of the patient's own serum to which whisky had been added – an interesting variant of the Lecoq approach.

1949 Drs J. W. Tintera and H. W. Lovell wrote from America about a new treatment for which revolutionary claims were made. Alcoholism was deemed to be due to a deficiency in the functioning of the adrenal cortex, and injections of adreno-cortical extract could work a cure.

1952 Dr C. O'Brien wrote from Milwaukee about 'Experimental Evidence in the Treatment of Alcoholism by Intensive Calcium Therapy'. This was not an approach which ever took the world by storm.

1953 Drs A. A. LaVerne and M. Herman claimed that the weekly administration of carbon-dioxide injections, given under the skin, constituted a cure for inebriety. In Russia, a Dr Lukashev was at about the same time using oxygen injections in this way.

1955 Dr M. M. Stern published in the prestigious *Journal of Nervous and Mental Diseases* a paper advocating the use of an antihistamine in the treatment of alcoholics. His eleven patients all reported a loss of desire for drink.

1958 Come the availability of LSD (lysergic acid diethylamide), it was probably inevitable that someone would give this drug to alcoholic patients in the name of treatment. Thus in 1958 the *Quarterly Journal of Studies on Alcohol*, a top-rank American specialist journal, published a paper by Dr C. M. Smith entitled 'A New Adjunct in the Treatment of Alcoholism: The Hallucinogenic Drugs'. A considerable literature emerged on LSD treatment for drinking problems.

1962 Drs V. K. Ibragimov and A. S. Udovichenko reported from Kazakhstan on a treatment for alcoholism which involved administration of nicotinic acid (vitamin B_3) three times a day for seven days, followed on the eighth day by five or six shots of vodka.

1966 Drs K. S. Ditman and D. Benor, writing from the USA, gave a description in an American journal of a single alcoholic patient treated with high doses of Valium on a maintenance basis. So great is the danger of creating a cross-dependence on Valium that today such an approach would probably lay a doctor open to risk of a malpractice suit.

1971 Again, the inevitable. In 1971 Dr J. Scher wrote in the *American Journal of Psychiatry* suggesting that cannabis should be used 'as an agent in rehabilitating alcoholics'.

A long sea voyage on an alcoholically dry ship was sometimes advocated, and, although there were difficulties set by the fact that not too many dry ships ever sailed the ocean, that must for many years have been a pleasanter and less dangerous cure than most other therapies proposed for the drinking habit. Listed one after the other, the entries presented in this chronology have about them a believe-it-or-not quality. Much the same effect would probably be created by listing the treatments which have at some time been advocated for many other rather intractable conditions.

In suggesting that the various nostrums once put forward for the treatment of alcohol dependence were at best useless and often rather worse than useless, one should of course be sensitive to the temporal context. Medical approaches to asthma, say, or rheumatoid arthritis, or cancer, often had that same kind of flavour during the long period when authority and assertion counted for more in therapeutics than did hard evidence. What is being identified here is the broad character of a transitional period leading up to the modern era of controlled trials and scientific assessment of efficacy and safety. Controlled trials are not a panacea, but the benefit to patients of a scientific appraisal of what treatments work, and with what attached risks, cannot be doubted.

Treatment gone badly wrong

Due understanding is owed to practitioners who were doing their best for a difficult condition without the benefit of modern research methods to inform them. It would be unwise and ungenerous to condemn that previous generation from the privileged position of hindsight. But every now and then a suspension of judgement becomes more hard. In the history of this particular field, there are rather too many techniques which look not so much like treatment as like punishment. As noted earlier, at the extreme what has been done in the name of treatment has shown a worrying resemblance to torture.

Under this heading should be put the use of electroconvulsive therapy (ECT) as treatment for alcohol dependence. Far from ECT being given only conservatively and in a way which might be viewed as unwise but not altogether out of tune with more general contemporary psychiatric therapeutic enthusiasm, a Dr W. L. Milligan in 1955 advocated the use of ECT with an intensity which even at the time must have been seen as unguarded. He gave up to two or three shocks on the first day of treatment, so as to put the patient into a state of total confusion. Further shocks were then given to keep the subject in a state of complete disorientation for seven to ten days. There never was, nor could there ever be, justification for such assault. Dr Milligan described the allegedly excellent results he obtained with fifty alcoholic patients treated in this way over a ten-year period, but the description carries no conviction.

Even more worrying are the several reports to be found in the literature of alcohol dependence being treated by brain surgery. Neurosurgery is by its nature irreversible, and surgically inflicted brain damage can cause disinhibition and a worsening in the drinking behaviour. Drs J. W. Watts and W. Freeman reported from America in 1946 on prefrontal leucotomies performed by them on three alcoholics, all of whom continued to drink. A well-respected British brain surgeon, Mr Geoffrey Knight, described in 1968 a technique in which he treated heroin and alcohol dependence by cutting nerve fibres which he believed to serve the psychological experience of tension. Dr D. Müller, who had previously in Germany used brain operations in treatment for 'sexual deviations', reported in 1973 on the application of his surgical methods to a thirty-year-old man with a drinking problem.

Mention should also be made of the method employed by a group of American investigators led by Dr C. H. Farrar. In 1968 they published a paper in the journal *Behaviour Research and Therapy* under the title 'Punishment of Alcohol Consumption by Apneic Paralysis'. 'Apnoea' means 'inability to breathe', and what these researchers did was inject their patients with suxamethonium. This drug is used in anaesthesia so as to produce total muscle paralysis, stop the patient's breathing, and let the anaesthetist temporarily take over. Dr Farrar's patients were, however, not anaesthetized. His idea was to give them an injection of the drug, hand them a glass of bourbon, tell them to think about a bad experience they had had with drink, and all this immaculately timed so that as they sniffed the drink their breathing would stop. Lying paralysed on a couch and finding oneself suddenly, inexplicably and totally unable to breathe must be one of the most terrifying experiences anyone could undergo. After a thirty-second interval, resuscitation was begun and, according to the investigators, total apnoea 'rarely exceeded 90 seconds'. The aim was to deceive the patients into believing that the apnoea had been brought on by the thought of alcohol and the presence of the bourbon. At twelve-month follow-up, only two out of nine patients were still off drink.

No ethical committee in the Western world would today be likely to countenance the use of ECT, brain surgery or apnoea aversion for the treatment of drinking problems in the ways described in these reports. In the modern world, anyone attempting such treatments would lay themselves open to risk of legal action – especially if patients had not given informed consent (the subjects in the apnoea trial were purposefully deceived rather than informed). There is no suggestion that any of the doctors concerned were other than well-meaning or were acting outside contemporary ethical expectations; however, that professionals in the relatively recent past could in good conscience have engaged in such practices suggests that there was at that time and in those settings something profoundly wrong with the medical profession's regard for ethical issues, together with an institutional failure to put due safeguards in place.

An ethical dilemma is set by the drug disulfiram (trade name Antabuse). Introduced into medical practice in 1945 by two Danish workers, it for a time enjoyed great therapeutic popularity, and it is still widely used in the treatment of alcohol dependence. If taken by mouth in tablet form, disulfiram will block the body's normal breakdown of alcohol at the stage when acetaldehyde is produced, and acetaldehyde will accumulate in the blood. If a patient who is on disulfiram takes alcohol, he or she will therefore experience over some hours an unpleasant bout of acetaldehyde poisoning. The symptoms are likely to include flushing, palpitations, nausea and vomiting. Collapse can occur, and there have been a few reports of death. The supposed rationale for this treatment is that the patient who takes the drug has a built-in chemical guard against impulsively taking a drink. According to a recent review by two British psychiatrists, Julian Hughes and Christopher Cook, there is very little research to support claims that Antabuse is an effective treatment. Doctors of good conscience, however, go on prescribing this drug, and it is a licensed product. But it is unusual in medicine to administer a drug which has as its intention the potential poisoning of a patient.

Treatment then and now

The delineation here of any distinct break point to divide the past from present times would be somewhat arbitrary. But, as in so many other sectors of medicine, what separates the historical past from present treatments is the absence then, and the presence now, of the knowledge gained from randomized controlled trials. Such research designs involve the comparison of treatment A against treatment B, with the statistical significance of any difference between treatment groups being objectively determined at six- or twelve-month follow-up.

In general medicine the first published report based on a fully random assignment to treatment groups was a 1948 Medical Research Council (UK) study on drug treatment for tuberculosis. As regards the application of a controlled-trial approach to the treatment of drinking problems, the first such study was probably that reported in a 1956 paper by R. S. Wallerstein, but that American work did not fully meet all the expectations of the technique. There are, however, many continuities between past and present. Identical attitudes towards the drunkards who betray their responsibility to handle this drug well, and who thereby insult the chemical of religious ritual, the national emblem, our belief that drink is fun, are as prevalent today as yesterday.

Looking back at the past two centuries, the conclusion must surely be for any of us that if, we were ever to develop a drinking problem, we would infinitely rather be treated by Dr Rush or Dr Trotter than by the doctors purveying any of the multitudinous therapies described in the previous sections. We might welcome the chance to consult either of those humane doctors of the Enlightenment, but we will surely shudder at the thought of the fate awaiting us if we had ever needed to consult many other good, kind doctors who over the many subsequent years were applying a leech behind the ear, any number of useless or dangerous drugs, ECT to total disorientation, brain surgery, the near-death experience of apnoea – all that and more – in the name of treatment.

Beyond any immediate and personal response we may have to this chronicle, there are three elements within the history which need to be identified. When brought into focus, they can make coherent a story with many shifts in therapies and therapists.

First, there is the theme of respect for the human worth of the drinking patient. That Trotter and Rush respected their patients was evident. They did not regard them as aliens or 'not like us'; rather, the inebriate was seen as worthy. Somewhere along the line that respect often came to be impaired or even lost. The alcoholic became someone not like us, and it was therefore permissible to do ill-advised or cruel things to this unworthy person. Behind the changing externals of treatment, there was the dark, continuing internal thread of a belief that those drinkers who misused this drug were not really ill at all.

They were people who had sinned and must be punished by treatment.

Second, and closely related to that first theme, there is a thread of ideas which is concerned with the patient's autonomy, as opposed to the doctor's right to impose. The Enlightenment physicians worked out their treatment plans in active collaboration with their patients; the asylum doctors wanted to shut up their patients and force treatment on them; and later there were all those enthusiasts for drugs and other physical treatments who drugged and otherwise did things to patients who seem to have been regarded as almost inanimate objects. Treatment in this area slid towards an attempt to alter human behaviour through application of the crudest kind of medical model – the doctor did things to the passively accepting or, at the extreme, to the disorientated patient.

The third and final theme is that of treatment as a crude and empirical non-science, as opposed to its being rooted in rationality and a proposed scientific model of the nature of the problem being treated. Rush and Trotter saw drunkenness as a habit to be comprehended within a psychological and theoretical framework, and this was the true beginning of science in this particular arena. Little bits of science may have been used to prop up the use of the Turkish bath, apomorphine, colloidal gold, Dr Lecoq's Curéthyl, and oxygen under the skin, and Shadel and Voegtlin derived their aversion treatment directly from Pavlovian theory. But for the most part, during the period we have been dealing with in this chapter, the doctors who treated drinking problems were rank empiricists, and anything went.

Put together that loss of humane respect for the patient, the medical desire to control, do, operate on the drinker as passive object, the willingness blindly to throw anything at the problem, and the resulting mix was at times all too likely to be a dangerous one.

The previous chapter traced out evolutions in what was done in the
name of treatment over a long previous period. Let's now continue
that story to the present day. This chapter looks at current treatments
for the habit of drinking, which is still the same human problem as
attracted medical attention two hundred years ago. We will approach
this matter through examination of a contemporary case history. The
material of the case is as much the doctor's response to the patient as
the patient herself.

The case of Mary M.

Mary M. had enjoyed a glittering university career. She acted, debated,
partied and had been a famous socialite. At the same time and without
seeming effort, she gained a first-class honours degree in politics.
Champagne was drunk out of her slipper on the day she came down
from university, and when she moved to London she quickly established
a presence in journalism and television. By her late twenties she was a
household name. Her personal life, however, was marked by repeated
and sometimes violent break-up of relationships. Aged thirty-three and
after yet another such trauma, she punched her right hand through a
window, with nasty lacerations resulting.

It was then that Mary M. faced up to the fact that her drinking had
become worrying. Sometimes she could take alcohol in a relaxed and
pleasurable kind of way. But, lunchtime or evening, if she drank, she
could not guarantee that, despite her intentions and resolves, she would
not get drunk. When she was drunk, her emotions would then be as
uncontrolled as her drinking. Amnesia for the previous evening had
become a frequent occurrence. In the mornings she would feel nauseous,

awful and full of self-revulsion, but she did not have shakes or need a morning drink.

After a visit to the Accident and Emergency department with her torn hand, and having sat around in late-night conditions of stench, mayhem and stressed nurses, Mary woke next day horrified at the stupidity, uncouthness and danger of her behaviour. The previous night she had been a drunk among all the others who were littering the A & E department. During the next few months she tried to control and ration her drinking, but amelioration was only short-lived. At a film première she again became drunk, loud-mouthed and abusive. Unfortunately, the papers reported the incident in unflattering detail. She knew then that her career was on the line. A colleague said, 'For God's sake, do something before it's too late!'

Mary was referred by her GP to Dr W., a psychiatrist specializing in alcoholism, who had a private practice in London's Harley Street. He was courteous and thorough, and they spent an hour together. His kindness caused her to burst into tears, and she talked about childhood trauma, the depths of her present misery, the glittering outer success, the inner emptiness, and how alcohol gave her good feelings and then made accessible awful waves of destructive anger. The anger was directed both at other people and at herself. She talked about depression and her ruminations on suicide.

At the end of the hour, Dr W. said, 'Well, we agree that alcoholism is the problem, don't we?' She said, 'No, the problem is me.' He said, ' "Me" always has a lot to do with it, but your problem is alcoholism.' Mary said, 'OK, what do I do about it?' He said, 'I'll admit you to my clinic, where we have an excellent twelve-step treatment programme, highly experienced counsellors and total immersion – no visitors for the first two weeks – and I expect you'll be in there for six weeks at a minimum. So I suggest that you clear your diary.' Mary said, 'Any alternative in your black bag? I'm not sure I can afford that amount of time. I don't think I need or want to go into hospital. Couldn't I see you again here in your consulting room? I'd like to meet you this way again.'

Dr W. put his hands together and gave his patient a firm message: 'No, there is absolutely no other way. Don't now go into denial. Denial can be dangerous – even fatal – and you know that. Come on. I'm willing to treat you as an in-patient; otherwise it's goodbye until you're able to open your eyes to the realities. I'm not going to flinch from confronting you with reality, even if that's not something you're used to, or much like.'

Mary M. went back to her office and got on miserably with the day's work. That evening she again got drunk. A year later Dr W. received this letter from her:

Dear Dr W.

You were so good as to give me an hour of your time when I came to see you exactly twelve months ago. We parted in disagreement, with you suggesting that I was 'in denial' because I would not accept your advice to go into hospital for a minimum of six weeks. That meeting was for me a turning point. I hope you won't think me abrasive if I say that the change point came about because of my anger at your talk of 'denial'. Even at that bleak moment I could see that the choice of this word was an attempt to manipulate me into accepting without question the imposition of your views on the nature of my problem – and your views of the treatment which I needed. You were going to slot me into a formula rather than help me to work within my own resources towards my own solution of my own problems.

I thought the idea that an abstract entity called 'alcoholism' was the problem threatened to overwhelm awareness of me as a person. And I felt you were shutting your eyes to the extent of my depression. So that visit forced me to realize that I myself am the person who has to get me straight. It was you who gave me that insight, and I'm grateful. I got hideously drunk the evening after seeing you. I have not altogether stopped drinking, but since that day I have been badly drunk only a few times. My GP has given me help with my depression. Life is a whole lot more manageable, but with plenty still to manage! Very sincerely, Mary M.

On headed paper which identified his several qualifications, Dr W. wrote back:

Dear Ms M.

I appreciate your kindness in writing to me, and am glad that life for you now seems more manageable. But I can't help but note that you are still drinking, and the news that you have been 'badly drunk' on several occasions does not seem to me reassuring. Do please make an appointment if you think it might be helpful for us to meet again.

Kind regards

In Mary M.'s records Dr W. entered the date and wrote, 'See her letter. Denial gross and unabated.'

What Dr W. believed

There are many sincere and competent present-day practitioners who are likely to interpret the encounter between Mary M. and Dr W. as forceful illustration of the problem which denial can set as a malignant block to recovery. They will view Mary's case as being one of denial writ large – of a woman refusing to face up to her alcoholism, rejecting the appropriate treatment, making 'depression' the excuse for her destructive drinking, and then blithely claiming improvement while continuing to get drunk. The patient was spurning excellent advice and expecting to dictate treatment on her own terms. An alternative analysis, however, would be that Dr W.'s understanding of this woman's needs was blocked by his fixed preconceptions.

Let's try to explore how this clinical encounter can help reveal the assumptions which influenced Dr W.'s response to his patient. We are looking at the attitudes displayed by one particular doctor, but his belief structure is representative of a large and important sector of the present-day alcoholism treatment world. And the continuities with the past will become very evident.

• *All patients who come to consult about a drinking problem are seen as suffering from one identical alcohol-related condition, namely the disease of alcoholism.* Mary M. was in Dr W.'s terms 'an alcoholic', and that would also be the view of her condition taken by the counsellors working at his clinic. Such a reflex and undiscriminating diagnosis blocks out the fact that different people will be experiencing different kinds of drinking problem to different degrees. Mary had a serious drinking problem, but she was not suffering from severe or well-established alcohol dependence. She retained an ability to drink at times in a social way, she did not experience withdrawal symptoms, and she did not need a drink in the mornings.

- *The disease of alcoholism becomes the central issue and shuts out the individual's definition of what for them is the problem.* Mary's attempt to talk about her depression was overriden. Frequently, and especially for women, depression can be mixed in with the drinking. Sometimes the depression is a consequence of the drinking, but at other times it can be a problem in its own right, and one which drives the drinking.
- *There is one treatment which is the panacea for all comers.* Here we seem to be straight back in the past. Whatever changes may have come and gone in therapeutic fashions, what still lives on in Dr W.'s beliefs is the notion that his treatment will do well for everyone – as a sort of philosopher's stone. Such an assumption has no support from research.
- *Treatments are believed to be better when they are more intensive.* Shutting up people in an inebriates' home for a year was believed to be a lot better than a more restricted stay, 231 lemons were more efficacious than any mere handful, and shocking people into total disorientation with ECT was better than any lesser use of the electrodes. Six weeks in-patient care is viewed by Dr W. and other advocates of the twelve-step approach as the benchmark. Two or three therapeutic groups each day are favoured over one or two such sessions a week. Intensive aftercare is mandatory. Everyone must affiliate with AA, and they are expected to attend 100 meetings in 100 days. But there is no research that supports the assumption that with treatment of drinking problems more and bigger is inevitably better. On the contrary, there is a good deal of evidence to suggest that much current treatment is excessive.
- *It is the twelve-step programme which is the prime instrument of the recovery, and patients are powerless to help themselves.* Again, that belief is the past relived. Dr W. will insist that his treatment programme is entirely concerned with helping people to make their own recovery. A critic, however, would suggest that he had left Mary M. with the message that his team was going to do something to her as a passive object, and she had better give herself into their hands and obey. Such a model of what treatment is about runs counter to a mass of research which

indicates that people with drinking problems need to have their own powers for recovery liberated, rather than having their helplessness reinforced.

Treatment as a useful but modest enterprise

There is evidence persuasively to suggest that treatment of various kinds can produce benefit. For example, several studies have demonstrated that when patients in general-practice settings are advised to cut down on alcohol, such a simple measure can lead to a reduction in their excessive drinking. Those kinds of study show something important about the malleability of excessive but non-dependent drinking, and there is also evidence that drinkers who have developed dependence on alcohol can often respond to fairly simple treatment interventions. About 50–70 per cent of patients who are treated in that low-key kind of way are likely to be showing significant and maintained improvement at the end of twelve months.

The research verdict on the efficacy of modern treatments is thus in sum reasonably positive, whatever the degree of the patient's dependence on alcohol. The conclusion to be drawn is not that all treatments are equally good – some approaches to treatment have been shown by research to be useful, while others rate less well. But what research tends also repeatedly to demonstrate is that a range of competently applied treatments, conducted from diverse theoretical starting points, are likely to give roughly the same kinds of success rate. The message is thus not that all treatments are equally good, but that many good treatments are equally good.

Although the packages may wear different labels, good treatments appear to have mysterious essences in common whatever the packaging, according to an important recent US study called Project MATCH. MATCH was a highly ambitious multi-site project which involved 25 senior investigators and 80 therapists, and randomized 1,726 subjects suffering from alcohol dependence to one of three treatments. That was many more patients than had ever before been recruited into a trial of this type. The three treatment arms were designated as *Twelve-Step Facilitation Therapy* (TSF), which was a model emphasizing the AA

approach and which sought to enhance engagement of patients in
AA; *Cognitive Behaviour Therapy* (CBT), which employed learning-theory
methods and taught patients practical skills which would help them to
avoid relapse; and *Motivational Enhancement Therapy* (MET), which sought
to strengthen and maintain commitment to making a change in drinking
behaviour.

At the end of a twelve-month follow-up of all treated patients, the
key finding to emerge from this extraordinarily painstaking study
was that across multiple measures of outcome there were very few
differences between the three treatment regimes. With TSF, CBT and
MET as the runners in this race, every one of them equally won first
prize.

And so back to the mystery of what inherently works in treatment.
The proper interpretation to be put on MATCH, and much other work,
must be that in large measure it is the covert or undeclared elements
which successful treatments have in common that facilitate the recovery.
But what constitutes those mysterious essences of treatment is a question
too often passed by in the busy rush, while the protagonists argue
about the merits of their preferred brand labels. The argument seems
too often to be about the packaging rather than about what might be
found if the packages were unwrapped and their common features laid
bare.

At the heart of the mystery may be the fact that treatments which
are useful have in common the capacity to catalyse and support *natural
processes of recovery*. What therapists and the treatment researchers have in
the modern era tended to forget is that many excessive drinkers get
better without ever going near a professional, a treatment agency or
AA. Treatment, we may conclude, is a worthwhile but modest facilitator
of natural recovery, an add-on element to what the patient can do
unaided, a timely nudge and wink which may help the individual to
the winning post quicker. But it is not a grand professional enterprise
in which individuals hand over captaincy of their souls to a professional
who will make the recovery for them. Treatment is an undertaking of
a kind very different from that enshrined in the beliefs of the professional
who insists that his or her therapy, if swallowed whole, is the one and
only gold cure.

Treatment essences

Important insights into the real nature of the recovery process have come from research conducted by George Vaillant. He followed up drinkers for forty years, and looked at how those who pulled out of their difficulties had succeeded. Some of his subjects were residents of inner-city Boston; others were Harvard graduates of the Kennedy generation. Some had received a great deal of treatment, while others had struggled on with their problems unaided. Similar British work conducted at the Addiction Research Unit in London followed treated subjects for a ten-year period. The aim both of the American and of the British studies was to achieve insights into what dependent drinkers themselves saw as the elements in their life experience which had assisted or frustrated recovery, and how treatment might have interacted with these processes. There are also several studies which have reported on drinkers who have shown 'spontaneous recovery' – an inaccurate term for what always turns out to be a far more complex and multiply-determined happening than anything evoked by the word 'spontaneous'.

There is thus no shortage of research bearing on how people get better from drinking problems. The challenge lies in discerning what consistent patterns emerge from diverse (and often fascinating) accounts of how people make and maintain their recoveries. Behind the abstract tabulations, one person will be found saying that he dealt with the hideous fears and loneliness of his initial period of sobriety by shutting himself away indoors, drawing the curtains, and not answering the door. Another may relate how she spent her early months of sobriety working all hours of the day at her job and then going round in the evenings to help at the local hospice. Yet another drinker may say that he got off alcohol only at the cost of contracting a bad tranquillizer habit. Listen to those and so many other stories and it is processes, life journeys, rather than miracle cures to which the speakers are most often referring. And when formal treatment can be seen as coming effectively into play, it is as something supportive of natural recovery. This research supports the view of treatment as something modest but worthwhile.

Here is an attempt to extract from all that research a summary of how people usually get better from drinking problems, and how treatment supports recovery. A good mix of these elements was probably present in all three MATCH regimes, despite their up-front focus on different aspects of the mix.

- *Feeling that it can be done.* Troubled drinkers who are going to get better must believe that they have it within their power to change their behaviour. In psychological language, that means that self-efficacy is the gateway to recovery. A skilled therapist will from the first meeting be seeking to enhance the patient's self-efficacy by everything which is said and implied.

- *Motivation.* Knowing that change is feasible is the foundation of recovery. The individual has then got to want personally to change. Motivation is therefore a further vital ingredient in recovery, and treatments have been designed which focus specially on its enhancement (for instance, MET within the MATCH experiment).

- *Stages of change.* Much attention has been focused in recent years on the idea that drinkers need to be differentiated according to their 'readiness to change'. Two American researchers, J. O. Prochaska and C. C. DiClimente, have distinguished the stages of pre-contemplation, contemplation, action, and maintenance. This sort of discrimination has been found to be helpful by many therapists in deciding on the appropriate timing and pacing of the help given.

- *Goal definition.* Recovery is movement towards a goal, and the individual has to define that goal and keep it in sight. The therapist can help with clarification of whether abstinence or moderated drinking is likely to be the better goal choice.

- *Avoiding relapse.* Staying off or moderating the drinking requires the deployment of certain distinct psychological skills. Some people hit upon the appropriate strategies spontaneously, but these are skills which are teachable (as in MATCH's CBT). They include avoiding unnecessarily dangerous situations, and rehearsing repeatedly and in an intentional way the benefits of sobriety and the disbenefits of a return to the old drinking habits.

- *Building supportive networks.* It makes sense for someone who is trying to stop drinking to establish a personal micro-environment which supports abstinence, rather than one which encourages drinking. AA in many countries provides that kind of microclimate. Therapy can help build an appreciation of what AA has to offer (as in MATCH's TSF).

• *Change must feel good for it to be held.* Few people stay sober if sobriety seems to them nothing but the loss of old friends, the warmth of the pub and the ready comfort of the drink. Sobriety experienced only in terms of loss and looking enviously backwards is likely to be fragile. An excuse for returning to drink will sooner or later be found. The essence of treatment therefore lies partly in helping people to work towards finding rewarding substitutes for the previous drinking. Breeding canaries, learning a foreign language, coaching the neighbourhood youth club's football team are the sorts of activity to which some people may find it helpful to turn. AA involvement and AA office-holding is a common and immediately available substitute. A career move or a new loving relationship can also give life fresh purpose and help consolidate recovery.

Those are the main psychological elements which research today identifies as the elements which are the effective content within the black box called 'treatment'. They constitute something a lot more complicated, subtle and naturally based than any blunt kind of single panacea.

Modern drug treatments

Much interest has recently been aroused by the emergence of a number of drugs which research suggests may be therapeutically useful in relieving craving for alcohol, and thus in reducing the risk of relapse. These agents include naltrexone, a drug which has also been employed in the treatment of heroin addiction, and acamprosate. The sales pitch made for some of these products by their manufacturers has at times seemed to get a little ahead of the evidence, and a review by two British researchers, Joanna Moncrieff and Colin Drummond, was markedly critical. Their position in turn attracted sharp criticism from those researchers who took a more bullish view of these developments. It is probably at present too early to decide whether these drugs are going to find a useful and accepted place within the therapeutic armamentarium. If they are proved to be useful, it is likely to be in the context of wider treatment, and no one is suggesting that they will constitute a pharmaceutical miracle cure for a condition which is deeply embedded in individual psychology and personal circumstance. Meanwhile, and without surrender to pessimism, Moncrieff and Drummond's historically informed caution against a too easy faith in any latter-day 'elixir of temperance' should be heard.

But was Mary in denial?

The way in which we have set up the discussion of Mary M.'s case would probably be viewed by Dr W. as uninformed and mischievous. One can hear him saying it: we have over-identified with this attractive, articulate, middle-class woman and have been lured into siding with her and sharing her denial. We are guilty of collusion. The twelve-step approach is the way and the truth.

Poor Dr W. – perhaps we have slandered him and he's not at all a descendant of those motley purveyors of sovereign remedies who were described in the last chapter. Dr W. may have a rather over-invested faith in the one approach, but the twelve-step model can be a vehicle for carrying forward exactly those essences of treatment which we have just been discussing. Dr W. was trying to strengthen Mary M.'s motivation, define her goal and get her moving in a therapeutic direction, and then his team would have taught her relapse-prevention skills and helped her see life as a journey. Perhaps after a fair-minded reappraisal we should conclude that Dr W. was right all along, and that Mary M. is in denial, stubborn, quite contrary. If we were her friend, would we really be happy to see her still sometimes getting drunk? All sorts of inner pains are probably unresolved, despite her constant outward glitter. That's not recovery but living in deep denial, Dr W.'s counsellors would say.

Perhaps Dr W.'s in-patient unit is a variant of a retreat, but with therapeutic groups substituted for golf and twelve-step study sessions the latter-day reincarnation of prayer meetings. (Only the Turkish baths have gone for ever.) To be fair, the argument has two sides. In the light of our best but still incomplete understanding of what works in the treatment enterprise, we do well to try to steer between the extreme and opposing views that would have us see either Mary as being in deep denial or Dr W. as a modern treatment professional hopelessly caught in antique ways of thinking.

Here is one way of splitting the difference. What Dr W. offered Mary M. was a possible vehicle for therapeutic change of some sophistication, and one which has worked for some people. At the time, however, it was not appropriate for Mary M., and Dr W. was handicapped by the belief that everyone who resisted his model of treatment was in denial. Mary M. is tasting and testing her capacity to change. If she could find the right counsellor, psychologist or psychiatrist, she might benefit at this point from help which assists her to make her changes more secure, incrementally cumulative, deeper, more rewarding, happier. The evidence suggests that there are professional inputs which can assist Mary and many people like her, and modestly help turn contrariness into the stuff of recovery.

'Once an alcoholic, always an alcoholic' is, as we suggested earlier, the absolute linchpin of the disease theory. For AA it is a non-negotiable belief born of shared and bitter personal experience. Acceptance of this belief is seen as the gateway to recovery, while any attempt to trim its validity is the hallmark of denial. Sooner or later – and probably sooner – says AA, the troubled drinker who experiments with a return to social drinking will be right back where he or she started from.

We will discuss in this chapter the origins of the idea that the badly troubled drinker (or in latter-day terminology 'the alcoholic') must accept that abstinence constitutes the only feasible and lasting pathway out of trouble. We will then examine some of the research findings which were reported from the early 1960s onward which suggested that science had shattered the validity of this belief in the necessity for lifelong abstinence. What happened during some disputatious years was interpreted by those on the revisionist side as science triumphing over prejudice. Alcoholism, declared this camp, was now and henceforth no more to be viewed as an 'incurable disease' than epilepsy was to be seen as a symptom of diabolical possession. Not just a few but perhaps all alcoholics could with the help of behavioural psychology go back to controlled drinking. The disease concept of alcoholism – Marty Mann's healing balm – lay in ruins as a discredited medical mythologizing of drunkenness behaviour. Yet within a few more years the evidence put forward in support of that revisionist position had itself begun to unravel. Later, out of a controversy which was marked at times by allegations of scientific fraud and much other noise of academic battle, came useful clarification of the issues in dispute. With the facts of the story recounted, this chapter will finally examine why scientific debate about the treatment of troubled drinking should have escalated into warfare.

Alcoholics can never go back safely
to drinking: the origins of a consensus

The more ancient origins of the belief that the person who has had a bad problem with drink must swear off alcohol completely are lost in the mists of time. It seems likely that over the centuries many people would have discovered by trial and error that this absolutist approach was for them the way to deal with their problem. Dr Samuel Johnson was, for instance, to be found personally favouring that solution back in 1773, as recounted by James Boswell in the following passage:

He [Johnson] has great virtue, in not drinking wine or any fermented liquor, because, as he acknowledged to us, he could not do it in moderation. – Lady McLeod would hardly believe him, and said, 'I am sure, sir, you would not carry it too far.' – Johnson. 'Nay, madam, it carried me. I took the opportunity of a long illness to leave it off. It was then prescribed to me not to drink wine; and having broken off the habit, I have never returned to it.

In the nineteenth century and under the influence of the temperance movement, the idea that the reformed drunkard should espouse total abstinence became widespread. The consensus which emerged derived entirely from the personal experience of drinkers, rather than from any discoveries of science. Observations to support this consensus were fed to the public in temperance lectures and through the stories about reformed drunkards which poured from the temperance presses. The following case history is quoted from the autobiography published in 1881 by one of the most famous of such lecturers, John B. Gough.

I have a letter before me from a minister of the gospel, who lost his church by his intemperance. A few of his members clung to him, and choosing him for their minister, started a new enterprise in a hall. Many put confidence in his repentance and reform. The new church was prosperous. The pastor was earnest and sincere. The Sunday-school was flourishing. The prospects were bright. Gradually he was gaining the confidence of the people of the town, as the increasing congregation declared. This went on for a year or more. The minister was appointed on a committee for procuring a Sabbath-school library, and was deputed to go to the city to select said library, the other gentlemen of the committee having perfect confidence in his judgement. I now quote from his letter:

> I had no desire for drink; the appetite was all gone. I was perfectly free. I
> went to ——, and called on an old classmate for information as to the best
> method of procuring the books I needed, as I was to pay cash for them to
> the amount of a hundred and fifty dollars, which I had with me. My friend
> invited me to dinner. He was a wine-drinker – strictly moderate. He asked
> me to take a glass of wine. I had no desire for it; and, thinking I might take
> one glass, and feeling perhaps a little sensitive at the thought that my
> classmate might suppose I could not take one glass with him, I did take
> that glass, and then another. How I got out of the house I cannot tell; but
> I woke from a drunken sleep four days after, ragged, penniless: the money
> held in trust for the books all gone; and now I am ruined . . . What shall I
> do? Where shall I go? I am heartbroken.

The story of that clergyman's sad disaster is one which would have resonated with Dr Lincoln Williams's patient whose testimony was quoted in Chapter 7. It is the sameness of the experiences reported over so many years which is convincing.

The experientially derived belief that abstinence offered the only safe goal for the person with a serious drinking problem had, however, by the end of the nineteenth century progressed beyond the status of folk wisdom. Here is Dr Norman Kerr, the foremost British authority on the treatment of inebriety at that time, defining abstinence as the professional edict:

Only one article should be excluded [from the inebriate's diet]. That article is intoxicating liquor of every kind and strength. The abstinence should be unconditional, with no exception in favour of birthday or other celebrations. Such exceptions have been the ruin of not a few, as has also the exception for religious purposes at the communion. Every intelligent and honest physician when asked as I have frequently been if it is safe for the reformed alcoholic to partake of intoxicating liquor in such circumstances, should at once reply, 'No, it is not safe.' This is a physical disease, a paroxysm of which is provoked by the application of an exciting cause . . . the purely physical effect of the sip of a sacramental intoxicant is sufficient in many cases to arouse to activity the latent disease . . . The great temperance orator John B. Gough, during his reform period of some forty years of abstinence, never would run this risk.

And in that last sentence we can see for ourselves the influence of popular belief on medical thinking, with the doctor quoting the temperance orator as authority. By this time the temperance movement's insistence that never could a drop of liquor safely be allowed to pass the reformed drunkard's lips was a message which had won public acceptance and, at least in Anglo-Saxon countries, had captured the high ground of medicine.

From then until right up to the early 1960s, no medical text would have done other than continue to assert that abstinence was the only medically advisable goal for the cure of alcoholism. There were a scattering of not too well observed reports in the journals which suggested that, around the margins of the case series, a few excessive drinkers might defy expectations and go back to moderate drinking. But those observations did not send so much as a tremor across the consensus. As mentioned in Chapter 7, E. M. Jellinek's *The Disease Concept of Alcoholism* was published in 1960. It seemed to provide the scientific basis for the consensus position. Jellinek identified a species of troubled drinker whom he designated as the 'gamma alcoholic'; with this type of drinker, he asserted, any resumption of drinking would inexorably result in a rekindled craving and 'loss of control'. Delta or 'inability to abstain' alcoholism was a further disease variant. The physiological roots of this disease lay in an adaptation of cell metabolism, and there were 'physio-pathological changes analogous to those in drug addiction'. Thus was the seal of science stamped by Jellinek upon Gough and the folk belief. Jellinek's authority was such that everybody knew as a given truth that alcoholics (of the gamma and delta variety) were, by reason of their disease, unable ever again to control their drinking if a drink was taken.

1962: Dean Davies rocks the consensus

In 1962, just two years after the appearance of *The Disease Concept of Alcoholism* Dr D. L. Davies, dean of the Institute of Psychiatry at the Maudsley Hospital, London, published a paper entitled 'Normal Drinking in Recovered Alcoholics'. It was as if someone had casually thrown a bomb at the established consensus. What forced the alcoholism world to take note was in part the simple fact that seven authenticated cases with a controlled-drinking outcome were being added to the previously scant literature on this topic. But what also must have affected the audience was the distinction of the author of this report, and the seemingly blue-chip quality of his research. Mark Keller, the then editor of the *Quarterly Journal of Studies on Alcohol*, the American journal which published Davies's report, later described his reaction when this paper came across his desk:

Out of 93 reliably diagnosed alcohol addicts treated in one of the best psychiatric hospitals in the world – the deservedly famous Maudsley Institute – 7 patients had returned to normal drinking. Not for any ridiculously insignificant 30 day period, but for a minimum of 7 years and ranging up to 11 years. The follow-up was as sound as the diagnosis and reporting, and the article was signed by the Dean of the Institute.

By the time of his death in 1984, Davies, although a modest man, must have tasted the satisfaction of knowing that his 1962 paper had become one of the most widely cited articles of post-war alcohol research. It had achieved the status of a classic, and was regarded by many people as having at a stroke revolutionized scientific understanding of an age-old problem. If 7–8 per cent of alcoholics could return to maintained normal drinking, that blew apart the previous consensus view of alcoholism as irreversible disease. Davies's report still only suggested that a rather small proportion of drinkers were defying expectations. But what was seen by doctors and researchers alike as vitally important was not the percentage but the principle. In principle, alcoholism could no longer be an irreversible disease. The linchpin had fallen out.

The 1970s and normal drinking
made an intentional treatment goal

Davies's patients had all been told by him to aim for abstinence. The seven who had regained control over their drinking had done so without professional help in support of the moderation goal. An obvious next step was for researchers to explore what would happen if alcoholics were invited to attempt a return to normal drinking, and given treatment specifically designed to support that intention.

Some work of that kind was published from Australia, but the most daring experiment took place in California. This project was conducted by a husband-and-wife team of psychologists, Mark and Linda Sobell. They allocated gamma alcoholics (Jellinek's terminology) between treatments which aimed either at abstinence or at controlled drinking. There was a further split according to whether subjects were given conventional or behavioural treatments, so the overall research design was such as to put the patients into four treatment groups. The content of the behavioural treatment package which aimed at controlled drinking was wide, but included inviting patients to drink in a bar which was set up within the hospital precincts. Electric shocks were administered if these subjects exceeded the advised intake limits and became drunk. Nothing more radically opposed to the practice and beliefs of the then conventional approaches could have been imagined. Gough and Kerr would have been aghast, and everyone who had signed up to the post-war disease consensus could be expected to see the Sobells' work as heterodox.

The Sobells published their findings in a series of meticulously detailed papers. The emphasis was on objectivity rather than an intentional stirring of controversy. In a 1976 report they concluded, on the basis of a two-year follow-up, that subjects who had been invited to attempt a controlled-drinking goal and had been put through a behavioural treatment programme had a very good chance of succeeding in that goal. They wrote:

Only subjects treated by IBT (Individualized Behavior Therapy) with a goal of controlled drinking engaged in a substantial amount of limited, non-problem drinking during the second year interval, and those subjects also had more abstinent days than those in any other group.

The results for this particular experimental group did indeed look good, both in comparison to the other research subjects and in absolute terms. In the final six months of follow-up, the controlled-drinking/IBT group 'functioned well' on more than 85 per cent of days. Most clinicians would regard that kind of result as an outstandingly positive outcome with this type of drinker. And here crucially was research which went beyond chance observation of a few patients who had been sent in the abstinence direction but who had in the event defied instructions. On the contrary, it was intentional research showing that alcoholics could regain control over their drinking as a majority outcome, if given treatment explicitly to support that goal. The Sobells did not, however, suggest that behavioural therapy was a panacea, or a return to normal drinking the preferred goal for all troubled drinkers.

1982: revolution meets backlash

By the early 1980s and in the light of the rapidly evolving march of research, it began to look as if the 'never let a drop pass their lips again' consensus was no longer tenable. We have referred here selectively to Davies's report and the Sobells' research as landmark contributions, but there was much other research which could be read as pointing to that conclusion. There was heady talk of a 'paradigm shift' and a 'scientific revolution'. The American alcoholism-treatment establishment appeared therefore to be stubborn when it continued to insist that alcoholics could never drink safely.

What had started out as a scientific debate within the specialist journals then suddenly spilled over into public controversy of the most vituperative kind. In July 1982, Mark and Linda Sobell found themselves under very unpleasant threat with the appearance of a report in *Science*, a leading American scientific journal, which suggested that their research was profoundly flawed. Controversy had that July morning gone beyond the level of even heated academic dispute, to accusations of a kind potentially to lead to destruction of research careers.

The *Science* article was written by three American researchers: Mary Pendery, Irving Maltzman and Jolyon West. By personal interview and record search, they claimed to have traced the twenty subjects in the behavioural-therapy/controlled-drinking group whom the Sobells had reported as doing so well at the two-year follow-up. The factual evidence now published appeared to attack the Sobells' competence or integrity, or both.

A review of the evidence, including official records and new interviews, reveals that most subjects trained to do controlled drinking failed from the outset to drink safely. The majority were hospitalized for alcoholism treatment within a year after their discharge from the research project. A 10-year follow-up (extended through 1981) of the original 20 experimental subjects shows that only one, who apparently had not experienced physical withdrawal symptoms, maintained a pattern of controlled drinking; eight continued to drink excessively – regularly or intermittently – despite repeated damaging consequences; six abandoned their efforts to engage in controlled drinking and became abstinent; four died from alcohol-related causes; and one, certified about a year after discharge from the research project, as gravely disabled because of drinking, was missing.

Pendery and her colleagues not only were suggesting that on longer-term follow-up the initial good outcome claimed by the Sobells fell to pieces: they were also asserting that the Sobells had neglected to report adverse outcomes experienced during the original two-year period. If true, that constituted a devastating indictment. The flavour of what Pendery and her colleagues claimed to have uncovered about the true fate of these patients was conveyed in a tabulation of case summaries which detailed the hospital readmissions these patients had undergone during the Sobells' follow-up period. Here, by way of illustration, is an extract from the table relating to just one of the thirteen subjects who were readmitted to Patton State Hospital (the clinical base for the Sobells' study) 'within approximately one year of their participation in the research project'.

Readmitted to Patton 3 months, 22 days after discharge. 'requests admission for treatment of alcoholism – was here previously . . . he thinks he might be close to DT's as he feels confused, sees pictures flash before his eyes and sees little moving objects on the floor . . . he is grossly tremulous.

Shortly before the *Science* article was published, a piece in the 28 June 1982 *New York Times* quoted one of the authors, Maltzman, as saying of the Sobells' research, 'Beyond any reasonable doubt it's fraud.' The same journalist had West referring to 'grave doubt on the scientific integrity of the original research'. The original manuscript submitted to *Science* had contained an explicit allegation that data had been fabricated, but this had been removed before the article went to print. In March 1983 *Sixty Minutes*, the coast-to-coast CBS current-affairs programme, carried emotive footage of a narrator standing by the grave of one of the Sobells' controlled-drinking subjects who had died.

Charges of fraud rebutted

Inevitably, the Pendery paper meant that the Sobells' employers would have to institute a formal inquiry to examine the damaging allegations which had been made. The Sobells had meanwhile moved from California to Canada, and had taken staff positions at Ontario's Addiction Research Foundation (ARF). At the request of the Sobells, the ARF convened a committee of inquiry under the chairmanship of Dr Bernard Dickens, a law professor at the University of Toronto. This committee worked quickly and reported back to the ARF in November 1982. Its findings were unequivocal: 'The Committee finds there to be no reasonable cause to doubt the scientific or personal integrity of Dr Mark Sobell or Dr Linda Sobell.' The Sobells were also cleared of all charges by an investigative group later set up by the American National Institute of Health, which had been a part-funder of their research.

Given the seemingly damning allegations which Pendery and her colleagues had deployed in their critique, the fact that the Sobells were acquitted of wrongdoing might at first appear curious, and perhaps arouse suspicions of a whitewash. How can the disparity between the Sobells' reported findings and the facts uncovered by Pendery be accounted for in terms other than wilful deception? In fact a dispassionate review of the evidence amply supports the conclusions of the Dickens committee.

With the smoke of battle blown away, it can be seen that the Sobells and Pendery and her colleagues were reporting the facts with equal honesty. But they were drawing different conclusions from the same material, because they were looking at it in different ways. The Sobells for the most part rested content with the relative abstractions of tabulated numerical data. Pendery went behind those figures to explore what the figures might actually mean, in human and clinical terms. The harshest judgement that can be made on the Sobells is that their methods of reporting – although technically flawless – accidentally failed to reveal the textured clinical truth. Equally, Pendery and her colleagues can be faulted for concentrating on one experimental group and failing to look at the fate of the controls (the ten-year mortality rate had been 20 per cent for the experimental subjects and 30 per cent among the controls). On that basis, Pendery, Maltzman and West went beyond objective criticism to launch a personal attack of a kind which was to no one's benefit.

Psychologists caught in the Skinner box

In 1983 Alan Marlatt, a psychologist and an alcohol researcher of considerable repute, published a commentary on the controlled-drinking controversy in *American Psychologist*, the journal of the American Psychological Association. He suggested that the Sobells' attempt to return troubled drinkers to normal drinking had in part to be understood within the context of an unrestrained confidence in behavioural treatment, which had over a period gripped American psychologists. Marlatt illustrated the atmosphere of that time with this anecdote:

I remember clearly an incident from my own clinical internship in 1968. Several of us were invited to visit a new behavioral treatment program for alcoholism at a sister state hospital in Mendocina County. Upon arrival at Mendocina State Hospital I was surprised to discover patients from the alcoholism ward sitting out on the lawn ... each with their own Skinner box, apparently shaping the behavior of rats to bar-press a food reward. The director of the program, a behavioral idealist, later told me that he was trying to teach his patients basic operant conditioning principles so that they could apply them after they left the hospital.

A Skinner box is a piece of laboratory apparatus used by psychologists in experimental analysis of animal behaviour. It is named after B. F. Skinner, a founding behavioural scientist. His intellectual brilliance seemed, however, at times to be coupled with a naive belief that all human conduct could be understood as conditioned behaviour and as the product of learning processes brought about by the stick and carrot of punishment and reward. That even the most 'idealist' behaviourist could believe that playing with rats in a Skinner box would shape later human behaviour may today seem bizarre. But Marlatt's evocative picture of the scene on that 1960s Californian hospital lawn speaks to the reality of the then contemporary confidence in behavioural solutions to human problems.

Having described the main events of the 'return to normal drinking' battleground, Marlatt went on in his review to give his interpretation of the motivations lying behind the dispute. In brief, his conclusion was that the Sobells and other researchers who believed in the possibility of a return to social drinking were factually right and the enlightened vanguard of a revolutionary scientific movement. Those who opposed them were factually wrong and a group of reactionaries suffering from entrenchment in outdated prejudices. He summed up his conclusions as follows:

To some observers, the diagnosis of alcoholism carries the moral stigma of a new scarlet letter. Such critics argue that the contemporary disease model of alcoholism is little more than the old 'moral model' (drinking as a sinful behavior) dressed up in sheep's clothing, or at least in a white coat. Despite the fact that the basic tenets of the disease model have yet to be verified scientifically . . . advocates of the disease model continue to insist that alcoholism is a unitary disorder, a progressive disease that can only be temporarily arrested by total abstention. From this viewpoint, alcohol for the abstinent alcoholic symbolizes the forbidden fruit (a fermented apple) and a lapse from abstinence is tantamount to a fall from grace . . . Anyone who suggests controlled drinking is branded as an agent of the devil, tempting the naïve alcoholic back into the sin of drinking . . .

Marlatt apparently left unconsidered that he might in his own way have
been engaging in a little casting of moral aspersions on those who did
not share his view of the nature of the light and truth.

The Dean revisited

Marlatt's piece in *American Psychologist* was dedicated to the memory
of D. L. Davies, who had recently died. Marlatt quoted Davies with
appreciation, and identified the 1962 paper as seminal. Unknown to
Marlatt, a patient who had been one of Davies's seven famous follow-up
subjects had subsequently been admitted to the Alcoholism Treatment
Unit at the Bethlem Royal Hospital, the sister hospital to the Maudsley.
The Bethlem and Maudsley Hospitals functioned in close liaison with
the Institute of Psychiatry, the academic arm of an overall university
and National Health Service clinical, teaching and research complex.
Davies had retired from his university and NHS positions in 1976, but
until shortly before his death he remained an active and respected figure
who was held in great affection on the Maudsley campus.

At this point it is inevitable that a personal note should be introduced.
Davies was the consultant psychiatrist for whom I worked on joining
the junior staff of the Maudsley in 1959. Come 1967, I had been
appointed consultant in charge of the newly established Alcoholism
Treatment Unit at the Bethlem. When Davies's 'return to normal drinking' subject was admitted to the Bethlem in the 1980s for the treatment
of his drinking problem, that patient came under my care.

On routine clinical history-taking, it became evident that this patient
had been drinking heavily during the years of Davies's follow-up. There
was no evidence that he had ever engaged in sustained normal drinking
of the kind which Davies's paper claimed. The patient's wife now told
us that she had given false information when Davies's research assistant
had called on her. She had done so because of the threat of violence
from her drunkard husband, who was at the time lurking menacingly
at the back of the family shop. The research assistant had never spoken
to the patient – if she had done so, his intoxication would probably
have been obvious. A variety of ancillary evidence suggested that the
dire account which we now assembled of the patient's drinking since

discharge from Davies's in-patient care was on strong balance of probabilities the truth of the matter.

Up to the time of this patient's fortuitous admission to the Bethlem,
none of us who knew Davies's work had imagined that the 1962 paper
might be open to question. His follow-up had seemingly involved a
painstaking check on what each patient said against the report of a
family member, in all seven instances. But, if the husband and wife
were to be believed, that had not happened with the patient who had
now accidentally come our way. Furthermore, a sight of the Maudsley
case file revealed that during Davies's actual follow-up period this
drinker had attended the Maudsley's out-patient department and had
talked freely to one of Davies's staff about the continuing drinking
problem. But that information did not get through to Davies when he
was writing up his research, and we now realized that he had never
used any kind of record search as a method of validation. So crucial
was Davies's 1962 paper to the evolution of post-war alcohol research
that I suggested to him in the light of this later finding that we might
together attempt a long-term follow-up of the other six cases in his
series. However, he had no memory of these patients' names, and we
could see no way of tracing the original files. But shortly before he
died, and entirely by chance, I was able to identify these missing six
subjects through papers stored in a by then abandoned office which
twenty years previously had housed records relating to discharges from
Davies's clinical unit. Old case files were traced, and an intensive
six-person follow-up project got under way.

Sadly, Davies's death occurred before he knew the results of this
project, which tracked his patients up to a point twenty-nine to thirty-
four years after their original Maudsley discharges. It was possible to
conduct lengthy personal interviews with five of them, one spoke only
on the telephone, and one was dead. Relatives were interviewed and,
with permission, GP and hospital records were examined.

In summary, the results of the new follow-up were as follows. For one
subject there was persuasive evidence for a pattern of social drinking
having been initiated after a brief initial period of abstinence, and that
pattern had been sustained up to the time of the interview. This was
'normal drinking' by any reckoning. But clinical assessment of this man

showed that, although he had at an earlier stage been drinking excessively, he had never been significantly dependent on alcohol. Within Davies's terminology he would thus never have qualified as 'an addict', and should not have been included in the original case series. By this time researchers had far greater ability to define and identify addiction (or the alcohol dependence syndrome) than had earlier been available to Davies.

There was one patient who had been severely dependent on alcohol when admitted to the Maudsley and who claimed to have stayed at a level of moderate social drinking ever after. His wife confirmed this story, and the medical records provided no indication of further drinking problems. However, he smelt of spirits at a mid-afternoon interview and refused a blood test, and he generously if somewhat surprisingly offered a drink to the researcher who called at his house.

In the five remaining cases, there was strong evidence that there had in each instance been a significant drinking problem both during Davies's follow-up period and subsequently, up to the time of the later interview. These patients included the man who had turned up at the Bethlem, who by the time of the later follow-up was as a result of his alcohol-related brain damage a permanent resident in a psychiatric hospital. The conclusions on these five men were supported by a confluence of interview data and evidence coming from medical records. In these five cases it was difficult to conclude other than that Davies's published claims were not supportable. However, there was no suggestion whatsoever that Davies had intentionally misrepresented his findings. Rather, the methods he employed, although acceptable at the time he conducted his study, were not adequate for determining the truth in a tricky type of inquiry where active concealment of the truth may for some subjects be the name of the game. The results of this further follow-up were published in 1985.

The war on the return-to-normal drinking front – how does it look now?

That question needs to be discussed from two different angles. There is first the question of what clinical and scientific consensus has emerged from this controversy. In the light of what we have learned, do we or do we not tell alcoholics that science says that it is safe and sensible for them to attempt social drinking? What should we be saying to a desperate clergyman like Gough's? Second, what does the inner story of this controversy, its clash and fury, tell us further about the nature of society's attitudes to the ambiguous and divisive alcohol molecule? The first question is about the science, the second about the arena, and let's now take them in turn.

So far as the science is concerned, the years since 1962 have seen considerable refining of the capacity to define what is being talked about. That has been important for the quality and meaningfulness of the argument. Davies's term 'alcohol addict' and the Sobells' use of Jellinek's phrase 'gamma alcoholic' were both acceptable at the relevant times, but these terms lacked precision as means for case identification. Within present-day thinking, case definition is best approached through the framework of the dependence-syndrome concept (Chapter 5). As already emphasized, that concept proposes that the dependent state is not a matter of all or nothing (addict or not addict), but something which can be experienced in varied and measurable degrees (more dependent or less dependent). Most experts would probably now agree that a drinker who has become heavily alcohol-dependent is unlikely afterwards to succeed in returning to social drinking. The conventional wisdom does to that extent seem to have scientific support. To suggest that drinkers of the kind who are attracted to AA should en masse and with a little Skinnerian help start drinking again, is a recommendation which would no longer be favoured by even the behavioural idealists. It is difficult to argue that those like Gough's clergymen should do other than accept that if they take the drink, the drink will take them.

With lesser degrees of dependence, return to normal drinking may be feasible. But the decision to attempt it will have to be made in the light of a detailed case appraisal and the patient's wishes. Younger patients may in general do better than older patients in achieving controlled drinking. Severe coexistent mental or physical illness, drug misuse and a propensity to self-harm or to violence towards others are among the factors which may speak against the wisdom of trying to return to normal drinking. However, for what are often called 'problem drinkers' – the non-dependent drinkers whom the GP will be advising

– a planned cutting back on the drink rather than an insistence on abstinence is a feasible and sensible goal which the patient is likely much to prefer.

Thus at the scientific level those years of controversy have, more than anything, led back to the eternally sound scientific insistence that before getting into an argument it is best to know what one is talking about, and to be able to define and measure that thing. Degree of dependence is not the only determinant of whether an individual will be able to drink again safely, but it is a factor of major significance. If we distinguish between, on the one hand, the severely dependent drinker and, on the other, the less dependent drinker or the person who is simply drinking too much, a lot of the heat disappears from the old controversy. However, the middle ground of dependence intensity can present difficult decisions which need to be made indi-vidually.

How, then, are we to understand the emotion which during a period of years was expended in this arena around the return-to-normal-drinking issue? Why did the Sobells think it timely to set up their clinical experiment? Why were they subsequently so pilloried, and why did that CBS television programme choose to film the grave of an experimental subject, but not that of any of the control subjects who had died? Why did Maltzman and West engage in such personal attacks? Those events constituted some quite considerable happenings in the play that went on around the science.

What we again seem strikingly to discover here is that ethyl alcohol is a drug capable of exciting passion. Some of the passion which it engenders is complex and atavistic, and undoubtedly relates to alcohol as symbol and mystery rather than to the drug as objective molecule. Stumble into any alcohol controversy and one may expect to disturb that kind of hornet's nest.

The dispute here was also perhaps about one rather specific and concrete ideological issue. Those who were defenders of the old belief that the troubled drinker can recover only through abstinence rooted their position in accumulated personal testimony or front-line clinical experience. To dismiss their belief as no more than repressive moralism would be a mistaken and ungenerous analysis: the belief that the alcoholic's recovery must involve permanent abstinence was a disease-based postulate, not a moral one. That position does, however, imply that recovery will mean acceptance of the disease, and in that sense acceptance by the drinker of his or her imperfection. For some people, that may involve the Christian idea of grace in accepting what one cannot change, and surrendering to God. And that is a very different ideological position from that of the behaviourist's belief that the rat in the Skinner box is a model and metaphor for infinitely malleable humankind, with the gamma alcoholic someone to be shaped by electric shocks in the mocked-up bar. That and other behavioural techniques reflect a faith in scientists' capacity to do things to people so as to make their behaviour change. The polarity between those two underlying ideologies may help to explain how controversy about the treatment of alcoholics escalated into bitter warfare.

This is what the author of an article recently published in the British *Medical Journal* had to say on alcohol as medicine:

People should be treated as adults and should be told the facts. These still need to be refined in detail, but in broad outline they are quite clear: in middle- and old-age some small amount of alcohol within the range of one to four drinks each day reduces the risk of premature death, irrespective of the medium in which it is taken.

The person making that statement was Sir Richard Doll, emeritus professor of physic (medicine) in the University of Oxford, and a researcher of great fame who did much to establish the link between cigarette smoking and lung cancer.

Debate about the alleged health benefits of alcohol has spread beyond the scientific journals and is a hot topic for the popular media. When an American television show suggested that red wine was a specific against heart disease, sales of that product went up hugely. The idea that alcohol is good for the heart is certainly good for the drinks industry. And quite a few doctors have begun confidently to translate the claimed research findings into patient-friendly advice at the clinical front line – 'Drink for your heart's sake, Mr and Mrs Smith. Alcohol is a good medicine, and you should be told the facts.'

But what facts? This chapter will first look briefly at the question of what gives the use of a drug the status of a medical use. Next we will describe the long, astonishing and largely forgotten story of the medical profession's scandalous love for alcohol as medicine. We will then scrutinize recent research on alcohol and coronary heart disease. Finally, supposing that the world were to accept in principle the proposition that alcohol is an effective prophylactic against heart disease, what would be the likely consequences for society of making alcohol into a medicine?

Drugs at the borders of medicine

With any mind-acting drug, what is to be deemed its recreational as opposed to its medicinal use is frequently akin to trying to determine where a blurred frontier runs on an uncertain map. And uncertainty is likely whether one is looking at the historical record or at present-day drug usage. Before turning to the special case of alcohol, let's for a moment broaden the focus and see what can be learned from an inspection of how drugs in general tend to pose questions about the frontiers between medicine and non-medicine.

Take, for instance, the nineteenth-century use of opium as one example of this kind of problem. In the early 1800s, each man, woman and child in Britain was on average consuming about 120 standard doses of opium each year. Access to doctors was limited – especially for the poor – and most of that opium was self-prescribed and bought across a shop counter without legislative restriction. It was purchased in pill form or, in an alcoholic solution, as laudanum. Much of its use was for self-treatment for common ailments, in an era when other symptomatic treatments for such complaints were lacking. There was, for instance, no other way of treating a cough. Self-medication it was, but do-it-yourself prescribing is also an important sector of therapeutics in the present day, as witnessed by the vast sale of non-prescription medicines. What began to worry nineteenth-century commentators was, however, not so much the free and escalating use of corner-shop opium prescriptions for the amelioration of common ills, but the rumour that labourers in Manchester were dropping opium into their beer and engaging in what was viewed as 'stimulant use' – or, in other words, taking opium for a recreational purpose. That behaviour crossed what was deemed the legitimate border. But the truth of the matter had probably always been that, although many people took their opium as medicine, they also at times swallowed it in the quest for a drug experience, or in the hope of relieving the misery of life. Opium could make existence in the mill towns transiently more bearable, and it also solaced those living in the dankness of the rural fenlands. The person with a box of pills or a bottle of laudanum was unlikely to have cared much for the niceties of the boundary question, and probably often blurred that boundary in a single dose.

There is a broad array of other drugs which can be called on to illustrate aspects of the shifting and multiple criss-crossing in perceptions as to whether a substance is or is not a medicine, or being used medicinally. Sometimes doctors seem to be picking up a folk drug and trying to turn its use towards a medical definition, as is today happening with debate over the medical use of cannabis. In the 1960s the medical profession briefly claimed ownership of LSD, with the suggestion that its use could open the doors of perception and give helpful insights in the process of psychotherapy. Valium seemed in the 1960s and 1970s to be recapitulating the story of opium. This minor tranquillizer rapidly became the NHS's best-seller, but the question of what proportion of this tranquillizer-prescribing was for any specific and identifiable medical condition, as opposed to making life in the tower block a little more bearable, was seldom asked.

The context within which to approach the medical use of alcohol should therefore be an awareness that what counts as the medical deployment of a drug is time-bound, arbitrary and often confused. We saw in Chapter 2 how society can dress this molecule with invented meanings. One such invention has for centuries involved clothing it in the garb of medicine.

The history of alcohol as medicine

So far as is known, the first treatise on the use of wine in the treatment of disease was written by Asclepiades (131–40 BC), a Greek physician who set up practice in Rome. Not long afterwards, St Paul was to be found urging Timothy to 'use a little wine for thy stomach's sake' (1 Timothy 5:23). That admonition subsequently caused embarrassment for temperance advocates, but was neatly dealt with by interpreting St Paul as implying that alcohol should now and then be rubbed on to the stomach wall as an embrocation. If the belief that alcohol is good for the human frame has this deep history, it is also a thoroughly modern belief, enshrined in contemporary lay wisdom. Whisky is a popular remedy for the common cold, and who would dare question the strictly medical motivations which cause the poor sniffing sufferer to pour a hot toddy? Brandy is widely considered to be a specific for shock. 'Guinness', a famous poster campaign told us, 'is Good for You.' Champagne will assist in recovery from almost any illness. A 'night-cap' is self-help sedation.

In the nineteenth century, alcohol attained a central and highly regarded place in the medical profession's therapeutic armoury. It was massively prescribed in the treatment of every kind of fever, including influenza, pneumonia, puerperal fever, malaria, typhoid, typhus and cholera. It was used in the treatment of diabetes, and advised as a remedy for snake bite and dog bite. Drink was the standard treatment for wasting diseases. When schoolboys were deemed to be weakened by growing too quickly, they would be given drink to slow down their sprouting.

An important stimulus to this medical enthusiasm for alcohol had occurred in 1780, when an Edinburgh physician, Dr John Brown, published his *Elementa Medicae*, which set out the principles of what came to be known as the Brunonian system. With pleasing simplicity, he proposed that all diseases could be classified as belonging to one of two categories. First there were the asthenic disorders, which were due to underexcitement in the system. Alcohol was viewed by Brown as a stimulant, and was therefore a sovereign remedy for all asthenic diseases. Second, and in contrast, sthenic disorders were due to too much excitement in the body's system. This overexcitement had to be subdued by bleeding, purging and the administration of emetics. It was inevitable that these procedures would often produce results beyond the intended mark, and then the patient would have to be stimulated by the pouring in of wine and brandy. Thus, by this alluring reasoning, alcohol – either as primary or as secondary remedy – became a panacea.

Dr Brown died in 1788 – apparently as the result of too large a dose of opium, which he had taken in accord with his belief that opium also was a medically advised stimulant. His system was, however, by then well launched, and was taken up enthusiastically by the majority of doctors. For much of the nineteenth century Brown's ideas dominated therapeutic practice. Their influence was to linger on long after the absurdities of the sthenic/asthenic dichotomy had been rejected. Thanks to Brown, the medical prescribing of alcohol was legitimized; doctors liked prescribing it, and patients liked having it prescribed to them. Well into the twentieth century, John Brown's alcoholic therapeutics went marching on.

Here are some remarks by Thomas Trotter on the subject of alcohol in the prevention and treatment of fevers, as given in his 1804 *Essay . . . on Drunkenness*:

While the body is under the influence of intoxication, it is surprising how it will resist impressions, that at other times would be fatal. This is particularly the case with respect to contagion . . . Men in this condition have certainly, on many occasions, been exposed to typhous contagion, and escaped. This being the case, a practice has been inculcated by some physicians, to swallow a little brandy when they approach the sick bed, by way of precaution. It is well known that a rigorous circulation of the blood, with that resolution and temper of mind which accompany it, is highly favourable to the resistance of contagion . . .

Trotter himself, however, did not favour this bedside practice. He thought that a doctor who drank before coming on the ward might set a bad example to the nurses. Instead, and as befitted a former naval surgeon, he declared himself 'partial to mental stimuli which spring from the desire of our duty'.

What is striking about the records of the medical profession's reliance on alcohol is the sense of extreme and unquestioning faith in this remedy, and the hyperbole of its praise. Brian Harrison in his book *Drink and the Victorians* described a doctor who in the 1850s prescribed to a patient six pints of brandy (3.2 litres) to be consumed in the course of seventy-two hours. Harrison suggested that the Prince Consort might have lived longer had he not been treated with similarly heroic doses of spirits.

And here is Dr Francis Hare, a well-known specialist in the treatment of inebriety, describing how, when working in Australia at an earlier point in his career, he had deployed alcohol in the treatment of typhoid:

I was in charge of the fever department of the Brisbane Hospital (Queensland) from 1885 until 1891. During the first eighteen months of this period I treated some six or seven hundred cases of typhoid by the ordinary expectant method, giving alcohol in the form of brandy or whisky, rather frequently and in some cases very freely – to the extent of 8, 12, 16 or more fluid ounces [16 fluid ounces equals a little over 400 ml] in the twenty-four hours – whenever it seemed necessary, as was the custom. The chief indication was the condition of the heart and pulse. Economical considerations, however, precluded the use of alcohol except for the purpose of saving life: it was never given as a luxury or placebo . . . the use was always abandoned toward the end of the febrile stage, that is, well before convalescence had commenced. Used with these limitations it was the decided opinion of all connected with the fever wards . . . that alcohol never led to inebriety. Indeed it was commonly remarked that the effect was rather to set up a distaste for alcohol . . .

In 1904 a remarkably thoughtful and clinically detailed paper on the treatment of '200 Cases of Acute Lobar Pneumonia' was published in the *Lancet* by Dr John Hay, a physician practising in Liverpool. He saw the public's faith in the therapeutic virtue of alcohol as unquestioning. He reported that an action for damages had recently been taken out against a physician who had not administered alcohol to a patient who had subsequently died.

Hay stated that, although the medical profession had at that time somewhat modified its views on the place of alcohol in the treatment of pneumonia, it was still very widely used by doctors in the treatment of that condition. One reason which he identified for this situation was the state of medical training. Few students had ever seen a severe case of pneumonia treated without alcohol. The second reason which he put forward to explain the profession's continued adherence to a practice which he viewed as outdated and irrational was the degree to which doctors were influenced by lay beliefs in the medical virtue of alcohol:

The greater public believe in brandy. It is 'the stimulant' and when a friend or relative is ill they are never happy until brandy or some other alcoholic drink is ordered. It takes a strong-minded medical man to withstand this and although one may not care to admit it, lay opinion on this matter cannot but have a far-reaching effect.

The strength of the medical profession's good opinion of alcohol, even at so late a period as the beginning of the twentieth century, can also be traced in many texts. Thus Dr Arthur Shadwell, in 1902, offering as evidence a poignant boyhood memory:

Once when at school I got a wound on the finger at cricket, which obstinately refused to heal. At last the surgeon, having exhausted his art, ordered me a glass of port wine every day. The place healed at once. I have seen many cases in which the moderate use of alcoholic liquor as an article of diet has been equally beneficial.

Although in the course of the twentieth century alcohol gradually lost much of its medical status, evidence can still be found of a determined rearguard action being fought by the older physicians some decades after Shadwell was writing. One can, for instance, find Dr Robert Hutchinson, MD, FRCP, physician to the London Hospital, writing on 'Alcohol as Medicine' in a textbook published in 1923. He recommended alcohol as a 'food and as of benefit in prolonged fevers and wasting diseases', and he suggested that it should be used in 'severe cases of diabetes in young subjects'. Alcohol was an aid to the digestion, and it could be prescribed in the treatment of heart failure. He also believed that alcohol was a widely useful tonic:

the red wines, such as Burgundy and Port [are] specially possessed of 'tonic' properties . . . It is in the building up of patients who are 'simply run down', who are neuralgic, or who are convalescing from acute disease that the tonic effects of alcohol are of special value.

Hutchinson signed off his chapter with the pleasing adage 'Wine is the milk of old age.' As a senior consultant at a London teaching hospital, he would have exerted on students a powerful influence of a kind to confirm Hay's worst fears.

Alcohol as medicine put away
The reasons why doctors finally gave up their enthusiasm for alcohol as a medicine were several. Quite early in the nineteenth century the medical profession began to be aware that promiscuous prescribing of

alcohol put patients at risk of alcohol dependence. 'Memorials', or public statements, containing such warnings were got up by certain members of the profession in 1839, 1847 and 1871, on each occasion with an impressive sprinkling of medical knights among the signatories. As quoted by George Wilson, the 1871 memorial gave the following opinion:

As it is believed that the inconsiderate prescription of large quantities of alcoholic liquids by medical men for their patients has given rise in many instances to the formation of intemperate habits, the undersigned, while unable to abandon the use of alcohol in the treatment of certain classes of disease, are yet of opinion that no medical practitioner should prescribe it without a sense of grave responsibility. They believe that alcohol, in whatever form, should be prescribed with as much care as any powerful drug, and that the directions of its use should be so framed as not to be interpreted as a sanction for excess . . . they hold that every medical practitioner is bound to exert his utmost influence to inculcate habits of great moderation in the use of alcoholic liquids.

A case reported by Francis Hare when he had returned from Australia and was treating people with drinking problems speaks vividly to the realities of the danger against which those memorials sought to warn:

A retired sergeant-major in the foot-guards had always been abstemious in his habits, though not an abstainer, until he contracted dysentery in South Africa. His illness was severe, and entailed his being kept in bed for five months. During the whole of this time, he states that he lived mainly, if not solely, on beaten-up egg with either brandy or port wine. Ever since his convalescence he has been a pseudo-dipsomaniac, that is to say, he has been unable to touch alcohol in any form, even a glass of light beer, without immediately plunging into a heavy drinking bout.

If the danger of medically induced dependence was an anxiety which began to tell against the profession's reliance on alcohol, the size of the drink bills which hospitals were incurring was another issue which began repeatedly to attract worried notice. In 1872, seven London teaching hospitals ran up between them a drinks bill totalling £7,712 – an astonishing sum for those days. In 1884 the four mental hospitals administered by the London County Council had a daily average bed occupancy of 7,246 patients, with 861 staff. Patients and staff between them consumed in that one year 8,529 pints of spirits, 6,687 pints of wine and what with touching accuracy was recorded as 255,486½ gallons of beer. And all of this was paid for by the public purse.

But what eventually killed off the profession's love of alcohol as medicine was the arrival of truly effective modern drugs. The doctor who prescribed alcohol for pneumonia had nothing worthwhile with which to treat the patient, and that was still as true in the 1930s as it had been for Asclepiades. The brandy was given to keep the relatives happy and to assuage the physician's sense of impotence, and in the process the mortality rate for the condition was made worse. Come the sulphonamides and penicillin, there were at long last drugs which worked. With the birth of scientific medicine and modern therapeutics, alcohol was put away.

Alcohol as medicine resurrected

Today's resurrected interest in alcohol as medicine centres around the suggestion that people who engage in a little bit of drinking are likely to live longer than abstainers. It was findings to this effect to which Richard Doll was referring in the paper which was quoted at the start of this chapter. With the notion of alcohol as medicine dead and forgotten for half a century, suddenly it seems to be alive and well, and very much with us again.

The first research of any scientific significance which explored the alcohol and longevity question was reported by F. G. P. Neison, and was published in the *Journal of the Statistical Society* as long ago as 1851. Neison's method was simple in the extreme, and involved the sending of questionnaires to doctors and asking them to give information on the age at death of patients whom they deemed to be drunkards. He calculated that, at any age, the rate of death among these excessive drinkers was 3.25 times that of the general population – a finding much in accord with modern studies of dependent drinkers. As he put it, 'If there be anything . . . in the usage of society calculated to destroy life, the most powerful is certainly the inordinate use of strong drink.'

Leaping from the pages of that 1851 paper comes another piece of information of extraordinary interest to contemporary debates about alcohol and life expectancy:

A few years ago Mr Munro, of Enfield, at much trouble and expense, procured returns from Rechabite societies, showing the rate of mortality and sickness experienced by the members, and the results, although not published, are known to exhibit as high a rate of mortality and sickness as is found to prevail among the members of other friendly societies. The facts collected by Mr Munro are of great value, and it is to be regretted that the societies furnishing them should, on account of the unfavourable nature of the facts arrived at, object to their publication.

The Rechabites were a friendly society which offered insurance only to total abstainers. So here was a suggestion that alcohol might confer no health disbenefit, dating from long before modern epidemiological research. This story stands as a sad and early example of research being suppressed because of the awkwardness of its conclusions.

In the early decades of the nineteenth century a number of investigators attempted to complement the findings on alcohol and longevity which had come from the study of human populations with research on animals which were exposed experimentally to alcohol. Most animals do not at all like drinking alcohol. The researchers' preferred method of administering it was to blow alcoholic vapour into the cages of the creatures, forcing them to engage in something rather equivalent to the heavy and prolonged sniffing of brandy. Thus a report published in 1918 in the *Journal of Experimental Zoology* by two American investigators, C. R. Stockard and G. N. Papanicolaou, on the effect of alcohol on guinea pigs:

A number of the guinea-pigs have now been treated with alcohol fumes almost to a state of intoxication six days per week from five to six years. Few guinea-pigs in captivity live so long a time. There were two males treated for over six years, one of which lived to be more than seven years old. So far as we know that is the longest reported for a guinea-pig . . . In no case when the treatment was begun on animals over three months old, could any injurious effects on its general welfare or length of life be discovered.

The 1920s saw some survey work published by Raymond Pearl, an American public-health doctor, suggesting that light drinkers would on average live longer than abstainers. That report caused little stir, alcohol as a medicine became an increasingly off-limits idea, and for fifty years the research question lay neglected. But in the late 1970s the silence was broken when a British medical team led by Archie Cochrane suggested that people living in wine-drinking countries had a lower death rate than people living in other countries of the developed world. First as a trickle and then as a rush, further papers on this topic then followed, and so far something over twenty such reports have appeared.

The evidence that light or moderate drinking is associated with lesser risk of heart disease is today viewed by most scientific commentators as very persuasive. They will be likely to see the statistical evidence for this pro-health relationship as being every bit as strong as the evidential basis for an anti-health relationship between cigarette smoking and lung cancer and heart disease. And these commentators are today also suggesting that there are good reasons for believing that behind the statistical association lies a true cause-and-effect relationship, with alcohol conferring its benefit through its action on blood-clotting mechanisms. The benefits are, however, restricted to groups such as men aged over forty and women of post-menopausal age, who are at high risk of heart disease. But that is still good news for countries where heart disease is a major killer.

So that is the way things today seem to many commentators conclusively to have gone. Alcohol is good for the heart. Poor Mr Munro of Enfield is after all these years vindicated. Those alcoholized guinea pigs were speaking to the human condition. Pearl was right despite the half-century of subsequent neglect. Cochrane's team stumbled again on the essential truth, although they were wrong in thinking that wine is uniquely protective. Modern science has now proved the matter up to the hilt. The continued snipings and mutterings from those who still want to question the strong evidence that alcohol protects against coronary heart disease are probably tainted by temperance prejudice. Add to this the views that drink may reduce mortality risk from the type of stroke which is due to blood clotting, can reduce risk of gall-bladder disease, may protect against one variety of diabetes and perhaps also decease risks for some kinds of depressive and neurotic disorder, and the conclusion must appear to be that it is time for Robert Hutchinson to give another lecture to the medical students.

Awkward findings

Or could it be that the cry to bring back alcohol as medicine is premature? Are the claims outlined above on the seeming pro-health impacts supported by really rock-solid evidence? Perhaps there are again some awkward findings being ignored, but this time it is not the Rechabites who are doing the ignoring. Let's examine some of the evidence and arguments which have recently challenged the 'alcohol is good for the heart' proposition.

The suggestion has been made that abstainers have a reduced life expectancy not because abstention is intrinsically bad for their health, but because in many cases illness has driven these people to stop drinking. They may, for instance, have got themselves into the abstention category because they have given up drink as a result of their alcohol dependence, or because of a recent heart attack, or even because of a terminal illness. No wonder, then, that light or moderate drinkers do better in the longevity stakes than abstainers. However, if the sick abstainers are taken out of the equation, the original statistical conclusion still holds. With the confounding-sickness question got out of the way, alcohol continues to be good for the heart.

But, with the 'sick abstainers' objection negated, the critics of the health claims for alcohol have more recently come back with another, and much stronger, argument. They suggest that the body of research which appears to show that abstainers are at heightened risk of heart-disease death is likely to be seriously if not fatally flawed by the failure to deal with the fact that abstainers radically differ from drinkers in certain very significant aspects of lifestyle. In 1998 an international research group led by an American researcher, Kaye Fillmore, published a series of three reports certain to shock anyone who believed that the question whether alcohol is good for the heart has been settled in the affirmative, and beyond reasonable doubt. Fillmore's research suggests that what had looked like an open-and-shut case should now be reopened.

What Fillmore and her colleagues did was to reanalyse all the material contained in the studies which are quoted in support of the claimed ability of alcohol to protect against death, but with corrections for subject characteristics such as social class, unemployment and depression. They did so in the belief that a significant proportion of abstainers may be people whose abstention is a marker for disadvantages of a kind which in their own right can enhance the risk of heart disease. With these corrections made, Fillmore's team appear to have shown that the heart benefits allegedly conferred by light or moderate drinking over no alcohol at all are clean washed away. The idea that alcohol is good for the heart appears to be challenged by their improved statistical handling of the data.

Quick on the heels of Fillmore's work has come a Scottish study which appears to confirm her conclusions. Carole Hart and her colleagues published in 1999 a twenty-one-year follow-up of 5,766 Scottish men. These men's drinking level at baseline was related to subsequent mortality with correction for multiple confounders. The investigators failed to find any protection against heart disease as a result of moderate drinking. For men who drank more than twenty-one units a week there was a significant increase in all-cause mortality. Furthermore, there was a strong positive relationship between alcohol consumption and death from stroke. Men who drank thirty-five or more units a week doubled their stroke mortality risk compared with abstainers.

What a jury might say

With the arguments of both sides represented as fairly as possible and put to a jury at an imaginary civil trial, what sort of verdict would we now expect to hear returned? The jury analogy is appropriate because what we have to do here is form a view on a balance of probabilities rather than hope for any kind of final proof – that's life, and, with this type of research, that's the nature of science. And at the end of the day it is the ordinary citizens, the jury and not the advocates, who have to determine the worth of the research evidence and the persuasiveness of the conflicting arguments, and decide whether they mean to drink for their health.

Here is one possible view of the conclusion which the jurors might be likely to reach. For men aged over forty and for women past the menopause, alcohol perhaps (or some might say 'probably') gives a degree of protection against heart disease. But in the light of Fillmore's and Hart's findings the jury would have to add a rider strongly advising caution. What until recently looked like a firm scientific consensus that alcohol is good for the heart now goes back to being a hypothesis rather than anything near a certainty.

And meanwhile outside the court room . . .

With our jury having reached their cautious verdict, what happens next? Do those among the jurors who are in the appropriate age group walk down the court steps and make for the nearest bar, there to take one for the heart? That 'what next?' question needs to be put to the government and to the medical profession, and then finally and most importantly it must be put back to society at large.

At the official level, should we expect to see Britain's chief medical officer and the US surgeon general now go on television and state with the authority of government that alcohol is somewhat good for the heart? Should education departments be expected to put out circulars advising teachers that, in their health-education classes, they should give prominence to the alleged health benefits of drinking? And should we expect the government to announce in the next Budget that taxes on drink will be lowered in the interests of the nation's health? Within this kind of scenario, a little further down the road one might perhaps see special alcohol concessions given to pensioners. Alcohol was removed from the British pharmacopoeia in 1932, but within this vision of the future it would be given back its rightful place. And, if alcohol is good for the heart, it would be logical to allow drinks manufacturers to tout the health benefits of alcohol in their advertising material. Perhaps the life-insurance industry should start to exclude abstainers from life cover or impose discriminatory weightings on them. Lest anyone should think that too wild a fancy, in 1840 Robert Warner, a Quaker and a total abstainer, found his application to a London life office met with the reply that he would have to pay an additional premium because abstainers had a shortened life expectancy.

Governments have a responsibility to let the scientific facts be known, but for the time being it seems improbable that we will see, as follow-through to the science, any radical shift in policies at the official level. What will probably continue to restrain governments from any too radical initiatives on this front is partly that the science is in reality much less certain than is sometimes suggested. And beyond that is the fear that anything which threatens to increase population alcohol consumption is a leap into the dark and a gamble with the nation's health which might prove economically and politically costly. On balance and despite the lures of populism, a policy which invited more drinking on health grounds is thus unlikely at present to be embraced by any prudent administration.

But, in face of the unguarded recent media messages on this topic, individual doctors are having increasingly to deal with patients coming into the practitioner's office for informed advice on whether a little of what they like will do them good. Here are two possible ways in which a doctor might today in good conscience respond to such a query:

First doctor: On my reading of what's been appearing recently in the journals, I think you should take a drink or two a day for your heart's sake. To my mind, the benefit for someone of your age is likely to outweigh any potential negatives.

Second doctor: Have a little of the stuff if you like it, but I can't in good conscience say that the evidence is so firm that I should tell you to drink alcohol for your heart's sake. If you want to avoid a heart attack, stop smoking, get your weight down, take some exercise, cut some of the fat out of your diet, and perhaps go on to half an aspirin a day. That's a more sensible health package than starting to use alcohol as a medicine on the basis of the still equivocal research.

The first of those two doctors may be sued if the patient subsequently experiences an alcohol-related accident, or develops alcohol dependence. Meanwhile, the second doctor may recapitulate history and, rather like the practitioner mentioned by Dr Hay, find himself facing an action because he or she has failed to prescribe a prophylactic medicine.

But now let's put the problem back to the people. What is the juror coming down the steps – the man or woman in the street – to make of the news that alcohol is supposedly a medicine? Despite much current amnesia about this fact, introducing to society today the idea that alcohol is medicine, even in the limited heart-disease context, would be reintroduction rather than innovation. It would mean edging towards renewed acceptance of the previously pervasive notion that alcohol, this deeply ambiguous molecule, has the special and reverential status which attaches to a medical substance. Medicines are good and, whether prescribed by a doctor or taken as a folk remedy, alcohol would have recovered that identity. Conferment of a therapeutic status on alcohol may in the doctor's view be rooted in the science of clotting mechanisms, but the medical verdict would be loaded with much wider implications. Government, doctors, people in the street – they are all one interacting culture, with everyone sharing in the shifting, multiple popular depictions of alcohol as blood of Christ, wrecker of altars, token of national virtue, devil to be cast out, addictive drug. Reinstate in that mix the idea that alcohol is a virtuous medicine, and profound shifts in the popular image of this drug may be created.

The debate which is in progress in the scientific journals on the protection which alcohol may give against coronary heart disease is thus in part dealing with objective, difficult and as yet not fully resolved questions of large potential clinical and public-health significance. But it is also a debate about symbolism, with a danger that the symbolic shift will get ahead of the science. There can be little doubt not only that Dr John Brown promiscuously dosed his patients with alcohol, but that the acceptance of his doctrines also and at the same time dosed society with a beneficent view of alcohol. It is the symbolism lurking in the idea of alcohol as medicine which should concern the jury. While weighing the modern science and scrutinizing the latest research report, they need to be aware of the depth and history of this thing. Alcohol as medicine could be a dangerous transubstantiation.

A dilemma is in essence a situation which presents two mutually exclusive choices, neither of which looks entirely good. That person in a dilemma has to weigh potential profit against possible loss and make a choice, with the conflicting outcomes never being entirely predictable. A dilemma has horns. Should we burden ourselves this morning with an umbrella, or trust that the rain will hold off? Go through the traffic light, or slam on the brakes and pray that the vehicle on our tail will also stop? Leap from the window of the smoke-filled room, or hold on a minute longer in hope of the fire brigade?

So to a man and woman sitting over their supper table. They have so far each enjoyed two glasses of wine with the meal. Now they confront the drinker's dilemma incarnate – shall they finish the bottle or stuff in the cork? Or perhaps they are even edging towards tacit agreement that opening a second bottle would not be a bad idea – not as a rule, mind, but just this evening: it's Saturday, been a hard week for both of them, don't need to drink it all.

Let's first identify the immediate positives, which are for them familiar and evident. Drink makes these people feel good, and they know from experience that in safe surroundings a few drinks more will make them feel better still. That kind of intoxication can for a little while open for them a magic territory of elation, talkativeness, laughter, loosened mental associations and emotional intimacy.

The short-term-profit side of taking a few more drinks is thus for these two people predictable. Drink gives them immediate gain, and they do not need an expert of any sort to convince them of this experiential truth. And as for the short-term losses, they are likely to be no worse than a bit of headache or sickness in the morning, regrets or recriminations over something stupid said, a wine glass knocked on to the floor, a slight edge of unease perhaps as to whether it was altogether sensible to open that second bottle. But, within the balance of only the short-term profit-and-loss account, it is likely that a hangover next morning will rate far lower than another drink poured at the supper table.

However, put into the reckoning the possible longer-term consequences of the evening's drinking, and before that couple pour another glass they will have to face up to a far more awkward dilemma than anything set by the simple calculation involved in weighing instant gratification against the shortly up-coming hangovers. How are they to balance evident short-term boozy pleasure against potential risks to health which may eventuate in the much longer term? Those seemingly innocuous extra few drinks sum towards each of the two individuals' lifetime exposure to alcohol, and hence bear on their lifetime risks for a raft of alcohol-related diseases. There's the drinker's dilemma.

This chapter will set out some of the scientific findings which are today available to help the drinking man and woman make, if they so wish, an informed personal decision in the face of their dilemma. To echo Richard Doll, there are facts involved which the consumer of alcohol has a right to know, and with which society should be better acquainted. Science here cannot promise certainties, but it can assist the risk analysis.

Alcohol and long-term risks to the drinker's health

In recent years a great deal of research has been directed at the relationship between the individual's habitual level of alcohol consumption and the likelihood of that person eventually developing certain kinds of disease. The questions which are being explored are not phrased in terms of a crude 'Does alcohol cause disease X – yes or no?' Rather, they are being cast in terms of mathematical estimates of risk. How does the *probability* of developing disease X increase with increased drinking?

To illustrate the sophistication of this sort of research, let's take as an example work which has explored the relationship between level of drinking and cancer of the female breast. Science here is based on large-scale and painstaking population surveys of drinking behaviour and health outcomes. In 1998 Dr Stephanie Smith-Warner and her colleagues at Harvard Medical School published a paper. They had put together and scrupulously reanalysed previously published studies from the USA, Sweden, Canada and the Netherlands which had reported on the relationship between drinking and breast cancer. Using the same type of approach that Kaye Fillmore had employed when trying to unravel the relationship between drinking and heart disease (see Chapter 12), the Harvard group put all this material into, as it were, one big analytical hopper. They then employed a statistical approach known as 'meta-analysis'. This is widely used in medical research where multiple studies are being published on the same topic and there is a need to determine through the fog of numbers whether any large and consistent truths are emerging across samples and between countries.

The advantage of meta-analysis is that, on a good day, it is an effective method for blowing away the fog and discovering what bare truths then stand out. For it to succeed, the different researchers must in their original reports have measured all important elements of observation in compatible ways, and the accuracy and trustworthiness of their measurement techniques must be of a high order. If these expectations are met, the pooling of material will result in a much bigger data set than is ever likely to be available to any single study, and hence to an analysis with far greater statistical power. The disadvantage is that this approach, if poorly handled, will result merely in nonsense in and nonsense out, on a grand scale.

The six data sets which Smith-Warner and her colleagues welded into their analysis met all necessary critical expectations. They had then in their frame the very large total of 322,047 women who had been followed forward from the study intake points for periods of between four and seven years. Interviewers had recorded these women's drinking habits at baseline, together with many other aspects of their health and lifestyle.

Over the follow-up, these six studies had reported between them a sad total of 4,335 women as having developed invasive breast cancer. The question then to be addressed was whether those who drank more alcohol were more likely to have developed cancer. That simple question is not, however, one where conclusions can be jumped at carelessly. All sorts of other factors besides the alcohol will have been criss-crossing and confusing the picture. For example, perhaps women who drink more eat a different diet from abstainers or lighter drinkers, or perhaps heavier drinkers smoke more heavily. A seeming relationship between drinking and breast cancer might thus in reality be spurious, with the real predictor being not the drinking but one or other of these confounders.

The Harvard study used statistical methods to correct for the possible influence of a wide range of possible confounders, including educational level, age at birth of first child, oral-contraceptive use, fibre intake, fat intake and smoking. With all these potential influences balanced out, the investigators found in their pooled sample a persuasive relationship between an individual's drinking and the risk of that person contracting breast cancer. Their conclusion was that a woman taking one drink per day (10 grams of alcohol) had a 9 per cent increased risk of developing breast cancer compared to a woman who was an abstainer, and this applied across a wide age band. A further 9 per cent of risk was added for each drink up to five drinks per day. The band consuming fewer than six drinks per day covered 99 per cent of the total surveyed population, and it is the implications of the findings for that range of drinking on which attention should be focused. At and beyond the six-drink level the relationship seemed to plateau out.

Through the fog, what walked towards these investigators was a simple straight-line and upward left-to-right graph. More drinking over a substantial and relevant range of alcohol intake goes hand in hand with a stepwise increase in risk of breast cancer. One drink a day is associated with greater risk than no alcohol, and then the line goes upwards at a steady 9 per cent increment for each drink up to the fifth drink. What needs to be emphasized is that this graph is dealing with common social levels of drinking, and not with flagrantly 'alcoholic' drinking. It is a graph which captures much ordinary drinking behaviour, including intake of a kind which is commonly termed 'safe' or 'sensible'.

The person who wants to dismiss these results as irrelevant may of course still insist that, even with confounders balanced out, a statistical association does not by itself prove a causal connection. The credibility of a causal assumption is, however, strengthened by the smooth 0–5 dose–response kind of relationship which looks more like cumulative effect than artefact. The relationship was consistent across all six original studies, and that adds a further degree of confidence. Most health scientists would probably draw a cautious conclusion in terms like: 'On current evidence, the quantity of alcohol drunk by a woman across the common range of social intake exerts a small and graded but significant influence on her risk for breast cancer. At higher levels of drinking the enhanced risk remains but tends to level out.' Within the limits of current knowledge, the answer to the question of whether alcohol causes cancer of the female breast is not 'Yes' or 'No', but 'Women who drink will experience a significant graded possibility of enhanced cancer risk.'

The medical conclusions on a topic of this sort are always more confident when it is possible to go beyond the statistical association and identify a plausible causal mechanism to explain the connection, and here there is a parallel with the debate around alcohol and protection against heart disease. The mechanisms by which alcohol might cause breast cancer are not at present established, but Smith-Warner put forward a number of reasonable if provisional suggestions. Alcohol raises levels of naturally occurring female sex hormone circulating in the body, and this could increase cancer risk; it may decrease elimination of certain cancer-producing substances, and it may make breast tissue more permeable to dangerous chemicals.

So that is what science tells about one particular risk with drink. The alcohol-and-breast-cancer story is news from the front line of this kind of research. There is older work which shows that, among both men and women, drinking increases the risk of developing cancers of the mouth, pharynx, tongue, gullet and liver, and possibly colo-rectal cancer is a risk for beer drinkers. There are, however, many other causes of cancer besides alcohol, and the cancer-inducing risk of this one substance should not be exaggerated. American research has suggested that in the USA about 3 per cent of all cancers are caused by drinking. And, as with breast cancer, what seems to be true with all these other cancers is that the enhancement of risk begins to take off at low levels of intake, with no guaranteed safe threshold.

Another important long-term health risk from drinking is cirrhosis of the liver. Historically, cirrhosis has often been given pride of place as the drinker's disease. It is a disorder in which the liver becomes scarred and damaged. Once established, cirrhosis is likely to progress and finally kill. The clinical connection between drinking and cirrhosis has been known for centuries, but it was not until 1978 that the first survey was published which showed a statistical relationship between the individual's level of drinking and the risk of cirrhosis. This work came from a group of French researchers led by Dr Georges Péquignot, and since then further studies on this topic have come from several countries. These reports indicate that, rather than there being in this instance a straight-line relationship between drinking and risk of the disease, for cirrhosis something like an exponential relationship exists. Thus, for men, the trajectory of risk begins to curve very steeply upwards at an intake of four or five drinks per day. For a man taking five drinks per day the cirrhosis risk is about five times that of the abstainer. At seven drinks per day men have a risk for cirrhosis of about ten to fifteen times that seen with abstainers. Similar research on female populations suggests that, for any level of drinking, women are at a greater risk of cirrhosis than men, with the curve bending upwards earlier and more steeply.

To round off this listing of long-term health problems where there is a known gradient of risk with increased drinking, let's add the following miscellaneous entries. Drinking is a common cause of raised blood pressure, and it is associated with the kind of stroke which is caused by bleeding into the brain. Heavy bout drinking puts up the risk of death from abnormalities in heart rhythm. Maternal drinking can cause low birth weight, impairment in childhood learning ability, and birth defects – and here again the heavier the drinking the greater the risk.

So much for the long-term physical-disease risks from alcohol where the existence of a dose gradient – or in simple terms the fact that more means worse – is information which the couple sitting at their supper table might want to take into the reckoning before filling up their glasses again. Pleasure now, but one more drink added to one more drink and yet another, and a risk that some years into the future the bet will turn out bad.

The view from the A & E department

Beyond the various long-term risks of physical disease, our drinking couple should also take into their calculations the relationship between drinking and accident. Neither of these people expects to fall off a chair and hit their head as they leave the table tonight. Their home is a much safer drinking environment than the factory floor, the street or a bar.

Here, however, are a few statistics on the alcohol-and-accident relationship. Something like 25 per cent of people injured in falls will have been drinking at the time, with the figure higher for fatal falls. In one American study of fractures due to falls, an average weekly intake of about twenty drinks was associated with a 54 per cent increased injury risk for women and a 26 per cent increased risk for men. We mentioned in Chapter 2 the relationship between drinking and death in accidental fires. Of less immediate concern to our drinking couple is the fact that alcohol is involved in about 20–30 per cent of fatal drownings, but they may like to bear this statistic in mind next time they have a boating picnic. Alcohol plays a part in about 50 per cent of road-traffic fatalities, and is a factor in a significant proportion of non-fatal traffic accidents and in pedestrian accidents.

Somewhere down the road from that supper will be a hospital Accident and Emergency department. It is there that the real-world statistics on the alcohol-and-accident relationship are being added up every day and night. Findings will vary according to geographical location, the population served and the day of the week, but a typical sort of finding would be that drinking will have made a contribution to the event in 20–30 per cent of injury patients attending an A & E department. Mary M.'s injuries (Chapter 10) were part of an ordinary night's work for these doctors and nurses. For the staff once more waiting for the ambulance to unload, the alcohol-and-injury connection is not an abstract statistic. It is a daily and continuing cause for frustration, grief and anger at the neglect of the problem.

And not forgetting the social consequences

Beyond the physical disease and accident risks, there is a range of adverse social consequences of drinking which should be taken into the audit around the drinker's dilemma. Social problems consequent on alcohol are common among drinkers, and about 5–10 per cent of men who drink will notch up one or more happenings of this kind during a twelve-month period (the rates among women are lower). Under this heading can be put debts and money problems, work problems, public disorder and fights, family upsets, broken relationships, and problems affecting children.

It would therefore seem sensible to put into the supper-table decision-making the fact that alcohol not only is a social lubricant, but can also be a social abrasive. And here too there is some evidence for dose-relatedness. A recent national survey conducted in Canada, with Robin Room as lead investigator, found that men or women with an average daily intake of 1½–2½ drinks doubled their chance of sustaining a social problem as compared with abstainers. If, however, these people saved up their ration so that, while maintaining the same average intake, they occasionally during the week took five drinks at a sitting, they put up their risk of a social problem not by a factor of two but by a factor of six.

Horns at the kitchen table

Back, then, to that evening's dilemma. Shall they fill their glasses again, with immediate and certain pleasure, and shut out of their minds the delayed and uncertain adverse consequences? Or put away the bottle, with instant disappointment guaranteed, but with possible long-term health advantage and perhaps a social mishap or accident avoided? And what about drink being good for the heart as another part of the actuarial assessment? Or drink being bad for the heart and one of those people having a sudden attack of fluttering pulse?

Neither of these two people sees themselves as having a drinking problem. They are in most people's terms social drinkers enjoying their conjugal bottle of wine. And the reality is that no couple at that sort of moment is going to be making their decision in the light of the detailed statistics which have been quoted in this chapter. To expect the decision as to whether the second bottle will be opened to be determined by what science says about the mathematics of risk is science fiction. This man and woman do not read the *Journal of the American Medical Association*, and meta-analysis is unlikely to be the subject of their evening's conversation.

One way in which many countries have in recent years tried to help drinkers to deal with their dilemma is to promulgate safe drinking limits. If that message can be put into the supper-table awareness, then, rather than having to digest a massive and complex literature before taking the next drink, this couple need only remember the shorthand message of safe limits in round numbers. Different countries give slightly different advice on this topic, but not more than three drinks a day for a man or two for a woman is the message currently favoured in Britain.

There is, however, a problem with that seemingly sensible approach, and a danger that it will in fact just take us back to science fiction. Realistically, around the table, the safe-drinking message does not stand much chance against the tempting pleasures of another convivial drink. The calculus of human decision-making is always likely to give heavier weighting to immediate and certain pleasure than to postponed and uncertain pain. The safe-drinking message that evening will in any case probably be forgotten with the third glass. Alcohol impairs sensible decision-making. Unsurprisingly, the research evidence suggests that the wide promulgation of the safe-drinking message has no significant effect on a population's drinking behaviour. Over a period of several years during which the British government made safe drinking a prominent health-education message, the number of people drinking beyond safe limits actually increased. The message was washed away by the greater social availability of alcohol.

Furthermore, at the scientific level the safe-drinking message is in several ways dubious. Say that the woman sitting at the table is aged thirty: two drinks will give her heart no benefit but will increase her risk of cancer. Perhaps after three drinks the man opposite her is called out on an emergency and has to drive his car. Safety is about context as well as the amount drunk.

What looks on the face of it like a sensible approach to advice on drinking, therefore, often does not work too well at table level. The very people who most need the advice may be those least likely to heed it. Perhaps the best overall public message on alcohol which we might hope to see reach the home is, Enjoy the drink, but less is generally better, getting intoxicated is never wise, drink is two-edged. That kind of open message is a more accurate representation of what science has to say than the spurious exactness of the drinking-limits formula.

But, even with that more scientifically informed phrasing of the advice, we are perhaps only swapping one ineffectual message for another. The drinker's immediate reality is the pleasure in drinking. The health message will seldom be so loud. The inevitable conclusion is that public statements alone are not enough. Society needs to put in place a range of external measures to support healthy drinking choices and to make excess less likely. The government had perhaps better meet society's wide and general dilemma over drink by making alcohol a little less lavishly available. That's a matter for the next chapter.

The ambiguities which have over time been generated by ethyl alcohol, C_2H_5OH, that stupid molecule, are, on the evidence, legion. Stand back and look at the picture which emerges. Christianity and Islam and the flattest of contradictions. St Bridget sipping at her lake of beer, and wretchedness stretched upon the pavement. Gin as the Lethe of the miserable, and today's toff's drink of gin and tonic with a slice of lemon and a chink of ice. The 'Mawdlen' drunk saying, 'By God, Captaine, I love thee', and the lion drunk drawing his dagger. The alcohol-dependent solicitor killing himself, and the vagrant drunk recovering. Prohibition, and afterwards repeal. What's your poison – or is it your medicine? Gough's sad wrecked clergyman, and D. L. Davies's 'return to normal drinking'. Mad and bad things done in the name of treatment. 'God *as we understood him*', and Skinner as understood by the behaviourists. Paradox piled on paradox – and that's not half of it.

At the centre of that inchoate, swirling mass of contradiction, there is, however, a very simple, two-part truth. Alcohol is in its being and essence an ambiguous molecule, an instrument of pleasure and at the same time of pain. And society's response to that molecule is, in all its dealings, and with total congruence, itself ambiguous. A congruence of ambiguities: that's the centre of the thing.

Having looked in previous chapters at many different aspects of that congruence, let's in this chapter try to make some predictions as to what might be the shape of humanity's future relationship with alcohol. We will start by exploring the possibility that people will sooner or later get so fed up with the pain in alcohol that they will replace it with a less ambiguous drug. Under the next two headings we will, in turn, examine the possibility of the world letting itself virtually drown in alcohol, with all controls on its consumption abandoned, and then the contrasting scene where people continue to drink but with alcohol going somewhat out of fashion and the drinking reduced. Finally, we will look at the scenario on which any sensible futurologist would surely want to put his or her money: a future of no great dramas, but hopefully of rather more rational handling of the problems intrinsic to the ambiguous coexistence with an ambiguous drug.

Could a safer recreational drug ever be found which will drive out alcohol?

Tea and coffee when they arrived in Europe may have succeeded in some degree in substituting for alcohol. But the recreational drug which has recently attracted most attention as a possibly feasible alternative is cannabis. A frequently heard argument supportive of the cause of those who favour the legalization of that drug is that no one has ever died of cannabis, whereas, as we earlier noted, alcohol each year is significantly implicated in about 40,000 deaths in the UK and over 200,000 in the USA. So look no further, say these advocates: we have ready to hand exactly the new and safer drug that can substitute for alcohol, if only governments will sensibly legalize it.

Cannabis has been widely used in parts of Asia and Africa for thousands of years, but Europeans for centuries knew little of it and got on with their drinking. A fascinating historical instance of alcohol meeting cannabis occurred, however, when the British established their presence in India.

The soldiers, civil servants and merchants who helped establish the Raj liked their drink. An alcohol-using culture was transported wholesale to a foreign clime. Prodigious quantities of wine and spirits were imported, and breweries were established. With a pleasant fusion of Hindi and King Edgar's ordinance, a small drink became known as a 'chota peg'. The official world, the regiment, club life, life in the remote districts had alcohol as much woven into the fabric as was the case in the distant homeland. But the drinking of the imperial caste was being conducted in a setting where the indigenous mix of races did not use alcohol, but in some sectors regarded cannabis as an acceptable recreational drug. They even gave this drug to their buffaloes to strengthen the field labouring of these beasts.

The British were aware of the Indian use of cannabis, and puzzled as to what to do about it. They decided to set up a committee of inquiry, the Indian Hemp Drugs Commission of 1893–4. This reported in terms remarkably favourable to cannabis:

Viewing the subject generally, it may be added that the moderate use of these drugs is the rule, and that the excessive use is comparatively exceptional. The moderate use practically produces no ill effects . . . The injury done by the excessive use is, however, confined almost exclusively to the consumer himself: the effect on society is rarely appreciable.

The East India Company established its first settlements in the subcontinent in 1609, independence was declared in 1947, and, by and large, during the whole of that period the British stayed with alcohol and the sections of India which had traditionally used cannabis (it was not a universally favoured Indian drug) stayed with their cannabis. The British did not bring cannabis back home with them, and, when they eventually left the subcontinent, an independent Pakistan was dry for religious reasons and India enacted prohibition into its constitution.

The key lesson to be drawn from that historical episode must be that the cultural embeddedness of an established recreational drug is likely to hold intact against any potential rival substance. If cannabis is to drive out alcohol, it will have to compete not just with a chemical, but with a symbolic substance deeply written into a culture and an economy.

But those who argue that cannabis is a feasible substitute for alcohol will no doubt contend that British India was a special case, and they will want to put in evidence from more modern times. Cannabis was virtually unknown in Britain until the 1940s or '50s. By the late 1990s, surveys were showing that in some parts of the country almost 50 per cent of young people had tried it at least once. How's that for market penetration – and a penetration achieved in the face of continued legal prohibition? Give cannabis a level playing field, argue the legalizers, and this safe and attractive drug will be the hands-down winner. The Indian Hemp Drugs Commission had it right: the effect of cannabis on society is rarely appreciable – in contrast with the toll of social problems associated with alcohol.

Those are alluring arguments. But, before levelling the playing field, there are two counter-arguments which need to be heard. First, the contention that cannabis would substitute for alcohol is not well founded. Nicotine did not drive out alcohol, heavy drinkers are often heavy cigarette smokers, and much the same might turn out to be the case with cannabis. In general, new drugs add to old patterns of drug use, rather than acting as substitutes. Second, over recent years research has been accumulating which suggests that cannabis is significantly addictive, can cause various types of health damage, and is not at all the harmless toy which it was previously made out to be. No health scientist would regard it as prudent to push cannabis as a safer alternative to alcohol. Rather than resulting in the substitution of a bad recreational drug by a good one, to go in that direction might only mean adding unrestricted exposure to a new bad drug on to entrenched exposure to the resident bad drug.

There is today no existing drug which could be reached down from the shelf and recommended as an alternative and safer substance to substitute for admittedly problematic alcohol. If society is ever to obtain a recreational drug which is all pleasure and no pain, it looks as if the chemists will have to get busy. If a government were to put the project out to tender, the specifications of this designer drug would include the following requirements. It will not be dependence-inducing. It will not impair coordination or reaction time. Its use will not lead to violence. There will be no or minimal long-term physical and mental health risks. It will not react adversely with common medicines. It will not be a ready instrument for suicide, or set risks of accidental poisoning. Its effects will be capable of being shaped by environmental and cultural pressures. To those demanding expectations would have to be added the need for it to produce its desired brain effects when taken by mouth (smoking and injection are intrinsically more dangerous modes of administration). It would have to be relatively bulky, to avoid too easy smuggling. To maximize the tax levied on this drug's commercial production, it should not be easily grown in the garden, or capable of production in a home laboratory. All that would be needed in addition would be a pretty name, some flavouring, the skilled attentions of the advertising and marketing experts, a few songs commissioned, an alliance forged with nationalistic sentiment, and the blessings of the bishops. And alcohol would then hopefully soon be remembered only as the loutish drug of a chemically unsophisticated yesterday.

Those specifications may one day be met. But neither in British India nor elsewhere across geography and time is it easy to identify an instance of a good drug driving out a bad. For the time being, the better drug than alcohol remains a tender for the science-fiction writers rather than for the chemists. And echoing in the air is the metaphorical warning contained in Gresham's Law: it is the bad currency which drives out the good.

The future for letting alcohol rip

Most western countries are at present drinking considerably less than they did in the nineteenth century. Furthermore, across the world there are industrial countries which are mean in their drinking compared to those at the top of the consumption league. France imbibes the equivalent of 11.8 litres of absolute alcohol per head annually, the USA 8.3 litres, the UK 7.8 litres, and Sweden about 4 litres per head. About 40 per cent of Italians expect to have a drink almost every day, but only about 10 per cent of Americans or the English and 2–3 per cent of Norwegians drink with that frequency. As regards the developing world, alcohol consumption is increasing in those regions, but it is still generally at a much lower level than in richer areas, and Islam remains for the most part dry.

Is it possible that the future will see these extraordinary present disparities vanish, and in their place a world in which all countries drink up to, or perhaps beyond, the level of the present league champions? There are certainly a number of forces conspiring to push consumption in the upward direction. The triumph of free-market capitalism, with its emphasis on deregulation and competition, is in many jurisdictions leading to the dismantling of the apparatus which had previously sought to put controls on drinking. Licensing hours have widely been relaxed. The numbers of drinking places and sales outlets have multiplied in countries which previously had been restrictive. Scandinavian countries have been forced to decrease the powers of their state alcohol monopolies in response to the demands for free competition set by the European Union. And hand in hand with this weakening in regulatory mechanisms is a shift in cultural attitudes to drinking. Lots of people are attracted to the idea of drink being an ordinary and easily accessible part of life. And, with political philosophy and the groundswell of culture as two strong forces working in alliance so as to encourage more drinking and a greater cultural acceptance of alcohol, there is also always the drinks industry waiting eagerly to seize and exploit every opportunity to expand its markets.

So will the future see the tide of alcohol let rip, with this drug treated as simply one more deregulated market commodity? Will alcohol be delivered to everyone's doorstep and be sold in every corner store? Will it be consumed every day by everyone, all the time, with the world's average consumption cheered on rejoicingly to a level which will reproach present-day France for its abstemiousness? That could happen; the world really could become awash with drink. In a hedonistic future the pains might be discounted, with all life becoming one sodden bacchanalia.

That could happen, but it is not likely to happen. What history suggests is that, when a population's drinking goes beyond a certain level, the consequences become so evidently damaging and offensive that the population rises against drink. Thus Islam, and also the reaction to the British gin epidemic in the eighteenth century, and the temperance reaction to America's 'alcoholic republic' in the nineteenth century. The level of drinking needed to precipitate a backlash will vary according to the historical and cultural context, but, in a modern society which has the capacity to estimate the costs of alcohol-related damage, few governments are likely to let alcohol rip absolutely. In the USA the total cost to society due to the adverse impacts of alcohol was estimated in 1995 at $60.5 billion, and for the UK the estimate for 1992 was £2.7 billion. Those estimates can only be approximate, but such figures must be worrying for any administration, and speak against the wisdom of encouraging a national bacchanalia.

If any government needed to be reminded of the dramatically awful consequences which can stem from unrestricted drinking, it would have to look no further than recent experience in Russia. Mikhail Gorbachev's attempt to cut down on Russian drinking, with the introduction in 1985 of a package of controls and a 45 per cent increase in the price of drink, appeared at first to be succeeding in its intentions. State alcohol sales in Moscow decreased by 38 per cent over the ensuing eighteenth months, and this was accompanied by a 33 per cent fall in the cirrhosis death rate. But by 1987 consumption and problems both again began steeply to rise, and a considerable sector of the production of alcohol was in the hands of criminal entrepreneurs.

In January 1992 Russia was hit by the full blast of market reforms, and in April of that year the state alcohol monopoly was abolished. In face of rampant inflation, the price of alcohol in relation to that of foodstuffs was considerably cheapened. Russia then woke to the realization that it was in the grip of what has come widely to be termed a death epidemic. Between 1992 and 1994, life expectancy in Russia fell by 3.3 years for women and 6.1 years for men. These highly alarming statistics were of a magnitude which might have been expected as a consequence of the epidemic outbreak of a virulent infectious disease. But there was no microbe to account for this disaster. Other factors related to the strains engendered by the market reforms may have made a contribution to the overall worsening in life expectancy, but recent analyses coming out of Russia suggest that it stemmed largely from a plague of alcohol-related deaths brought about by the upswing over a few years in alcohol consumption. Cirrhosis death rates in Moscow stood in 1995 at almost three times the level which had pertained before the Gorbachev campaign. The already considerable life-expectancy disadvantage for Russians in comparison to those living in western Europe and the USA was exacerbated, and in 1994 a Russian could expect to die 16.5 years younger than the average citizen of an EU country. The same kinds of loss in life expectancy have occurred in several other republics of the former USSR, including Latvia, Estonia, Lithuania and the Ukraine.

Letting alcohol rip is thus not a likely future for the industrialized world, even in an age of ripping free-market economics. But it can hardly be doubted that if poor countries become richer they will be urged by the industry to drink up to the level of the rich.

Could the future see alcohol go significantly out of fashion?

In the section above, reference has been made to background changes in regulatory controls and national culture which have recently tended in some countries to help drive alcohol consumption upwards. France has for long been probably the country in which alcohol is most linked with the national way of life. The citizens of France, until recently, have as a consequence held the dubious distinction of heading the world in cirrhosis death rates. Wine – *Mon docteur le vin* – has, as we have seen earlier, been flaunted as a symbol of all that is glorious in France. The French have often been naively admired by other countries for their apparent ability to use alcohol well and for the absence of street drunkenness, with the cirrhosis deaths, the alcohol-related cancers and the prevalence of foetal abnormalities all equally invisible to the café tourists.

Similarly unremarked by these visitors is the fact that alcohol has, over recent decades, gradually but progressively become less fashionable in France. Between 1962 and 1992 per-capita consumption of wine almost halved. The drinking of beer and spirits marginally increased, but the overall result was that between those years annual per-capita consumption expressed in terms of summed absolute alcohol fell from 17.2 litres to 11.8 – a decline of about 31 per cent in the average citizen's drinking. The French still drink heavily in comparison to many other nations, but their alcohol consumption is much lower than it was in the recent past.

Over the same period, Italy, another great wine-drinking nation, has also seen its alcohol consumption slide quietly downwards. In 1962 consumption was at 12.5 litres absolute alcohol per head, but in 1992 it had fallen to 8.9 litres – a cut of almost 29 per cent. And it is again the wine drinking which has seen the decrease.

What are the likely explanations for these untrumpeted changes in the drinking habits of two countries which have for so long regarded wine as a condiment at every main meal, the stuff to be put into the workman's dinner bag, the casually inevitable accompaniment for all social intercourse, and even at times in watered form the liquid on which to wean the baby? No one predicted this sea change. The best guess is probably that alcohol in France and Italy has simply slid a bit out of fashion. Fitness and physical appearance have become more important than for the previous generation, while intoxication even of a social kind has begun to seem unattractive, old-fashioned and handicapping. Jobs no longer go well with heavy day-time drinking. Self-control and self-actualization have become more imperative, and alcohol does not fit comfortably with those kinds of psychological need. These changes in the level of alcohol consumption and in ways of thinking about drink were led by the urban middle-classes and the well-educated young. Those groups started to define not drinking at all, or drinking only beer, as modish.

EU policies which have cut down on wine production, national taxation policies, intentional public-health initiatives of various kinds and heavy advertising of beer may also have contributed to the decline in wine drinking. But the central and enormously powerful change agent which has caused drinking to tumble by about 30 per cent across this extensive stretch of Latin Europe has almost certainly been the invisible force of fashion. So here is evidence further to support the pervasive truth that alcohol is not only a chemical, but also a symbol, an image created, and an instrument in the creation of images.

Italy and France are special cases, in that the decline in their drinking was from remarkably high starting points. The question must therefore be asked, Are the experiences of France and Italy aberrant, or are they likely to have a generalizable relevance to the alcohol future? The story of drink becoming less fashionable in these two countries could be matched by the experiences of many other parts of the world in which alcohol has, over recent years, become distinctly more fashionable. To be modern in Scandinavia can mean the purposive use of alcohol to define a lifestyle where the aspiration is to be more 'Continental', and which may involve drinking wine rather than throwing back the shot of raw spirits in the way practised by an older generation. It would be a mistake to suppose that fashion has alcohol on the run worldwide.

But the central fact is still true: that fashion can be a force in determining what happens to drinking. Across much of the world, work conditions, leisure patterns, income distribution, self-definitions, relationships between the generations and the sexes, and a host of other visible and invisible dimensions of life are in a state of flux. The future of alcohol is something which is likely to be carried to a significant degree on the tide of those changes. Fashion is currently running strongly against tobacco as the twin recreational drug to alcohol. It is not unthinkable that the future will see a wider international tendency for people to turn against patterns of heavy alcohol use as old-fashioned. France and Italy may today look like the exceptions, but it is possible that their reduction in drinking will in the long run prove to have been the shape of things to come.

What turned sentiment against tobacco was the research which showed that cigarettes were the cause of a death epidemic of lung cancer. Tobacco has also been shown to be a substantial cause of other diseases, including bronchitis, emphysema and heart disease. How much further evidence on alcohol-related harm would be needed to turn fashion radically against alcohol in a future world in which expectations of good health and longevity may have become ever more salient? Supposing it is confirmed that alcohol even in moderate quantities can increase the likelihood of a woman developing cancer of the breast: what does that do for fashion? As research methods become yet more powerful, there is the likelihood any day of further bad news on the drinker's doorstep. That is the stronger probability than more news to say that alcohol is good for the drinker's heart.

In Georgian England, it was fashionable for gentlemen to slip comatose under the table at a certain stage in the evening. But in Victorian times that behaviour ceased to be regarded as genteel, and it died out. For anyone wanting to predict the future of alcohol, the advice must in part be, Look at nouvelle cuisine.

A future with the ambiguities ameliorated

And now to the question of what societies in the near future might do practically to shape their handling of a substance which is likely to go on being the favourite recreational drug, even if fashion takes its consumption down a peg. How are we to go on with alcohol as our pleasure drug, while ameliorating the pain? Honesty requires an open admission that it is only amelioration that can be talked about. So long as people chose to use alcohol, there will be alcohol-related pain and that is inescapable. The hope that the day will dawn when everyone across the whole population drinks at a safe, sensible level is a delusion.

There is convincing research to indicate how the harm done by alcohol can be reduced if people so wish, and governments so act. Research does, however, suggest that there is no likely single ameliorating device, no one master stroke which can be recommended as panacea; rather, there is a set of remedies which between them are, on the evidence, capable of reducing the pain in alcohol. Some of those measures concentrate on defined target problems, as these arise in particular drinking situations. Bar staff can be trained not to serve evidently drunken customers or be made legally responsible for the adverse consequences which may result from serving such people. An obvious way to reduce the danger of a broken beer mug being pushed into someone's face during a drunken brawl is to make the mugs out of unbreakable glass, and, given that the annual cost of replacing broken glassware in British pubs currently runs at about £100 million, enlightened self-interest is likely to accord with the aims of injury prevention. Drunk-driving legislation, if strictly enforced, can prevent injury and save lives on a large scale. Despite increased road usage, sustained and vigorous efforts against drunk driving in Britain over the period 1978–98 brought down the number of road-traffic deaths in which alcohol was involved to about one-third the starting level. Policies targeted at drinking in the workplace, at drinking around sporting events, at drinking in city-centre public spaces provide further examples of that type of focused action. Such remedies can often lie with a local community, if it cares to empower itself and act on the local drink problem, and enforce existing statutory provisions.

Beyond those targeted kinds of action, there is then the question of whether broad health benefits can be achieved by keeping the overall population alcohol consumption in check and making society somewhat drier. The intuitive expectation might be that, if average per-capita consumption were reduced, social drinkers would drink a little less while heavy but dependent drinkers would probably cut back on other items of spending or rob their families and then go on drinking at their habitual level. Such intuitions are, however, contradicted by a considerable body of research which shows that the intake level of the average citizen and the overall harm done to the population by drink tend to go hand in hand. Here are some examples of findings which support that contention.

- *Paris in the Second World War.* The German occupation of Paris in 1940–45 constituted a kind of accidental public-health experiment. Wine was rationed and the alcohol supply was greatly curtailed. Concurrently, the cirrhosis death rate fell over those five years by a dramatic 80 per cent. Life in Paris was at that time abnormal in many ways, and one should therefore interpret these data cautiously. But when after the war drinking went back to its old level, so did cirrhosis deaths. There really can be no reasonable doubt as to the interpretation to be put on this 'experiment' – population alcohol consumption is related to population death rate for a health problem which is an indicator of heavy drinking. Solly Ledermann, a French demographer, analysed these findings in a 1964 report which is today widely regarded as a classic of the research literature.

- *The alcohol supply and further research on deaths from specific causes.* Ledermann's work was on cirrhosis deaths, and subsequent studies from many other countries and relating to many different time periods have confirmed that population drinking and population cirrhosis mortality are likely to go hand in hand. Similar research has shown a significant relationship between the amount a country drinks and death rates for alcoholic psychosis, 'alcoholism', pancreatitis and some cancers. In a number of countries a relationship between per-capita alcohol consumption and suicide has been demonstrated. Bring the drinking level down, and all those problems are ameliorated.

- *Alcohol consumption and mortality across twenty-five European countries.* In 1998, Minghao Her and Jürgen Rehm, two researchers working at the Addiction Research Foundation in Toronto, published an analysis of the relationship between per-capita alcohol consumption and deaths from all causes for twenty-five European countries between the years 1982 and 1990. What these Canadian researchers found was that on average a 1 litre change up or down in per-capita consumption was accompanied by a corresponding 1.3 per cent change in overall mortality. This suggests that if a country over time brings down its annual per-capita consumption by 3 litres of absolute alcohol (a quite feasible real-world shift), its overall death rate would be cut by almost 4 per cent, with a huge number of lives saved.

The findings which have been summarized here on the relationship between alcohol consumption and harm provide merely an indication of what is to be found in a very wide international research output which bears on this topic. There are exceptional cases, but what most stands out is the sheer weight and repetitiveness of the core and general finding across time, across countries, across problems: measures which bear on the quantity drunk are likely to ameliorate the harm done by alcohol. A sentence from a 1975 World Health Organization report written by Kettil Bruun (a Finnish alcohol researcher) and his colleagues deserves to be quoted as encapsulating with force and truth the key message which they drew from the evidence available to them at the time, and which has since become much strengthened by further research:

Changes in the overall consumption of alcohol beverages have a bearing on the health of the people in any society. Alcohol control measures can be used to limit consumption: thus, control of alcohol availability becomes a public health issue.

Science must thus unequivocally recommend to any government which intends to reduce the national burden of alcohol-related problems that measures which check or reduce alcohol consumption are an essential part of the effective policy mix. Control of supply is not an alternative to more targeted measures, but is rather to be seen as providing a supportive context for those focused approaches. But let the alcohol supply run high and out of control and the benefits from all the more targeted and local efforts are likely to be washed away in that tide. Regrettably, sections of the drinks industry have sought over recent years to discredit the research on which these policy recommendations are based, and have attacked independent scientists while hiring their own industry-funded researchers. The similarities with aspects of the tobacco industry's behaviour are close and are likely in the long term to be equally counter-productive. In 1995 the Portman Group, a British drinks-industry lobby, scored an own goal when it offered £2,000 to each of six researchers to take part anonymously in an industry-sponsored attack on the WHO report *Alcohol Policy and the Public Good* and these machinations were exposed in the press.

If one accepts the premise that control over supply is part but by no means the totality of the needed public-health policy there is then the question of what means may be available to a government to achieve that control. One such mechanism is the use of taxation to support the health interest. A mass of economic research shows that alcohol is a commodity which is responsive to price, and the research also suggests that heavier at least as much as lighter drinkers are likely to cut back if they have to pay more for their drink. A few pence tax increase on beverage alcohol is thus one of the most readily available and widely effective policies for ameliorating alcohol-related harm. Conversely, letting the real price of alcohol drift downwards is likely to result in consumption drifting upwards, with all sorts of damage indicators moving in the same upward direction. And for governments the good news is that a tax increase need not necessarily reduce the revenue generated. Less will be drunk, but that will be compensated for by the higher tax take on whatever is bought.

Another way of influencing consumption is to make it that little bit harder for the consumer to buy the next drink. There is a health advantage in liquor stores not being on every corner or open all day, and in non-alcoholic drinks being more easily available. Those kinds of policy together mean that alcohol is not so pushed at everyone all the time. Licensing provisions are good for the public health. Their role is to make healthy choices easier, and less healthy choices a shade more difficult.

School education and public education are not directly effective strategies for reducing the harm done by alcohol, and a recent review by David Foxcroft and his colleagues of an astonishing total of 500 research reports on this topic was overwhelmingly negative in its conclusions. There may, however, be indirect positive effects as a result of such educational efforts making drink a more important issue in the public mind. Research increasingly suggests that drinks advertising not only affects brand loyalty, but can also help to build a positive image for alcohol and promote overall consumption. If further studies strengthen that conclusion, one would hope to see governments having the courage to ban alcohol advertising. In America there has been debate on whether health messages on beverage strength carried on drinks containers are likely to be beneficial, but the efficacy of this approach has not yet been much researched.

Better and earlier access to advice and treatment should be part of the ameliorative policies. A strengthened medical response must, however, mean all doctors being more willing to talk about alcohol with all their patients as a health and lifestyle issue, often, rather than treatment being focused only on the late case and the woman who has fallen downstairs.

Put those various measures together within intentional and integrated national policies, and countries will have less pain with their drinking. Drinking decisions are an individual's responsibility, but the vision of the future being presented here is also guided by the evidence that, for better or for worse, drinking choices are shaped by society. Handling alcohol well is thus society's as well as the individual's responsibility. Alcohol is a social issue. In suggesting that some degree of control over consumption will have to be part of any effective policy package, the proposal is not control for control's sake or a return to prohibition. Control is legitimate only in so far as it is socially acceptable and demonstrably to the public good.

Some years on . . .

So what will the picture be some years on? Standing in the street, sitting at the supper table, over at the A & E department, how will drinking look? What will be alcohol's myths and images and fashions, as well as the statistics on litres of absolute alcohol consumed? With all that drinking history and the litter of accompanying ambiguities stretching behind, what really is likely to happen to the relationship between societies and their drink around the next corner?

What happens to the future coexistence with alcohol is properly a matter for citizens themselves to determine, rather than the issue being left to the experts, to the lobbyists for vested interests, or to accident and political whim. That said, it must be likely that the people themselves will increasingly ask their governments for policies on alcohol which better support the public interest than has up to now often been the case. For the individual, less alcohol is better – and that message will perhaps become increasingly fashionable. And the assertion that less is better is equally and congruently true for the population as a whole. Around the next corner, the only readily available and substantial way to ameliorate alcohol's painful ambiguity is both for the individual and the state to take less of it. At the end of some millennia's experience with this drug, that is the truth staring us in the face, unambiguously.

Sources and Further Reading

The bibliography which follows is offered in the hope that it will be of practical use to readers whose interest has been sufficiently aroused for them to want to go somewhat deeper into the matters discussed in this book. Identified by an asterisk are a number of key entries most of which are likely to be available fairly easily through a library. The remaining entries are for anyone who wants to identify quoted sources in academic fashion or to pursue matters further. Some chapters are of necessity more densely referenced than others.

1 Alcohol, What is It?

Diethelm, O. (1965) Chronic alcoholism of Northern Europe. *Akta Fragen Psychiatrie und Neurologie*, **2**, 29–38.

Edwards, G., Marshall, E. J., and Cook, C. C. H. (1997) Alcohol as a drug. Chapter 2 (pp. 21–30) in *The Treatment of Drinking Problems*. 3rd edn. Cambridge: Cambridge University Press.

*Nutt, D. J., and Peters, T. J. (1994) Alcohol, the drug, pp. 5–17 in G. Edwards and T. J. Peters (eds.), *Alcohol and Alcohol Problems*. British Medical Bulletin 50, No. 1. Edinburgh: Churchill Livingstone.

2 Alcohol, Myths and Metaphors

Aye, J. (1934) *The Humour of Drinking*. London: Universal Publications.

Baasher, T. (1983) The use of drugs in the Islamic world. Chapter 2 (pp. 21–34) in G. Edwards, A. Arif and J. Jaffe (eds.), *Drug Use and Misuse, Cultural Perspectives*. London: Croom Helm and the World Health Organization.

Boswell, J. (1998) *Life of Johnson* (1791), ed. R. W. Chapman. Oxford: Oxford University Press.

Brown, B. Meredith (1948) *The Brewer's Art*. London: Naldine Press for Whitbread & Co.

Cherpital, C. J. (1992) The epidemiology of alcohol-related trauma. *Alcohol Health and Research World*, **16**, 191–6.

Clark, P. (1983) *The English Alehouse: A Social History*. London: Longman.

Davies, D. G. (1965) *The Early Christian Church*. London: Weidenfeld & Nicolson.

de Silva, P. (1983) The Buddhist attitude to alcoholism. Chapter 3 (pp. 31–41) in G. Edwards, A. Arif and J. Jaffe (eds.), *Drug Use and Misuse, Cultural Perspectives*. London: Croom Helm and the World Health Organization.

Derys, G. (1936) *Mon docteur le vin*. Paris: Draeger Frères.

Dickens, C. (1996) *Bleak House* (1853), ed. Nicola Bradbury. London: Penguin.

Furst, P. T. (ed.) (1972) *Flesh of the Gods: The Ritual Use of Hallucinogens*. London: Allen & Unwin.

Lair, P.-A. (1800) Essai sur les combustions humaines, produites par un long abus des liqueurs spiritueuses. *Journal de physique*, **50**, 115–28. English translation reproduced in *Philosophical Magazine* (1800), **6**, 132–46, as 'On the combustion of the human body: produced by the long and immoderate use of spirituous liquors'. A translation was also published in *Quarterly Journal of Studies on Alcohol*, **2**, 806–15.

Macnish, R. (1834) *The Anatomy of Drunkenness*. 5th edn, Glasgow: M'Phun.

Mass Observation (1943) *The Pub and the People: A Worktown Study*. London: Victor Gollancz.

Monckton, H.A. (1969) *A History of the English Public House*. London: The Bodley Head.

Richardson, A. (ed.) (1969) *A Dictionary of Christian Theology*. London: SCM Press.

Roth, C. (ed.) (1972) *Encylopedia Judaica*. Vol. 10. Jerusalem: Keter Publishing House.

Rudgley, R. (1993). *The Alchemy of Culture*. London: British Museum Press.

Selley, E. (1927) *The English Public House as It is*. London: Longmans Green.

Snyder, C. R. (1958) *Alcohol and the Jews: A Cultural Study of Drinking and Sobriety*. Glencoe, Ill.: The Free Press.

*Sulkunen P. (1997) Images and realities of alcohol. *Addiction*, **93**, 1305–12.

Trotter, T. (1804) *An Essay, Medical, Philosophical, and Chemical, on Drunkenness, and its Effects on the Human Body*. London: T. N. Longman and G. Rees. Facsimile reproduction 1988, with an introduction by Roy Porter, London: Routledge.

3 **A Short History of Drunkenness**

Booth, W. (1890) *In Darkest England and the Way Out.* London: International Headquarters of the Salvation Army.

Bridgett, T. E. (1876) *The Discipline of Drink: An Historical Enquiry into the Principles and Practice of the Catholic Church Regarding the Use, Abuse and Disuse of Alcoholic Liquors.* London: Burns & Oates.

Clark, P. (1983) *The English Alehouse: A Social History.* London: Longman.

Evelyn, John (1959) *The Diary of John Evelyn* (1631–1706), ed. E. S. de Beer. Oxford: Oxford University Press.

French, R. V. (1884) *Nineteen Centuries of Drink in England: A History.* London: National Temperance Publication Depot.

Glatt, M. M. (1958) The English drink problem – its rise and decline through the ages. *British Journal of Addiction,* **55**, 51–67.

*Harrison, B. (1971) *Drink and the Victorians.* London: Faber and Faber.

Lecky, W. E. H. (1890) *History of England in the Eighteenth Century.* Vol. 1 of 8 vols. London: Longmans Green.

McKinlay, A. P. (1948) Ancient experiences with intoxicating drinks: non-classical peoples. *Quarterly Journal of Studies on Alcohol,* **9**, 388–414.

Partridge, G. E. (1912) *Studies in the Psychology of Intemperance.* New York: Sturgis & Walton.

Select Committee of the House of Commons (1834) *Report of Committee on the Prevailing Vice of Drunkenness* [chairman J. S. Buckingham]. London: House of Commons.

Shadwell, A. (1902) *Drink, Temperance and Legislation.* Chapter 2 (pp. 14–42) Drink in the past. Chapter 3 (pp. 43–74), The decline of drunkenness. London: Longmans Green.

Smollett, T. B. (1840) *The History of England, from the Revolution in 1688 to the Death of George the Second.* Philadelphia: M'Carthy & Davies.

Spring, J. A., and Buss, D. H. (1977) Three centuries of alcohol in the British diet. *Nature,* **270**, 567–72.

The Statutes at Large, Passed in the Parliament Held in Ireland: from 1310 to 1786. Vol. 1. Dublin.

Warner, J. (1992) Before there was 'alcoholism': lessons from the medieval experience with alcohol. *Contemporary Drug Problems,* Fall, 409–29.

—— (1997) Shifting categories of the social harms associated with alcohol: examples from late medieval and early modern England. *American Journal of Public Health*, **87**, 1788–97.

Warner, J. F. (1997) The naturalization of beer and gin in early modern England. *Contemporary Drug Problems*, **24**, 373–402.

Williams, G. Prys, and Brake, G. Thompson (1980) *Drink in Great Britain: 1900 to 1979*. London: Edsall.

Wilson, G. B. (1940) *Alcohol and the Nation*. London: Nicholson & Watson.

—— (1941) The liquor problem in England and Wales: a survey from 1860–1935. *British Journal of Inebriety*, **38**, 142–65.

4 Thomas Nashe's Menagerie

Edwards, G. (1974) Drugs, drug dependence and the concept of plasticity. *Quarterly Journal of Studies on Alcohol*, **35**, 176–95.

*Graham, K., Leonard, K. E., Room, R., et al. (1998) Current directions in research on understanding and preventing intoxicated aggression. *Addiction*, **93**, 659–76.

Heath, D. B. (1958) Drinking patterns of the Bolivian Camba. *Quarterly Journal of Studies on Alcohol*, **19**, 491–508.

Hillier, A. (1902) quoted in C. Harford (1904) The drinking habits of uncivilized and semi-civilized races. *British Journal of Inebriety*, **2**, 92–103.

*MacAndrew, C., and Edgerton, R. B. (1970) *Drunken Comportment: A Social Explanation*. London: Nelson.

Nashe, T. (1592) *Pierce Penilesse. His Supplication to the Diuell*. Quoted in E. M. Jellinek (1943–44) Classics of the alcohol literature. The observations of the Elizabethan writer Thomas Nash on drunkenness. *Quarterly Journal of Studies on Alcohol*, **4**, 462–9.

Norström, T. (1998) Effects on criminal violence of different beverage types and private and public drinking. *Addiction*, **93**, 689–700.

Stockham, G. H. (1888) *Temperance and Prohibition*. Oakland, Calif.: Pacific Press.

Trotter, T. (1804) *An Essay, Medical, Philosophical, and Chemical, on Drunkenness, and its Effects on the Human Body*. London: T. N. Longman and G. Rees. Facsimile reproduction 1988, with an introduction by Roy Porter, London: Routledge.

5 Alcohol is a Drug of Dependence

Ball, D. M., and Murray, R. M. (1994) Genetics of alcohol misuse, pp. 18–35, in G. Edwards and T. J. Peters (eds.), *Alcohol and Alcohol Problems*. British Medical Bulletin 50, No. 1. Edinburgh: Churchill Livingstone.

Cloninger, C. R., Bohman, M., and Sigvardsson, S. (1981) Inheritance of alcohol abuse. *Archives of General Psychiatry*, **38**, 861–8.

Dawson, D. A., Harford, T. C., and Grant, B. F. (1992) Family history as a predictor of alcohol dependence. *Alcohol Clinical and Experimental Research*, **16**, 572–5.

Edwards, G. (1990) Withdrawal symptoms and alcohol dependence: fruitful mysteries. *British Journal of Addiction*, **81**, 447–61.

Edwards, G., and Gross, M. M. (1976) Alcohol dependence: provisional description of a clinical syndrome. *British Medical Journal*, **1**, 1058–61.

*Edwards, G., Marshall, E. J., and Cook, C. C. H. (1997) The alcohol dependence syndrome. Chapter 3 (pp. 31–54) in *The Treatment of Drinking Problems*. 3rd edn. Cambridge: Cambridge University Press.

Fleming, J., Mullen, P. E., Sibthorpe, B., et al. (1998) The relationship between childhood sexual abuse and alcohol abuse in women – a case study. *Addiction*, **93**, 1787–98.

Goodwin, D. W., Schulsinger, F., Hermansen, L., et al. (1973) Alcohol problems in adoptees raised apart from alcoholic biological parents. *Archives of General Psychiatry*, **28**, 228–43.

Helzer, J. E., and Pryzbeck, T. R. (1988) The co-occurrence of alcoholism with other psychiatric disorders in the general population and its impact on treatment. *Journal of Studies on Alcohol*, **49**, 219–24.

Kaij, L. (1960) *Alcoholism in Twins*. Stockholm: Almquist & Wiksell.

Levine, H. G. (1978) The discovery of addiction: changing conceptions of habitual drunkenness in America. *Journal of Studies on Alcohol*, **39**, 143–74.

Mello, N. K. (1972) Behavioral studies of alcoholism. Chapter 9 (pp. 219–92) in B. Kissin and H. Begleiter (eds.), *Biology of Alcoholism Vol. 2*. New York: Plenum.

Mendelson, J. H. (ed.) (1964) Experimentally induced chronic intoxication and withdrawal in alcoholics. *Quarterly Journal of Studies on Alcohol*, Supplement 2.

Schuckit, M. A. (1985) Ethanol-induced changes in body-sway in men at high alcoholism risk. *Archives of General Psychiatry*, **42**, 375–7.

6 The American Prohibition Experiment

*Blocker, J. S. (1989) *American Temperance Movements: Cycles of Reform.* Boston: Twayne.

Burnham, J. C. (1993) *Bad Habits: Drinking, Smoking, Taking Drugs, Gambling, Sexual Behavior and Swearing in American History.* New York: New York University Press.

Daniels, W. H. (1878) *The Temperance Reform and its Great Reformers: An Illustrated History.* New York: Nelson & Phillips.

Dobyns, F. (1940) *The Amazing Story of Repeal: An Exposé of the Power of Propaganda.* Chicago, Ill: Willett & Clark.

Gough, J. B. (1881) *Sunlight and Shadow or, Gleanings from My Life Work.* Hartford, Conn.: A. D. Worthington.

Gusfield, J. R. (1986) *Symbolic Crusade: Status Politics and the American Temperance Movement.* Urbana, Ill.: University of Illinois Press.

Kerr, K. A. (1985) *Organized for Prohibition: A New History of the Anti-Saloon League.* New Haven, Conn.: Yale University Press.

Levine, H. G. (1992) Temperance cultures: concern about alcohol problems in Nordic and English-speaking cultures. Chapter 2 (pp. 15–36) in M., Lader, G. Edwards and D. C. Drummond (eds.) *The Nature of Alcohol and Drug Related Problems.* Oxford: Oxford University Press.

Maxwell, M. A. (1950) The Washingtonian Movement. *Quarterly Journal of Studies on Alcohol,* **11**, 411–15.

Rorabaugh, W. J. (1979) *The Alcoholic Republic.* New York: Oxford University Press.

Sinclair, A. (1962) *Prohibition: The Era of Excess.* London: Faber and Faber.

Tyrrell, I. (1979) *Sobering up: From Temperance to Prohibition in Antebellum America, 1800–1860.* Westport, Conn.: Greenwood.

—— (1997) The US Prohibition experiment: myths, history, and implications. *Addiction,* **92**, 1405–9.

Warburton, C. (1932) *The Economic Results of Prohibition: Studies in History, Economics and Law,* edited by the Faculty of Political Science of Columbia University, New York. New York: Columbia University Press.

7 Calling Alcoholism a Disease

*Jellinek, E. M. (1960) *The Disease Concept of Alcoholism.* New Brunswick, NJ: Hillhouse Press.

Mann, M. (1950) *Primer on Alcoholism.* New York: Rinehart.

Page, P. Booth (1997) E. M. Jellinek and the evolution of alcohol studies: a critical essay. *Addiction,* **92**, 1619–37.

Shadwell, A. (1902) *Drink, Temperance and Legislation.* London: Longmans Green.

Williams, L. (1956) *Alcoholism: A Manual for Students and Practitioners.* Edinburgh: E. & S. Livingstone.

—— (1960) *Tomorrow will be sober.* London: Cassell.

8 Alcoholics Anonymous

Alcoholics Anonymous (1953) *Twelve Steps and Twelve Traditions.* New York: Alcoholics Anonymous World Services.

*—— (1976) *Alcoholics Anonymous: The Story of How Many Thousands of Men and Women have Recovered from Alcoholism.* 3rd edn. New York: Alcoholics Anonymous World Services.

Edwards, G. (1996) Alcoholics Anonymous as a mirror held up to nature. Chapter 14, (pp. 220–39) in G. Edwards and C. Dare (eds.), *Psychotherapy, Psychological Treatments and the Addictions.* Cambridge: Cambridge University Press.

*Kutz, E. (1991) *Not-God: A History of Alcoholics Anonymous.* Center City, Minn.: Hazelden.

Levine, H. G. (1992) Temperance cultures: concern about alcohol problems in Nordic and English-speaking cultures. Chapter 2 (pp. 15–36) in M. Lader, G. Edwards and D. C. Drummond (eds.), *The Nature of Alcohol and Drug Related Problems.* Oxford: Oxford University Press.

McCrady, B. S., and Miller, R. W. (eds.) (1993) *Research on Alcoholics Anonymous: Opportunities and Alternatives.* New Brunswick, NJ: Rutgers Center of Alcohol Studies.

Mäkelä, K., Arminen, I., Bloomfield, K., et al. (1996) *Alcoholics Anonymous as a Mutual Help Movement: A Study in Eight Societies.* Madison, Wis.: University of Wisconsin Press.

Miller, W.R. (1990) Spirituality: the silent dimension in addiction research. *Drug and Alcohol Review*, **9**, 259–66.

Robinson, D. (1974) *Talking out of Alcoholism: The Self-Help Process in Alcoholics Anonymous*. London: Croom Helm.

9 **In the Name of Treatment**

American Association for the Study and Cure of Inebriety (1893) *The Disease of Inebriety from Alcohol, Opium and other Narcotic Drugs*. Bristol: John Wright.

Berridge, V. (1990) The Society for the Study of Addiction 1884–1988. (special issue), *British Journal of Addiction*, **85** 983–1087.

Bloomberg, W. (1941) Further report on the use of amphetamine (benzedrine) sulfate as an adjuvant in the treatment of alcoholism. *Archives of Neurology and Psychiatry*, **45**, 899.

Blumberg, L. L. (1978) The American Association for the Study and Cure of Inebriety. *Alcoholism: Clinical and Experimental Research*, **2**, 234–40.

Cooper, J. W. Astley (1913) *Pathological Inebriety: Its Causation and Treatment*. London: Baillière, Tindall & Cox.

Dent, J. Yerbury (1949) Apomorphine treatment of addiction: some recent developments. *British Journal of Addiction*, **46**, 15–28.

—— (1950) Discussion following Dr Spenser Paterson's paper. *British Journal of Addiction*, **47**, 16–30.

Ditman, K. S., and Benor, D. (1966) Diazepam (Valium) very high dosage: longitudinal and single case study. *Western Medicine*, **5**, 109–10.

Farrar, C. H., Powell, B. J., and Martin, L. K. (1968) Punishment of alcohol consumption by apneic paralysis. *Behaviour Research and Therapy*, **6**, 13–16.

House of Commons (1904) Inebriates Acts 1879 to 1899. Regulations, made by the Secretary of State for the Home Department. London: HMSO.

Hughes, J. C., and Cook, C. C. H. (1997) The efficacy of disulfiram: a review. *Addiction*, **92**, 381–96.

Ibragimov, V. K., and Udovichenko, A. S. (1962) On the treatment of alcoholism with nicotinic acid. *Zdravookhr. Beloruss*, **22**, 30–33.

Kelynack, T. N. (1907) The arrest of alcoholism. Chapter 15 (pp. 261–88) in T. N. Kelynack (ed.), *The Drink Problem in its Medico-Sociological Aspects*. London: Methuen.

Kerr, N. (1888) Inebriety, its Etiology, Pathology, Treatment and Jurisprudence. London: H. K. Lewis.

Knight, G., and Strom-Olsen, R. (1968) Stereotactic surgery. Journal of Alcoholism, 9, 78–91.

LaVerne, A. A., and Herman, M. (1953) Carbon dioxide maintenance therapy in neurosis and alcoholism: preliminary report. Diseases of the Nervous System, 14, 316–18.

Lecoq, R. (1949) Alcoolisme chronique et désintoxication alcoolique. Gazette medicale de France, 50, 573–81.

Lemere, F. (1987) Aversion treatment of alcoholism: some reminiscences. British Journal of Addiction, 82, 257–8.

Macy, F. S., and Silkworth, W. D. (1938) Colloidal gold and colloidal iodine in chronic alcoholism. Lancet, 58, 291–2.

Medical Research Council (1948) Streptomycin treatment of pulmonary tuberculosis. British Medical Journal, 2, 769–82.

Milligan, W. L. (1955) The use of intensive ECT in the treatment of chronic alcoholism. International Journal of Alcoholism, 1, 42–6.

Müller, D., Roeder, F., and Orthner, H. (1973) Further results of stereotaxis in the human hypothalamus in sexual deviations: first use of this operation in addiction to drugs. Neurochirurgia, 16, 113–26.

O'Brien, C. (1952) Experimental evidence in the treatment of alcoholism by intensive calcium therapy. Journal of the American Osteopathy Association, 51, 393–4.

Pareja, C. A. (1947) Treatment of alcoholism by means of alcoholized human serum (Abstract). Quarterly Review of Psychiatry and Neurology, 2, 299.

*Rush, B. (1790) An Inquiry into the Effects of Ardent Spirits on the Human Body and Mind, with an Account of the Means for Preventing and of the Remedies for Curing Them. 8th edn (1814). Brookfields: E. Merriam. Reprinted in Quarterly Journal of Studies on Alcohol, 4, 325–41.

Scher, J. (1971) Marijuana as an agent in rehabilitating alcoholics. American Journal of Psychiatry, 127, 971–2.

Shilo, B. F. (1961) On the treatment of chronic alcoholics with lemon juice. Zdravookhr. Beloruss, 7, 54–5.

Smith, C. M. (1958) A new adjunct in the treatment of alcoholism: the hallucinogenic drugs. Quarterly Journal of Studies on Alcohol, 19, 406–17.

Smith, J. J. (1953) Modern orientation in alcoholism. Nursing World, 127, 18–19.

Stern, M. M. (1955) Antihistamine treatment of alcoholism. *Journal of Nervous and Mental Diseases*, **122**, 198–9.

Tintera, J. W., and Lovell, H. W. (1949) Endocrine treatment of alcoholism. *Geriatrics*, **4**, 274–80.

*Trotter, T. (1804) *An Essay, Medical, Philosophical, and Chemical, on Drunkenness, and its Effects on the Human Body*. London: T. N. Longman and G. Rees. Facsimile reproduction 1988, with an introduction by Roy Porter. London: Routledge.

Wallerstein, R. S. (1956) Comparative study of treatment methods for chronic alcoholism: the alcoholism research project at Winter VA Hospital. *American Journal of Psychology*, **113**, 228–33.

Watts, J. W., and Freeman, W. (1946) Prefrontal leucotomy *Southern Medicine and Surgery*, **108**, 241–7.

*White, L. W. (1998) *Slaying the Dragon: The History of Addiction Treatment and Recovery in America*. Chapter 4 (pp. 21–31), The rise and fall of inebriate homes and asylums. Chapter 7 (pp. 50–63), Franchising addiction treatment: the Keeley Institutes. Bloomington, Ill.: Chestnut Health Systems/Lighthouse Institute.

10 **The Mysterious Essences of Treatment**

*Addiction (1999) Commentaries on Project MATCH: matching alcohol treatments to client heterogeneity. *Addiction*, **94**, 31–69.

Cook, C. C. H. (1988) The Minnesota Model in the management of drug and alcohol dependency: miracle method or myth? Part 1. The philosophy and the programme. *British Journal of Addiction*, **8**, 625–34.

Edwards, G., Marshall, E. J., and Cook, C. C. H. (1997) *The Treatment of Drinking Problems*. 3rd edn. Cambridge: Cambridge University Press.

Institute of Medicine (1990) *Broadening the Base of Treatment for Alcohol Problems*. Washington DC: National Academy Press.

Marlatt, G. A., and Gordon, J. R. (1985) *Relapse Prevention: Maintenance Strategies in the Treatment of Addictive Behaviour*. New York: Guildford.

*Miller, W. R., and Heather, N. (eds.) (1998) *Treating Addictive Behaviors*. New York: Plenum.

Moncrieff, J., and Drummond, D. C. (1997) New drug treatments for alcohol problems: a critical appraisal. *Addiction*, **92**, 939–47.

Prochaska, J. O., and DiClimente, C. C. (1984) *The Transtheoretical Approach: Crossing Traditional Boundaries of Therapy*. New York: Daw-Jones Ireven.

Project MATCH Resource Group (1999) Summary of Project MATCH. *Addiction*, **94**, 31–4.

Sobell, L. C., Sobell, M. B., and Toneatto, T. (1991) Recovery from alcohol problems without treatment, pp. 198–242 In N. Heather, W. R. Miller and J. Greeley (eds.), *Self Control and the Addictive Behaviors*. New York: Pergamon.

*Vaillant, G. E. (1983) *The Natural History of Alcoholism*. Cambridge, Mass.: Harvard University Press.

11 **Once an Alcoholic . . .**

Davies, D. L. (1962) Normal drinking in recovered alcoholics. *Quarterly Journal of Studies on Alcohol*, **23**, 94–104.

Edwards, G. (1985) A later follow-up of a classic case series: D. L. Davies's 1962 report and its significance for the present. *Journal of Studies on Alcohol*, **46**, 181–90.

—— (1994) D. L. Davies and 'Normal drinking in recovered alcohol addicts': the genesis of a paper. *Drug and Alcohol Dependence*, **35**, 249–59.

Gough, J. B. (1881) *Sunlight and Shadow or, Gleanings from my Life Work*. Hartford, Conn.: A. D. Worthington.

*Heather, N., and Robertson, I. (1981) *Controlled Drinking*. London: Methuen.

Johnson, S., and Boswell, B. (1984) *A Journey to the Western Isles of Scotland (1775) and The Journal of a Tour to the Hebrides (1785)*. London: Penguin.

Keller, M. (1977) A nonbehaviorist's view of the behavioral problem. Section 5, Chapter 1 (pp. 381–98) in P. E. Nathan, G. A. Marlatt and T. Lørberg (eds.), *Alcoholism: New Directions in Behavioral Research and Treatment*. New York: Plenum.

Kerr, N. (1888) *Inebriety, its Etiology, Pathology, Treatment and Jurisprudence*. London, H. K. Lewis.

Marlatt, G. A. (1983) The controlled drinking controversy: a commentary. *American Psychologist*, **38**, 1097–1110.

Pendery, M. L., Maltzman, J. M., and West, L. J. (1982) Controlled drinking by alcoholics? New findings, and a re-evaluation of a major affirmative study. *Science*, **217**, 169–75.

Sobell, M. B., and Sobell, L. C. (1973) Alcoholics treated by individualized behavior therapy: one year treatment trial. *Behaviour Research and Therapy*, **11**, 599–618.

—— (1976) Second year treatment outcome of alcoholics treated by individual behaviour therapy: results. *Behavior Research and Therapy*, **14**, 195–215.

—— (1984) The aftermath of heresy: a response to Pendery et al.'s (1982) critique of 'individualized behavior therapy for alcoholics'. *Behaviour Research and Therapy*, **22**, 413–40.

—— (1995) Controlled drinking after 25 years: how important was the great debate? *Addiction*, **90**, 1149–53.

12 **Molecule as Medicine**

Berridge, V., and Edwards, G. (1986) *Opium and the People. Opium Use in Nineteenth-Century England.* London: Allen Lane, 1981. Paperback edn: New Haven, Conn.: Yale University Press, 1987.

Brown, J. (1795) *The Elements of Medicine*, trans. T. Beddoes from *Elementa Medicae* (London: 1780). London: J. Johnson.

Doll, R. (1997) One for the heart? *British Medical Journal*, **315**, 1664–8.

Fillmore, K. M., Golding, J. M., Graves, K. L. et al. (1998a) Alcohol consumption and mortality. I. Characteristics of drinking groups. *Addiction*, **93**, 183–203.

—— (1998b). Alcohol consumption and mortality. III. Studies of female populations. *Addiction*, **93**, 219–29.

Hall, J. (1904) 200 cases of acute lobar pneumonia. *Lancet*, **1**, 1643–8.

Hare, F. (1912) *On Alcoholism: Its Clinical Aspects and Treatment.* London: J. & A. Churchill.

Harrison, B. (1971) *Drink and the Victorians.* London: Faber and Faber.

Hart, C., Smith, G. D., Hold, D. J., et al. (1999) Alcohol consumption and mortality from all causes, coronary heart disease, and stroke: results from a prospective cohort study of Scottish men with 21 years of follow-up. *British Medical Journal*, **318**, 1725–29.

Hutchinson, R. (1923) Alcohol as a medicine. Appendix 1 (pp. 177–82) in E. H. Starling (ed.), *The Action of Alcohol on Man.* London: Longmans Green.

Leiino, E. V., Romelsjö, A., Shoemaker, C., et al. (1998) Alcohol consumption and mortality. II. Studies of male populations. *Addiction*, **93**, 205–18.

Neison, F. G. P. (1851) On the role of mortality among persons of intemperate habits. *Journal of the Statistical Society*, **14**, 200–219.

Pearl, R. (1923) Alcohol and mortality. Appendix 3 (pp. 213–86) in E. H. Starling (ed.), *The Action of Alcohol on Man*. London: Longmans Green.

*Puddey, I. B., Rakic, V., Dimmitt, S. B. et al. (1999) Influence of pattern of drinking on cardiovascular disease and cardiovascular risk factors – a review. *Addiction*, **94**, 649–64.

Rimm, E. B., Williams, P., Fosher, K., et al. (2000) Moderate alcohol intake and lower risk of coronary heart disease: meta-analyses of effects on lipids and haemostatic factors. *British Medical Journal*, **318**, 1523–33.

St Leger, A. S., Cochrane, A. L., and Moore, E. (1979) Factors associated with cardiac mortality in developed countries with particular reference to the consumption of wine. *Lancet*, **1**, 1017–1020.

Shadwell, A. (1902) *Drink, Temperance and Legislation*. London: Longmans Green.

Stockard, C. R., and Papanicolaou, G. N. (1918) Further studies on the modification of germ cells in mammals: the effect of alcohol on treated guinea pigs and their descents. *Journal of Experimental Zoology*, **26**, 119–226.

Trotter, T. (1804) *An Essay, Medical, Philosophical, and Chemical, on Drunkenness, and its Effects on the Human Body*. London: T. N. Longman and G. Rees. Facsimile reproduction 1988, with an introduction by Roy Porter. London: Routledge.

Warner, J. H. (1980) Physiological theory and therapeutic explanation in the 1860s: the British debate on the medical use of alcohol. *Bulletin of the History of Medicine*, **54**, 235–57.

Wilson, G. B. (1940) *Alcohol and the Nation*. London: Nicholson & Watson.

13 **The Drinker's Dilemma**

*Edwards, G., Anderson, P., Babor, T., et al. (1994) The individual's drinking and degree of risk. Chapter 3 (pp. 41–74) in *Alcohol Policy and the Public Good*. Oxford: Oxford University Press in association with the European Office of the World Health Organization.

Péquignot, G. (1975) Rations d'alcool consomées 'déclarées' et risques pathologiques, pp. 23–40 in R. J. Royer and J. Levi (eds.), *Symposium Franco-Britannique sur l'alcoolisme*. Paris: INSERM.

Romelsjö, A. (1995) Alcohol consumption and unintentional injury, suicide, violence, work performance and inter-generational effects. Chapter 5 (pp. 114–142) in H. D. Holder and G. Edwards (eds.), *Alcohol and Public Policy: Evidence and Issues*. Oxford: Oxford University Press.

Room, R., Bondy, S. J., and Ferris, J. (1995) The risk of harm to oneself from drinking, Canada 1989. *Addiction*, **90**, 499–513.

*Smith-Warner, S. A., Spiegelman, S. S., Yaun, P. A., et al. (1998) Alcohol and breast cancer in women: a pooled analysis of cohort studies. *Journal of the American Medical Association*, **279**, 535–40.

14 Ambiguous Futures

Bruun, K., Edwards, G., Lumio, M., et al. (1975) *Alcohol Control Policies in Public Health Perspective*. Helsinki: Finnish Foundation for Alcohol Studies in association with the European Office of the World Health Organization.

*Edwards, G., Anderson, P., Babor, T., et al. (1994) *Alcohol Policy and the Public Good*. Oxford: Oxford University Press in association with the European Office of the World Health Organization.

Foxcroft, D. R., Lister-Sharp, D., and Lowe, G. (1997) Alcohol misuse prevention for young people: a systematic review reveals methodological concerns and lack of reliable evidence of effectiveness. *Addiction*, **92**, 531–7.

Gual, A., and Colom, C. (1997) Why has alcohol consumption declined in the countries of Southern Europe? *Addiction*, Supplement 1, S21–S32.

Her, M., and Rehm, J. (1998) Alcohol and all cause mortality in Europe 1982–1990: a pooled cross-section time-series analysis. *Addiction*, **93**, 1335–40.

*Holder, H. D. (1998) *Alcohol and the Community: A Systems Perspective for Prevention*. International Research Monographs in the Addictions 1. Cambridge: Cambridge University Press.

*Holder, H. D., and Edwards, G. (eds.) (1995) *Alcohol and Public Policy: Evidence and Issues*. Oxford: Oxford University Press.

Indian Hemp Drugs Commission (1894) *Report* 7 vols. Simla: Government Central Printing Office.

Jernigan, D. H. (1997) *Thirsting for Markets: The Global Impact of Corporate Alcohol*. San Rafael, Calif.: Marin Institute.

Kalant, H., Corrigall, W., Hall, W., et al. (eds.) (1999) *The Health Effects of Cannabis*. Toronto: Centre for Addiction and Mental Health.

Ledermann, S. (1964) *Alcool, alcoolisme, alcoolisation: mortalité, morbidité, accidents du travail* (Alcohol, Alcoholism, Alcoholization: Mortality, Morbidity, Accidents at Work). Institut National d'Études Démographiques, Travaux et Documents, Cahier 41. Paris: Presses Universitaires de France.

Mosher, J. F. (1997) What place for alcoholic beverage container labels? A view from the United States. *Addiction*, **92**, 789–92.

Nemstov, A. V. (1998) Alcohol-related harm and alcohol consumption in Moscow, during, before and after a major anti-alcohol campaign. *Addiction*, **93**, 1501–10.

Österberg, E. (1995) Do alcohol prices affect consumption and related problems? Chapter 6 (pp. 145–63) in H. D. Holder and G. Edwards (eds.) *Alcohol and Public Policy: Evidence and Issues*. Oxford: Oxford University Press.

Shepherd, J. (1998) The circumstances and prevention of bar-glass injury. *Addiction*, **93**, 5–8.

Shikolnikov, V., Mesle, F., and Valin, J. (1995) Health crisis in Russia 1: recent trends in life expectancy and causes of death from 1970 to 1993. *Population*, **4–5**, 907–44.

Simpura, J. (1998) Mediterranean mysteries: mechanisms of declining alcohol consumption. *Addiction*, **93**, 1301–4.

Skog, O.-J. (1987) Trends in alcohol consumption and deaths from diseases. *British Journal of Addiction*, **82**, 1033–41.

*Society for the Study of Addiction (eds. R. Raistrick, J. Hodgson and B. Ritson) (1999) *Tackling Alcohol Together*. London: Free Association Books.

Index